DEFAMED!

'I sometimes think that the price of liberty is not so much eternal vigilance as eternal dirt.'

George Orwell, *The Road to Wigan Pier*

DEFAMED!

FAMOUS IRISH LIBEL CASES

A.J. DAVIDSON

Gill & Macmillan

Gill & Macmillan Ltd
Hume Avenue
Park West
Dublin 12
with associated companies throughout the world
www.gillmacmillan.ie

© A.J. Davidson 2008

978 07171 38036

Typography design by Make Communication
Print origination by Carrigboy Typesetting Services
Printed by Nørhaven Paperback A/S, Denmark

The paper used in this book is made from the wood pulp of
managed forests. For every tree felled, at least one tree is
planted, thereby renewing natural resources.

A CIP catalogue record for this book is available from the
British Library.

1 3 5 4 2

For David

CONTENTS

CONTENTS

ACKNOWLEDGMENTS

With deepest thanks to Consultants Chris Pigeon and John Caird, and the nursing staff of Richmond Neurosurgical ICU and Acute Wards, Beaumont Hospital.

INTRODUCTION

It was a ferocious physical assault on a defenceless man. Three youths were being chased by a garda in the Deanrock area of Togher, on the southside of Cork City. An unidentified assailant picked up a large lump of concrete and threw it at the unprotected head of Garda James Grogan. His aim was good and the young father of two crashed to the ground, unconscious. One of the three, Finbarr Hill, stepped forward and landed a series of kicks to the head and groin of the helpless garda. The other two youths joined in the frenzied beating. It was one of the worst attacks ever endured by a serving member of the Garda Síochána.

Grogan suffered a broken skull and was on a life-support machine for a fortnight; he underwent two emergency operations. For a while it was not clear if he would survive the appalling attack. In the event he did recover, but not fully; he was left with partial paralysis on the left side of his body.

Nineteen-year-old Finbarr Hill was arrested and charged for his part in the savage attack. He was sentenced to three years in prison. His companions were also imprisoned, though there was an outcry over the leniency of the sentences they received, which were seen as an insult to the brave men and women of the Garda Síochána. Most observers thought that was where it ended, but as it transpired, Hill had not seen the last of a courtroom.

On 25 October 1995, a photograph of Hill taken in Cork prison was published in the *Cork Examiner*. The related article read that he was being kept in isolation in the C-wing, where sex offenders were housed. The journalist went on to point out that the wing also accommodated prisoners who needed to be separated for their own protection. A month later the newspaper published a statement making it clear that Hill had not been charged or convicted of any sexual offence.

Hill sued the newspaper for libel, accusing it of portraying him as a sex offender, child molester or rapist. The *Cork Examiner* defended the libel action in the High Court in November 2000, claiming that the article was not capable of defaming Hill because his character being so flawed, he could not be defamed. Unfortunately for the defence, the judge imposed a strict limitation as to what evidence it could adduce: there would be no testimony concerning the nature of the offence of which Hill had been convicted, i.e. that he and two others had come close to beating a garda to death.

The jury found that Hill had been defamed and awarded him damages of £60,000. A year later, the Supreme Court upheld that verdict and the amount of damages awarded. Despite agreeing that Hill had a somewhat imperfect reputation and that the damages award was at the higher end of an appropriate range, the Supreme Court was not prepared to allow the newspaper's appeal.

While the verdicts reached in the Hill libel action case will appall some people, those in the know will not be surprised by it. Libel litigation is about reputation – its preservation or its destruction. Hill's reputation had already suffered grievously from his arrest and subsequent conviction, therefore he had nothing to lose but everything to gain (or £60,000, to be precise).

There are lessons to be learned from Hill's case, both for litigants and the media. If you do not want to have your dirty linen aired in public, avoid taking a libel action into court. The greater your fame, or indeed notoriety, the more intense will be the public scrutiny of your life. The defendant's legal team will place you under a microscope and every humiliating blunder or idiotic mistake you have ever made will be dissected in a very public manner. Even if you do have the stomach for all that a libel case will entail, the sorry truth is that there are few winners in a libel court: secure victory and it may prove hollow; lose, and it could ruin you. Oscar Wilde certainly had time in jail, and later in exile in Paris, to regret his decision to sue the Marquess of Queensberry. Jonathan Aitken and Jeffrey Archer are two more recent litigants who should have known better than to tempt fate.

On the other hand, in the Hill case the *Cork Examiner* assumed it had nothing to fear from a man, a convicted thug, whose reputation was already in tatters. It should have known, however, that nothing can ever be taken for granted in a libel court. An oversight that cost it a lot of money. Unfortunately, all too often, the economics of defending a libel suit in Ireland, no matter how strong the case, mean that a pre-trial settlement offer is the preferred route. A newspaper can win a libel action yet still be enormously out of pocket due to unrecoverable costs.

Yet, in spite of all this, the libel courts of Ireland are rarely empty. What motivates these cases? What drives these people to gamble on the vagaries of a jury? Perhaps it stems from a genuine desire to clear their name. If so, that is a naive attitude considering the amount of mud-raking and mud-slinging to which the litigant will be subject in a high-profile libel hearing. Perhaps it is the headline-grabbing size of the damages awarded that proves seductive? If so, the wounded party has been misled, as most awards are paltry compared to those for even relatively minor personal injury. What, then, is the impetus? Could it be that Ireland's creaking libel laws excessively favour the plaintiff?

The Defamation Act 1961 set the current legislative framework for libel and slander litigation in Ireland. It repealed a number of obsolete laws, some of which dated from medieval times, when appropriate punishments included cutting off a slanderer's ears to whipping a libeller and parading him around the city. Today, more than a few public faces might believe our forefathers had the right idea.

The 1961 legislators were faced with a dilemma that even their best efforts did little to resolve. Article 40.3.2. of Bunreacht na Éireann (the Irish Constitution) holds that the State shall, by its laws, protect as best it may a citizen's good name. However, Article 40.6.1 protects the right of citizens to freedom of speech. This quandary recurs in Article 10 (1) and Article 10 (2) of the European Human Rights Convention. Thus it fell to the Irish judiciary, and in particular the Supreme Court, to navigate a course through the choppy waters of defamation litigation.

The 1961 Act did not provide a definitive description of defamation, but the courts currently hold it to mean 'a statement which tends to lower the reputation of the subject in the eyes of right-thinking people'. In the 1970s, the courts decided that in order to be actionable, a defamatory statement must be false, must refer to the plaintiff and must be published to a third party. The offended person does not necessarily have to be named, so long as his/her identity is obvious. The most common form of 'publication' is in a radio or television broadcast, a newspaper, periodical or book, but there are others. A waxworks' proprietor, for example, was sued for displaying an unflattering image of a celebrity. A policeman won an action after a cartoonist revealed his identity by mocking his prominent eyebrows and large ears.

Most defamation is classified as a tort, that is, a civil wrong. Criminal libel is rare and differs in that no prosecution may be brought until an order has been obtained from a High Court judge, who will hear the application *in camera*. Slander has also become a rarity in the courts because modern technology ensures that most defamatory statements are recorded by one means or another, and are therefore classed as libel. Defamation is a 'strict liability' offence, which means the intention of the offender is irrelevant and therefore anyone involved at any stage of its publication is liable to be sued, from author, to editor, to publisher, to owner and distributor. Perhaps in an effort to even up things, it was determined that only a living person can sue for libel.

Those who drafted the 1961 legislation were attempting a delicate juggling act – striving to protect the innocent citizen on the one hand, while allowing certain freedoms on the other. It is no disgrace that they did not achieve all they had hoped for. What is reprehensible is the sluggishness of successive governments to deal with the inequalities exposed by the implementation of the Act.

Acceptable defences against a charge of defamation are clearly delineated in the Act, with fair comment, privilege and justification being the most frequently cited in litigation actions. Less well-known forms of damage-limitation are apology, consent and accord and satisfaction.

Fair comment is the articulated opinion of the defendant, as, for example, a sports journalist writing: 'The referee had an off day and made several howling errors, which dramatically affected the final score.' Justification is where the defendant can prove the veracity of that which was stated.

Privilege is split into two types: absolute and qualified. Deputies speaking in Dáil Éireann have absolute privilege and therefore may level allegations of improper conduct without the fear of being sued. The same privilege protects judges and barristers in the performance of their legal duties. Qualified privilege, on the other hand, affords protection to the informant as long as he/she has a legal, moral or social duty to communicate the information and the recipient has a justified need to learn of it. Publishing details of an adulterous affair would not fall under qualified privilege unless, of course, the man happened to be Minister for War and the woman was also dating a Russian spy, as was the case in the British Profumo affair. However, even this privilege could be ruled invalid if malice is proved.

The decades since the passing of the Defamation Act 1961 have exposed its many inherent flaws. It is most frequently criticised for being biased in favour of the plaintiff, a charge that is easy to sustain. As the law stands, litigation may be initiated up to six years after the publication of the offending statement. This is twice the limitation period set for a personal injury action. Indeed, in certain circumstances this may be extended for longer than six years. In effect, this means that if, for example, a book with an offending statement is purchased years after its original publication, the plaintiff could argue that the limitation period commences from the date of purchase and not the date of publication.

The other distinguishing factor in libel cases is that juries still hear High Court libel actions; they have been dispensed with in other civil actions. The jury is responsible for awarding damages, but receives little guidance as to appropriate amounts. The enormous damages awarded by British juries to successful plaintiffs, like Jeffrey Archer and Elton John, did much to hasten the introduction of guidelines on damages for British juries. This measure greatly reduced the awards made to successful plaintiffs. Despite a number of large awards in Ireland, no corresponding guidelines have been put in place, despite some bizarre results that point to the need for same. For example, businessman Denis O'Brien saw his 1999 libel damages against the Mirror Newspaper

Group overturned because the Supreme Court considered the €317,000 award to be excessive. When the case was reheard in November 2006, the High Court jury awarded O'Brien €750,000. (Should the Mirror Group win another appeal, as seems likely, this libel action may well be heading back to the High Court for a third hearing.)

In a libel action instigated in the Irish courts, the plaintiff has no requirement to prove that the offending statement is defamatory; the court will presume that it is. Equally, in certain cases the plaintiff does not need to prove any financial loss or damage, does not have to sign a statement or swear an affidavit specifying actual damage incurred, nor is limited in how many actions he/she can bring regarding the same defamation.

On the other side of the coin, the defendant cannot lodge money into court – a method of limiting exposure in the event of costs being awarded against him/her – without an admission of liability on at least part of the claim; until 1999, one had to admit liability on the claim in its entirety. A similar punitive restriction means no apology for an error can be made without an admission of liability. If a defendant decides to fight a libel action, he/she risks having to pay aggravated damages for the additional harm done to the plaintiff's reputation during the course of the action. Should he/she win, the chances are that he/she will fail to collect some, or all, of the costs, as the expense of a prolonged legal action is so great.

Robert Maxwell, the business tycoon, took advantage of the similar British libel system to intimidate and terrorise journalists for decades. His corrupt business practices may well have been exposed years earlier if it had not been for the protection afforded him by libel laws. The same thing has been happening in Ireland: persons harbouring unsavoury secrets have used the threat of libel action to prevent exposure. The unwholesome reality is that time and time again, small publishers and broadcasters are often forced to spike stories after a solicitor's letter lands on their desk, knowing that to proceed could end in bankruptcy.

Regrettably, even when they have irrefutable proof, the larger media organisations have realised that it is often more prudent to settle out of court. This shameful situation of bullying and frivolous litigation will continue until the libel laws are reviewed and revised. Irish publishers have been calling for reform of the Act almost since its inception. Despite the Law Reform Commission's 1991 recommendations – in particular that a defendant be allowed to plead that he/she had exercised reasonable care prior to publication – and a string of politicians' promises, new legislation remains frustratingly just out of reach.

That brings us to our litany of libel lows and highs. Although it is clear that pursuing a libel case could end in a spectacular disaster, both in terms of public profile and personal finances, there are still a large number of hardy souls who sail forth into battle. Their outflanking manoeuvres, rallying cries, sallies and killer-blows provide us with a fascinating insight not just into the law, but into the very heart of human nature. These are the stories of the wrong-doers, and the wronged.

01 | THE LEGAL EAGLES SOAR:
P.J. MCGRORY v TODAY & ORS [1990]

The shooting dead of three IRA volunteers by soldiers of the Special Air Service (SAS) in Gibraltar on 6 March 1988 sparked an explosion of jingoistic headlines in the British press. The exact circumstances of the killings were unclear at first, but that did not stop the tabloids from indulging in xenophobic jubilation at the news. Since their successful storming of the Iranian embassy in London during a siege in 1980, the press had portrayed SAS soldiers as supermen. Therefore, any IRA incursion onto the iconic Rock of Gibraltar that was met with 'ultimate force' was certain to be greeted with approval.

Two days after the shootings, Spanish police found 141 lbs of Semtex in the boot of a car in an underground car park in Marbella, on the Costa del Sol. The British authorities claimed that the three IRA volunteers – Mairéad Farrell, Daniel McCann and Seán Savage – were planning a car-bomb attack, timed to go off during the changing-of-the-guard ceremony at Ince's Hall, Main Street, Gibraltar, on 8 March 1988. It was alleged that their visit to the Rock on 6 March was a reconnaissance mission in preparation for this attack. The trio did not know that the SAS and other military and police units had been following the active-service unit for some time. A spokesman said that a decision had been taken to stop and arrest the three IRA members, but that they had made movements which had led the soldiers to believe their lives were in danger, therefore they opened fire.

Before long the broadsheet press was beginning to question exactly what had happened at the scene of the shooting – a Shell petrol station on Winston Churchill Avenue. The stories being told by the eyewitnesses suggested a different picture from the one given by Sir Geoffrey Howe, British Foreign Secretary, to the House of Commons. It soon became clear that the three IRA members were unarmed and were killed execution-style by the SAS soldiers. Thames Television filmed a documentary, *Death on the Rock*, which highlighted some of the inconsistencies in the version of events supplied by the authorities. Thames came under extreme political pressure to withdraw it from the schedule, but the programme was broadcast on 28 April 1988.

The British government was embarrassed by the revelation that Spanish intelligence and police services had been co-operating extensively with their British counterparts. The intelligence that had been gathered on the three was so comprehensive that the British government must have known they were on a recon-naissance mission and therefore that they posed little danger at the time of their killings. The ensuing controversy, denials and debates raged all summer.

The Gibraltar inquest into the three deaths commenced on 6 September 1988. Paddy J. McGrory, a Belfast solicitor, leading criminal lawyer and civil rights campaigner, agreed to represent the families of the three IRA members on a *pro bono* basis. McGrory had studied law at Queen's University, Belfast and opened his own practice in 1948. In the late 1960s he became voluntary legal advisor to the Civil Rights Association and was involved in many high-profile legal cases, most notably the Burntollet compensation cases and the supergrass trials.

During the four-week inquest in the Gibraltar coroner's court, McGrory led the cross-examination of more than ninety witnesses – a mammoth task. His performance was all the more extraordinary considering the obstacles that were placed in his path: witnesses were threatened; expert opinion was denied to him; even the cost of the daily transcript of the court proceedings, which had been 50p a sheet, was raised to £5.00 a sheet. McGrory became known as the man who took on the SAS single-handedly, a profile that inevitably attracted a lot of adverse comment from the press . His determined pursuit of the facts of the case ensured that the British authorities could not bury the truth. McGrory alluded to Hemingway's *Death in the Afternoon* when he said: 'Those who killed publicly enough in the sunlight should not be allowed now to seek the shadows.'

The Belfast solicitor was a wily old fox who would have known that he was unlikely to win the first battle, but that perseverance would tell in the end. The inquest jury found by a majority of nine to two that the three had been killed lawfully. Undaunted, McGrory took a case to the European Commission of Human Rights, arguing that the killings violated Article 2 of the European Convention for the Protection of Human Rights. He was supported in this by the National Council for Civil Liberties and Amnesty International. In its ruling, the Commission found by a ten to nine split vote that excessive force had been used and referred the case to the European Court of Human Rights.

The first libel case to result from the imbalanced press coverage of the Gibraltar killings was when eyewitness Carmen Proetta sued the *Sun* after it published allegations in April and May 1988. The British tabloids had vilified Proetta in an effort to discredit her as a witness. The *Sun* described her as 'The Tart of Gib', claiming she was a former prostitute who ran an escort service. The newspaper further claimed that she was married to 'a sleazy drug peddler' and that her dislike for the British was so intense, she had fabricated her witness testimony. In fact, Proetta was a well-respected translator for two Spanish legal firms.

Acting for Proetta, Oscar Beuselinck told Mr Justice Potter in the High Court, London, on 16 December 1988 that his client and her children had suffered hurt and distress as a result of the untrue allegations. The *Sun*'s solicitor told the court that editor Kelvin MacKenzie and journalists Michael Fielder and Martin Smith now accepted that Proetta had not been involved in criminal activity and that she did not hate the British, as was alleged. The *Sun* agreed to pay Proetta substantial damages (an estimated £50,000) and all legal costs.

On 15 April 1989, Proetta received a further 'substantial' award from the Mirror Group Newspapers and an apology for articles published in the *Daily Mirror* in April and September 1988. The newspaper had alleged that Proetta's account of events contained in *Death on the Rock* was fabricated. Brian Hepworth, counsel for the newspaper, said that its story, which had been provided by a third party, was published in good faith, but that the newspaper and its editor now realised it to be incorrect. He added: 'They recognise that her statement and evidence to Thames Television, and subsequently to the inquest were an honest and credible account of the events she saw.'

McGrory had received much the same treatment at the hands of the British newspapers, who demonised him for daring to act for the families of the deceased. One newspaper published scurrilous allegations about him months before the inquest even commenced. His courage in challenging the evidence given by the SAS soldiers during the inquest made him a target for the worst kind of patriotic ranting in the tabloid press. As a result, over the following years, while McGrory continued his fight for truth for the victims' families, he also had to fight a rearguard action mounted in the libel courts.

The first of McGrory's litigation actions was heard in a Belfast High Court on 13 February 1990, in front of Mr Justice McCollum and a jury. The *Today* newspaper (a subsidiary of News (UK) Ltd, part of the Murdoch publishing empire) had published two articles on 6 July 1988, subsequent to a ruling by the Gibraltar coroner that the SAS soldiers who had shot dead the three IRA volunteers would have to give evidence at the inquest. The headline read: 'SAS Soldiers Must Face Provo Lawyer Says Coroner'. In the editorial, the newspaper argued against the soldiers appearing at the inquest: 'To expose undercover British soldiers to lawyers, who are effectively promoting the IRA's propaganda war, would be to condemn these men and their families to a lifetime under constant threat of IRA revenge.'

In his opening address, Michael Lavery QC, counsel for McGrory, advised the jury members that although they might have strong feelings about what had happened in Gibraltar, they must put those feelings out of their minds. He stated that it was important to have lawyers who were prepared to take on unpopular cases and that they should be able to do so without being accused of condoning the alleged crimes of their clients: 'Mr McGrory has given a lifetime of service in this regard and these libels impugn everything in which he believes. They were a most vicious attack on him and have caused annoyance, upset and real fear.'

McGrory regarded sectarianism as the ultimate obscenity and had always represented both sides of the community in Northern Ireland. In the present case he felt he had an obligation to the three victims because they were the children of former clients. He received no payment for his work at the inquest nor or at any other with which he was involved. The Gibraltar inquest was, in McGrory's opinion, an important case with regard to the rule of law. He regarded it as a challenge, which attracted him in the professional sense.

When asked to describe how he felt after reading the articles, McGrory replied: 'Here I was after forty years in practice being told I was not a lawyer, but some sort of creature, a hack of one particular group. That upset me very much.'

There were other, more sinister effects of the newspaper's allegations, however. McGrory had started to receive abusive and threatening phone calls at his home. His family had tried its best to shield him from these calls because he suffered from a heart complaint, but occasionally a call would get through to him. He was called a 'Provie bastard' by one anonymous caller.

McCrory and his colleague Pat Finucane, were targeted by the Ulster Freedom Fighters (UFF), a dangerous Protestant paramilitary group that disagreed with the principled stand both men took with regard to the law. After Finucane was killed in 1989, the Royal Ulster Constabulary (RUC) issued McGrory with a personal protection firearm. (It would emerge years later that Brian Nelson, an undercover British agent in the Ulster Defence Association (UDA), had targeted both Finucane and McGrory.) In effect, the newspaper articles relating to the Gibraltar killings had transformed McGrory's life; he could have gone anywhere without a threatening word before the *Today* allegations.

The newspapers agreed to publish an apology, but failed to reach an agreement with McGrory on the wording. McGrory explained: 'I don't think they came to grips with just how serious the matter was, and I thought their editor, who comes from Northern Ireland, might have had a bit more sense.'

Desmond Boal, a Queen's Counsel and well-known figure in Northern Ireland, gave evidence as to McGrory's professionalism. McGrory had often instructed Boal on behalf of both Roman Catholic IRA and Protestant UVF clients, but at no time, Boal insisted, had McGrory strayed into the area of identifying with his clients: 'Never once had I the slightest suspicion that his attitude was other than purely professional.'

Today's editor, David Montgomery, denied that any attempt had been made to connect McGrory with the IRA. He did not accept that the articles were defamatory. He did recognise that McGrory had a grievance, but argued that the newspapers had responded appropriately by offering to publish an apology. He did not regret publishing the articles and had done so in a spirit of fairness.

Mr Justice McCollum asked Montgomery what he understood was the plaintiff's grievance, to which Montgomery replied, 'He believes that we have branded him as a cohort of Sinn Féin, but I believe the meaning is entirely different.'

The hearing was destined to be a short one. Shortly after lunch on the second day, both sides announced that a settlement had been agreed. Frazer Elliott QC told the court that the newspaper now accepted that the articles were defamatory and acknowledged that Paddy McGrory was a man of the highest professional integrity: 'In acting on behalf of the next-of-kin of the deceased at the Gibraltar inquest, he was doing so properly in the exercise of his duty as a solicitor.'

The settlement agreed between the parties included contributions from the *Sunday Express* and the *Star* newspapers. McGrory's action against the two other newspapers, which had also published defamatory articles about him, had been listed for hearing the following week in the High Court. Elliott added: 'As an earnest of its apology the defendant has agreed to pay to the plaintiff a substantial sum by a way of damages together with his costs in the case.'

It was estimated that the total amount of damages accepted by McGrory was a generous six-figure sum, reflecting the fact that his life had been put in danger. Outside the courtroom Montgomery was asked how he felt after the settlement. He told the reporters that he had done nothing wrong and had apologised when asked to do so.

McGrory also spoke to the waiting press: 'These papers tried to steal my good name as a lawyer and I have got it back. I am perfectly happy.' He claimed that the *Today* articles had been part of a larger disinformation campaign over the Gibraltar killings.

'Are you accusing the British government?' a reporter asked.

The old fox, a veteran of a quarter-century of Troubles-related judicial skirmishing, smiled as he replied, 'I never accuse anybody'.

Unfortunately, McGrory did not live to see the European Court of Human Rights ruling (25 September 1995), which declared the Gibraltar killings to be unlawful. He died the year before.

* * *

In an analogous case, Donagh McDonagh, the barrister appointed by the Irish government as an observer at the Gibraltar inquest, also brought a libel action against the *Sun* newspaper. Most legal pundits considered it a case of relatively minor importance, so nobody foresaw the devastating blow the verdict would deal to the Irish publishing industry. The case was listed for a Dublin High Court on 26 June 1991, to be heard before Mr Justice Lynch and a jury.

McDonagh's appointment to represent the Irish government at the Gibraltar inquest was not one awarded lightly. Such was the nature of the role, and the degree of controversy expected to ensue, that only a person of the highest standing within the legal profession could have been considered – something the newspapers should have borne in mind.

The *Sun*, which operated under the umbrella of News Group Newspapers Ltd, published an article on 12 September 1988 under the heading: 'Leftie Spies Pack SAS Gib Inquest'. The article read:

> Members of Leftie groups have been given privileged seats at the inquest into the shooting of three IRA terrorists so they can draw up bulky dossiers for their leaders.
>
> The watchers: 1, National Council of Civil liberties; 2, Amnesty International; 3, Inquest (anti-police); 4, Irish Government; 5, Left-wing Eire MP.

Although not named, McDonagh was incensed by this description. He had received many briefs from the Director of Public Prosecutions and from the State, all of which he had performed in an exemplary fashion. He felt his professional reputation had now been maligned by the newspaper. He claimed that the article insinuated that he was a left-wing spy, that his function at the inquest included spying for left-wing groups, that he attended the inquest for purposes other than the fair and accurate reporting of the evidence and proceedings, that he would not prepare a fair and accurate report for the Irish government and that he sympathised with terrorist causes.

McDonagh was first alerted to the article, and its effect, on the day it was published. He caught a taxi to the inquest court in Gibraltar, and the driver asked if he was the Irish government's representative. When he confirmed this, the driver proceeded to barrack him. Later that day a staff member in a restaurant refused to serve him, while in a second restaurant he was asked if he represented the Irish government before being told that he was not really welcome. The humiliation heaped on McDonagh was not just from Gibraltarians. A friend of McDonagh's had also commented on the article and, when back in Dublin, the barrister had visited a pub on St Stephen's Green and overheard the remark: 'Here comes the spy.'

McDonagh insisted that he had done as professional a job as he could in carrying out the duties and functions assigned to him by the Irish government. He repudiated the allegation that he was a leftie spy.

The *Sun* offered no defence – a strategy it would have cause to regret – other than admitting that the words had been published, but denied that they referred to, or were understood to refer to, McDonagh. Mirror Group Newspapers also denied that the words bore, or were understood to bear, any of the meanings claimed by the plaintiff.

Mr Justice Lynch charged the jury on the second day of the hearing that they were not concerned with the newspaper's circulation of four million copies in Britain. They were to consider only its circulation in Ireland. Although no evidence had been presented as to the Irish circulation, it could not be denied that it existed. The jury had to consider the alleged harm to the plaintiff's reputation in Ireland and any hurt endured. Should the jury find for the plaintiff, the damages should be such as it found fit and proper to compensate McDonagh for the unwarranted disparagement of reputation and the hurt, humiliation and upset incurred by the publication. The jury was instructed that damages had to be fair, just and reasonable to both parties and within the boundaries of common sense.

The jury took just over an hour to return a verdict. It found in favour of McDonagh and answered 'Yes' to all seven questions on the issue paper: whether the words meant, or were understood to mean, that McDonagh was a left-wing spy; attended the inquest for purposes other than the fair and accurate reporting of the evidence and proceedings of the inquest; his report would be biased and influenced by extraneous and irrelevant left-wing views or ideologies; was a sympathiser with terrorist causes; was unsuited for and incapable of performing the functions for which he was appointed by the government; his conduct was such as to cause outrage to army officers charged with combating terrorism; and was biased, lacking in integrity and incapable of exercising sound judgment.

That the jury found for the plaintiff was no great surprise – after all, the *Sun* had offered no evidence in defence. The amount of damages awarded, on the other hand, did shock many in the courtroom. McDonagh was awarded £90,000 in compensation and costs. It was a decision that transformed libel litigation in Ireland and caused many sleepless nights for Irish publishers over the next decade. To the *Sun*, £90,000 may not have been a great deal of money – especially when compared to some libel awards given in England – but to many small, independent Irish publishers, the prospect of paying such a vast sum meant extinction. Accordingly, few could now risk defending a case in the High Court because a losing verdict, award and costs would drive them into bankruptcy. Mr Justice Lynch allowed a stay on the award in the event of an appeal, on condition that one-third was paid within two weeks.

Mirror Group Newspapers felt confident that it would manage to have the award reduced on appeal to the Supreme Court. The article had been defamatory, but had McDonagh really suffered that much? Prior to publication of the article he had been a successful barrister and he was still a successful barrister. Nobody disagreed that he had endured a few off-colour comments as a result, but then a prerequisite for being a barrister is a thick skin. As the award was tax-free, it was equivalent to earnings of £180,000: surely the Supreme Court would rein in this extreme generosity, as it had done in other cases?

The Supreme Court heard the appeal in November the following year. Mirror Group Newspapers argued that the High Court judge had misdirected himself in refusing to discharge the jury on the grounds that the case was unduly exaggerated and inflammatory and therefore a fair trial could not be secured. It was also argued that the trial judge was mistaken in leaving to the jury the question as to whether or not the words bore, or were capable of bearing, the meaning that McDonagh was a sympathiser with terrorist causes. The newspaper countered that McDonagh had not been mentioned by name and the damages were excessive.

The appeal was denied. The Supreme Court upheld the award of £90,000, which would not be topped until the *De Rossa* case, seven years later. The Chief Justice, Mr Justice Finlay, held that while the award was at the top of the appropriate range, it was not so great that the Supreme Court should interfere with it. He stated that in Ireland there were few defamatory accusations that could be considered more serious than to be called a sympathiser of terrorist causes. The seriousness of the accusation was exacerbated by the fact that McDonagh had a key role in the administration of justice. Taken as a whole, the accusations had the effect of levelling a charge of professional misconduct. In the judge's estimation, that was something that could not be tolerated.

Donagh McDonagh continued to practise law successfully and was appointed a judge in 2004.

* * *

No chronicle of Irish libel cases brought by our 'legal eagles' would be complete without mention of the 'éclair affair'. A Belfast journalist who wrote a short comical story, hoping to raise a laugh or two, found out to his cost that the punchline was far from amusing. At first sight the story seemed fairly innocuous, but the consequences illustrate the perils of running a story that is entirely fictitious.

The *Sunday World*, a Dublin-based newspaper, published an article about two leading Northern Ireland barristers in its 'Who?' gossip column of 13 September 1987. It was meant as a humorous piece, a sort of 'Lawyers Behaving Badly' snippet of tittle-tattle. Robert McCartney QC and Desmond Boal QC were reported to have had words over who had first seen the remaining chocolate éclairs in a bakery shop in Holywood, Co. Down. The bun story had an extra layer of tempting icing in that both men had been involved in opposing unionist political parties: Boal had been a Democratic Unionist Party MP; McCartney was an Ulster Unionist Party stalwart. As it happened, the *Sunday World* had been misinformed; the alleged incident had never occurred.

Despite the publication of an apology two weeks later, the newspaper had to defend its action a year later, on 13 October 1988, in a Belfast High Court. Mr Justice Carswell presided over the six-day hearing in front of a jury. Such was the interest in the action that the public benches were filled with lawyers who had no direct involvement in the case. McCartney and Boal sat next to each other at the front of the court.

John Gillen QC, acting for McCartney, began his opening address to the jury by handing out copies of the defamatory article. He told the jury that the *Sunday World* had admitted there was no truth to the story, which had portrayed the two plaintiffs as a couple of petulant, ill-judged clowns, prepared to disgrace themselves in public over something as trivial as an éclair. Gillen condemned the article as being 'nothing short of a complete and utter tissue of lies from beginning to end'.

McCartney was the youngest member of a family of eight children born on the Shankill Road in Belfast. He had come from a humble background and certainly wasn't born 'with a silver spoon in his mouth'. He had been the only one of the family who had attended university and had gone on to reach a level of excellence in his profession.

McCartney had been deeply affected by the story because the tone of the article intended to show him as a ridiculous and contemptible clown: 'When you have put so much effort, as I have, into achieving a position as a respected, I hope, and reputable QC, then to be portrayed in a totally pernicious and lying article as some form of contemptible, senseless clown who would make an exhibition of himself in a bakery shop made me very distressed and very angry.' McCartney stated that he had spent twenty years pursuing excellence in his career and had a sense of duty for politics: 'I live in a home with bullet-proof windows; I examine my car underneath every day and I can't go everywhere I would like because it's believed I would be assassinated. That's what being a politician means.' The article was likened to a cancer eating into McCartney's career: it would grow and grow and could not be excised.

McCartney was also scathing about the newspaper's printed retraction, published a fortnight later. To his mind, it was a flippant and insincere article representing an apology which had done more harm than good: 'To have your professional career and whatever you offer as a politician sneered at in a lying, untruthful article in a gutter journal, is very wounding indeed.'

Gillen told the jury that when it came to awarding damages, the members should bear in mind that McCartney's high reputation was dependent on his judgment and the same applied to his politics: 'This newspaper must be shown that it can't behave in this way. As a jury you can say that it must pay dearly. It was mean and nasty journalism in order to boost circulation because the *Sunday World* accepts that there was not a word of truth in this article.'

Alan Commerton QC, counsel for the *Sunday World*, cross-examined McCartney. He asked the co-plaintiff if he ever 'had words' with people, or had wagged his fingers at them, or spoken in a loud voice. McCartney said he felt sure he had on occasion. He provoked some laughter when he admitted having had 'hot words' with political rivals like Rev. Ian Paisley, as well as colleagues in court.

In explaining why he had brought the action, McCartney said, 'I was seeking to ensure that the perpertrators of the lying article were brought to court and exposed.'

Desmond Boal QC, Northern Ireland's leading criminal lawyer, took the witness-box on the second day of the hearing to give his evidence. He said that the article was 'garbage'. It was a classic example of holding a man up to ridicule, a man whose very stock in trade depended on being regarded as a person having sound judgment. He described how, the morning after the article was published, he had been the object of many jocular remarks about buns and éclairs: 'I was hugely embarrassed to see myself canvassed as an ass. I got the impression from those around me that they were confident there was something in it.' If his colleagues could think that of him, he pointed out, what were others going to think? They were going to believe that it was true.

Ivan Martin, a freelance journalist and host of a breakfast show on Downtown radio, was the author of the article. He was asked if he regretted writing the story: 'If I had known it was untrue, I would never have submitted it in the first place and now I regret it as I do not like being associated with anything that is untrue.'

'Did you make it up?'

'Absolutely not.'

Martin told the court how the *Sunday World* had twice asked him to check that the facts supplied by his source were correct. He had done so and received assurance that the information was true.

Jim Campbell, Northern editor of the *Sunday World*, insisted that it was not the newspaper's policy to publish lies. Its policy was to tell the truth. On the subsequent printed apology, Campbell said: 'We said clearly we had got it wrong and I don't think that it was half-hearted.'

He agreed that the newspaper had been poking fun at Boal and McCartney, but argued that it had done so in the nicest possible way. Being men of great stature, Campbell felt a humorous little item in a gossip column would not cause the two lawyers any harm. It was clear that he thought the entire affair was of the 'storm in a teacup' variety.

Regrettably for Campbell, no attempt had been made to contact the two lawyers to check the facts of the story. Although in truth, it would not have been normal practice to do so with such a minor story – it was just a matter of a few cream buns, after all.

In his final address, Commerton advised the jury not to be overawed by the case, warning that high-powered people could not come into court showing great emotion in order to bully the jury into awarding substantial damages.

Nonetheless, it soon became apparent that the jury had few sympathies with the newspaper and its failure to check facts. After two hours' deliberation, an award of £50,000 was made to each plaintiff – an amount sure to offer some crumbs of comfort to the two maligned legal men. Costs were also awarded. Informed sources estimated a bill of £60,000 in legal fees.

The newspaper lodged an appeal, but on 30 June 1989 counsel for the *Sunday World* told the Lord Chief Justice in the Court of Appeal that the appeal had been abandoned. The éclair affair was wrapped up.

02 | A REVERSAL OF FORTUNE:
TURKINGTON & ORS v THE TIMES & ORS [1996]

Few events during the Troubles triggered as great an avalanche of emotive newspaper articles as the prosecution and eventual successful appeal of British paratrooper Lee Clegg. The case fiercely divided opinion, both in Ireland and Britain, with few people maintaining an even-minded approach. It was therefore inevitable that of the million words written about the case, some would be defamatory.

The event that led to Clegg's arrest and prosecution occurred in September 1990. A stolen Vauxhall Astra driven by 'joyriders' sped through a British Army checkpoint on the Glen Road in Belfast. Some of the soldiers opened fire on the vehicle, with the result that two of the occupants were killed: seventeen-year-old Martin Peake and eighteen-year-old Karen Reilly.

Paratrooper Lee Clegg, a young man of twenty-four, was convicted by a Belfast court of murdering Reilly and wounding Peake. He was jailed for life and also handed a concurrent term of four years. In the wake of this decision, his supporters, who included several British MPS among their number, fought a vigorous campaign for an appeal. Clegg was transferred from a prison in Northern Ireland to Wakefield prison in Yorkshire, close to his mother's home. His release on licence in June 1995, approved by Secretary of State Sir Patrick Mayhew, provoked some of the worst riots ever seen on the streets of Northern Ireland.

Clegg's first appeal against the two convictions failed: both the Appeal Court and the House of Lords rejected his challenge. After his release on licence, Clegg mounted a second appeal on the grounds of fresh ballistic evidence. The Court of Appeal granted him a re-trial in 1999, which acquitted the paratrooper of murdering Reilly, but found him guilty of wounding Peake. This conviction was appealed successfully in November 1999. Lord Chief Justice Sir Robert Carswell stated that the accuracy and reliability of a RUC constable's recollection of events had been shown to be suspect.

Nationalists were appalled at Clegg's exoneration. Sinn Féin president, Gerry Adams, described the verdict as 'the final insult' to the families of the victims and to the nationalist community.

Almost as a side-show to the Clegg legal manoeuvres was a concurrent series of libel actions brought by a firm of Belfast solicitors. Yet the significance of this litigation cannot be over-emphasised because it was pivotal in defining press freedom in the UK. Ironically, the final result owed much to the House of Lords judgment handed down in the Albert Reynolds libel action.

On 23 January 1995, after the House of Lords had upheld his conviction, Lee Clegg's supporters held a press conference at the Yorkshire home of Lord St Oswald to announce the launch of a campaign to free the paratrooper. It was the first of many such press conferences of a campaign led by MPS and former officers of the Parachute regiment. *The Times* reported on the press conference and published a front-page article on 25 January, which was headlined: 'MPS demand release of jailed Para'. The report, written by *The Times*'s Northern correspondent, Paul Wilkinson, included comments critical of the Belfast firm of solicitors, McCartan, Turkington and Breen, which had acted for Private Lee Clegg. Most of the unfavourable comments made in the article related to the firm's handling of the defence at trial and appeal.

The legal firm considered the comments to be defamatory and initiated a libel action. *The Times* pleaded a defence of qualified privilege under the Defamation Act (Northern Ireland) 1955, asserting that the press conference was a public meeting and its article 'was a fair and accurate report of the meeting'.

The case reached Belfast High Court in October 1996, but the newspaper's case was dealt a severe blow when Mr Justice Girvan was asked by the plaintiffs to make a ruling on a point of law. Judge Girvan held that the mere presence of people who were not journalists did not make the press conference a public one. He further held that the newspaper article drew on matters (a press statement) that occurred after the formal closure of the meeting, thus could not be considered a report on the proceedings of a public meeting. The judge explained his reasoning thus:

> What makes a meeting a public meeting as opposed to a private or non-public meeting is the absence of any particular nexus between those organising the meeting and those taking part. Where a person or group organises a meeting at which persons are invited not as members of the public but because some other relationship between the invitor or the invitee the meeting does not arise from the fact that the invitees are members of the public.

This left the newspaper without a defence, which meant John Thompson QC, for the newspaper, had no option but to apologise on behalf of his client. The only task the jury then had to decide was the amount of damages. The firm of solicitors was awarded £145,000.

Human rights campaigners were appalled by this extravagant sum. A spokesman for the Derry-based Pat Finucane Centre called for a fundamental review of a system that ensured that 'injurious words count for so much more than the loss of a human being.' He went on to say:

> There are obvious discrepancies in the justice system where solicitors for a convicted murderer received nearly half-a-million pounds in libel claims against various newspapers, while the family of the murder victim Karen Reilly is paid a

paltry sum in compensation for the death of their daughter. The family of Karen Reilly has suffered enough. First they lose a daughter, learn that a celebratory mock-up of the car is hung on the wall of the regimental gym, watch in disbelief as Clegg is released, and now discover that her death is worth at least 25 times less in monetary terms than defamatory words about the solicitors who defended the murderer.

The newspaper appealed the decision, but in October 1998 the Court of Appeal Northern Ireland dismissed the appeal, although it did reduce the damages award to £75,000. However, Lord Chief Justice Carswell ruled in favour of a second point brought by the newspaper's counsel. The Appeal Court judges agreed that a passage in the contentious article that had been taken from a press release amounted to a 'report' of the proceedings of the press conference.

Encouraged by this reversal on a point of law, the newspaper decided to take its appeal to the House of Lords. Anthony Whitaker, legal consultant to *The Times*, explained why:

> This case is of vital importance not just to *The Times* and to the press, but to the whole of the media and the public at large. It raises a point of law of importance to the operations of the media – a point which has been unclear and undecided for decades and we hope it will be decided in favour of free speech.

The House of Lords appeal judges heard the crucial test appeal on 5 October 2000 – coincidentally, the same day the Human Rights Act came into force in full. This appeal would therefore be the first challenge to come before the House of Lords under the Human Rights Act 1998. Under Article 10 of the new Act, *The Times* could argue that the media should be protected by 'qualified privilege' when reporting material arising from press conferences.

Lord Lester of Herne Hill QC was retained by Theodore Goddard, the solicitors acting for *The Times*. Lavery QC would act for the Belfast solicitors. In the previous year, Lord Lester had acted for *The Sunday Times* in the House of Lords appeal in the

Albert Reynolds action. In that appeal, Lord Lester had also invoked Article 10 of the Human Rights Act, albeit with only partial success for the appellants.

In the McCartan, Turkington, Breen appeal, Lord Bingham of Cornhill headed the panel of five lords who heard the case, which also comprised Lord Steyn, Lord Hoffman, Lord Cooke of Thorndon and Lord Millett.

Lord Lester opened for the newspaper by criticising the construction of section 7, paragraph 9 of the 1955 Act, which reads: 'a fair and accurate report of the proceedings at any public meeting held in the United Kingdom, that is to say, a meeting bona fide and lawfully held for a lawful purpose and for the furtherance or discussion of any matter of public concern, whether the admission to the meeting is general or restricted.'

Counsel claimed that as interpreted by the High Court judge and Appeal Court, these words were narrow, technical and liable to infringe the freedom of expression which should be enjoyed by the press. He suggested that a broader, more realistic and contemporary understanding was required, one that was in line with common and statue law, the European Convention and the Human Rights Act 1998. While the right to freedom of expression could never be absolute, Lord Lester argued, the protection afforded by paragraph 9 went too far.

Lavery QC, for the solicitors, argued that the High Court and the Appeal Court had interpreted paragraph 9 correctly and that the European Convention and the Human Rights Act had no bearing on it. Indeed, far from curtailing free speech, paragraph 9 was extending that right. Counsel reminded the Law Lords that while both the Faulks Committee in 1975 and the Irish Law Reform Commission in 1991 had recommended the extension of statutory qualified privilege to cover press conferences, neither recommendation had been given legislative effect. It was not for the courts to grant a privilege that Parliament had declined to grant, despite an opportunity to do so in the Defamation Act 1996.

In finding for the newspaper, Lord Bingham, Lord Steyn and Lord Cooke referred to the ruling in *Reynolds v The Sunday Times* [1999]. Although it had come too late for the High Court and

Appeal Court hearings, that ruling's interpretation of qualified privilege had to be taken into consideration now, especially as it had been buttressed by the Human Rights Act and the European Convention. The Law Lords were unanimous in finding for the newspaper and quashing the High Court and Appeal Court judgments. Lord Bingham held that press freedom was of cardinal importance and the restriction of that freedom had to be proportionate and no more than was necessary to promote the legitimate aim of the restriction. It was a sentiment that many court observers had never expected to hear from the mouth of a Law Lord. Lord Bingham added that a modern, developed society required free, active, professional and inquiring media if the majority were to participate in public life.

The partners in the Belfast firm had seen their £145,000 damages slashed to £75,000, before finally being reduced to zero. The reversal of fortune in the House of Lords took the sheen from an estimated £500,000 they had been awarded in other actions against the *Daily Telegraph*, *Daily Express* and *Sunday Express*.

It was not all bad news, however, as just a few months later the *Daily Telegraph*'s application for an extension of time to appeal was rejected. The newspaper had had damages of £130,000 awarded against it in an action brought by the firm of solicitors in May 1996. Following *The Times*'s House of Lords decision, the *Daily Telegraph* had thought the courts might look favourably on its submission. The application was heard in the Belfast Appeal Court and the reserved judgment was handed down on 5 April 2001. Lord Justice Campbell ruled that when *The Times* had appealed in 1996, the *Daily Telegraph* could have asked for an extension of time, but instead had chosen to do nothing and had remained silent. It would be unjust to McCartan, Turkington and Breen to allow the paper to re-open the proceedings now, five years after the award had been made. In other words, the newspaper had missed the boat. It was bad news for the *Daily Telegraph* – yet another black eye suffered at the hands of McCartan, Turkington and Breen.

In November 1998, the newspaper lost a second libel action brought by the firm of solicitors. In this instance the Belfast firm was acting for two Scots Guardsmen who were convicted of murdering Peter McBride, an eighteen-year-old youth from the New Lodge area of Belfast. *The Daily Telegraph* published a letter on 19 August 1997 from Lt. General Sir David Scott-Barrett in support of a campaign to free the two Guardsmen. The contentious passage read: 'I have grave reservations over the absence of crucial military evidence at the trial. While I intend to pursue these omissions, the investigation must not be allowed to delay the release of the two soldiers, compounding the injustice.'

The letter did not mention the name of the solicitors' firm nor any of the partners, but a libel action was duly initiated by the firm, seeking aggravated damages. The firm claimed that *The Daily Telegraph* had acted out of malice and a desire to 'get its own back' after the earlier libel award. It was also claimed that there had been 'significant and sinister alterations' to the letter prior to publication.

The Daily Telegraph's letters editor, David Twiston Davies, denied that he had doctored the letter as part of a vendetta by the newspaper. He said that there had never been any intention to defame the solicitors and the publication had been a 'horrible coincidence'. He insisted that he had learned the identity of the solicitors in question only at a later date.

In his reserved judgment of 13 November 1998, Mr Justice Sheil said that he did not accept that publication of the letter had been part of a vendetta against the firm, but was satisfied that the six partners had been defamed. He also castigated the newspaper's solicitors for an allegation of 'money-grabbing' made in a letter to the firm. Consequently, an award of £65,000 was made, although the claim for aggravated damages was rejected.

03 NOT A PENNY MORE:

ALBERT REYNOLDS v THE SUNDAY TIMES & ORS [1996]

It is ironic that while the antiquated Irish Defamation Act 1961 ended the twentieth century unscathed by any serious political effort at amendment, it was an Irishman's libel action in the Old Bailey in London that led to a major overhaul of its British counterpart. That the Irishman involved was former Taoiseach Albert Reynolds only added to the irony.

On 20 November 1994, *The Sunday Times* published a front-page article entitled: 'Goodbye Gombeen Man. Why a Fib Too Far Proved Fatal for Ireland's Peacemaker and Mr Fixit'. A gombeen man is an usurer, i.e. someone who profits excessively at the expense of those who can afford it least. The derogatory term had been widely used during the Irish Famine to describe a speculator in corn prices. As the headline suggested, it was a hard-hitting story. Perhaps not unsurprisingly, it was published in the British edition of the paper only, not in the Irish edition. Reynolds's eldest daughter, Miriam Fogarty, was living in Scotland at the time and read the article. She immediately telephoned her father to draw his attention to the piece, which was written by the newspaper's Irish editor, Alan Ruddock:

In another age Albert Reynolds could have been the classic *gombeen* man of Irish law – the real fixer with a finger in every pie. His slow fall last week, his fingernails scratching down the potential cliff-face, has been welcomed with a whoop of delight by many Irish people who want to see their country dragged out of the past. The full story of this eclipse, however, has sullied Ireland's reputation, damaged its Church, destroyed its peacemaking and provided its unionist neighbours with a fistful of new reasons to avoid the contamination by the South.

The article concerned that week's resignations of Taoiseach Albert Reynolds and the recently appointed president of the High Court, Harry Whelehan, which signalled the disintegration of the Fianna Fáil and Labour coalition, the government that had been in power since February 1992. It had been an extraordinary week in Irish politics, brought live to the nation by RTÉ broadcasts. The newspaper alleged that Reynolds's fall was directly attributable to his 'fibs'.

A less aggressive article, ascribed to journalist Vincent Browne, was published in the Irish edition of the newspaper, in which Reynolds was portrayed as a victim of circumstance. The headline in that article was: 'House of Cards'. A side-bar asked: 'What do you call a northsider without an anorak? Taoiseach.'

That the coalition had been proceeding fitfully for some time was beyond argument. The contrasting styles of Reynolds and Tánaiste Dick Spring were always going to make them uneasy partners. The Beef Tribunal had seen them at loggerheads, as had the 'money for passports' débâcle and the granting of a second tax amnesty just a few years after the first. Spring had been described as morally bankrupt for allowing Reynolds to do much as he pleased, but, to be fair, Reynolds often seemed to have luck on his side as he took outrageous gambles time after time and came away a winner. No doubt Reynolds's supporters would attribute his survival against all the odds to his astute political acumen.

The final rift came from an unexpected source – what should have been a storm in a teacup was what brought an end to Reynolds's era as Taoiseach. In a manner typical of political scandals, it was not the facts that did the harm, it was how the facts emerged into the public arena.

Fr Brendan Smyth, by this time in jail in Northern Ireland, had committed sexual abuse against children over a twenty-four-year period between 1964 and 1988. The RUC had earlier requested his extradition, but the then Attorney General, Harry Whelehan, took seven months to reach a decision on the matter. Whelehan would later blame the delay on the complexities of the case, yet the extradition to England of another sex offender, former cleric John Duggan, had been accomplished without the need for any lengthy ponderings.

Reynolds upset his coalition partner once again when he announced his intention to appoint Harry Whelehan as president of the High Court – the second most senior position in the Irish judicial system. It was an unusual move by any standard, as most previous presidents had first served as High Court judges. Nonetheless, Reynolds forged ahead, despite heavy opposition from Dick Spring, and defended the appointment in the Dáil. Reynolds would have known there was a chance that Whelehan would have to resign from the post after just a few days, but what he had not foreseen was that he himself would have to go first.

The Sunday Times claimed that Reynolds had essentially been the author of his own downfall. It was well known that he was a risk-taker and had misled the Dáil on 15 November 1994 regarding the Duggan extradition, thereby denying his coalition partners and the opposition the opportunity to examine Whelehan's explanations for the delay in the Fr Brendan Smyth case. The newspaper also claimed that Reynolds had misled the coalition Cabinet ministers by holding back information between 14 November and 16 November, and that he had been economical with the truth over the timing of when information concerning the Duggan extradition had first come to his attention.

Reynolds was no stranger to the libel court. Indeed, his earlier forays had been so successful that a house he had bought had been christened 'Litigation Lodge' by backbench wags in the Dáil. He had accepted £60,000 in an out-of-court settlement with *The Sunday Times*, £50,000 in total in two actions against *The Irish Times* and £10,000 from the publishers of *The Guinness Book of Political Blunders*. As the action against *The Sunday Times* was being heard, a further £20,000 would be paid into the Reynolds's coffers by Radio Tara, a Co. Meath radio station. It was quite a tally by any measure.

The Dáil was keen to learn the truth about how much Reynolds had known, and when he had known it. A Select Committee of the Houses of the Oireachtas was set up to look into the Whelehan appointment and it published its report in March 1995. At the release of the report, the committee chairman, Mr Justice Liam Hamilton, said that Reynolds was completely vindicated and had acted honourably at all times. Shortly after that, Reynolds issued a writ for libel in England. The case would come to court in October 1996, before Mr Justice French, the judge who had presided over the libel case brought by cricketers Ian Botham and Alan Lamb against Imran Khan earlier that year.

The fact that Reynolds opted to sue in an English court, rather than in the plaintiff-friendly Irish courts, came as a surprise to many. Of course, it was not that British courts could be described as plaintiff-unfriendly: Richard Branson had been awarded £500,000 against British Airways; Elton John had won £350,000 from the *Sunday Mirror*; and politicians Rupert Allason and George Galloway had been awarded £230,000 and £150,000, respectively, from MGN, the parent group of the *Mirror*. The much-publicised damages awards had led to London being described as 'Sue City' by successful libel litigants. The record Irish libel award at that time was £90,000, and though it was upheld by the Supreme Court in 1993, it was with the caveat that it was at the top of the permissible range.

In London and in Dublin, the Reynolds hearing was keenly anticipated. It was quite a line-up: the 'Longford Slasher', as some deputies called him, taking on the mighty Murdoch Corporation. The last Irish leader to defend his reputation against Times Newspapers was Charles Stuart Parnell in the nineteenth century. It would be an entertaining scrap, that much was sure.

Reynolds was in court when the hearing opened, accompanied by his wife, Kathleen, and their eldest daughter, Miriam. His chief counsel, Lord Williams of Mostyn QC, made it clear that an 'absolute and base minimum' of between £45,000 and £125,000 in damages would be sought. The one thing his client and *The Sunday Times* agreed on was that the newspaper had called Albert Reynolds a liar. Lord Williams went on to describe how the article had 'damaged [Reynolds's] reputation, attacked his good name, upset the peace and tranquillity of his mind and wounded his heart'.

The jury members were having trouble getting their heads around the Irish names and titles. Williams patiently explained the meanings of Taoiseach (prime minister), Tánaiste (deputy prime minister) and Dáil (parliament). Fianna Fáil and Fine Gael also took some time for the jury to fully grasp. During the hearing, even anglicised names were occasionally confused, the plaintiff being addressed at Fitzreynolds and Dick Spring being referred to as Stone.

Once the Gaelic terms had been explained, Williams continued to outline Reynolds's case for the court. It boiled down to one significant point of timing: the newly appointed Attorney General, Eoghan Fitzsimons, had discovered that Harry Whelehan had dealt with the Duggan extradition personally, therefore it would have been wrong for Reynolds to defend in the Dáil his appointment of Whelehan on the basis that the delayed extradition of Smyth had been caused by lack of precedent. The burning question was at what time *exactly* did Reynolds receive that information from Fitzsimons?

Reynolds claimed that he had not received the information until after he had left the Dáil chamber and had had something to eat on the evening of 15 November. 'Not a man, woman or donkey from *The Sunday Times* asked him that,' Williams explained. Reynolds had asked *The Sunday Times* for an apology for the article, but the newspaper had refused. He had brought the case to force the newspaper to say sorry and to ask for damages from the jury.

John Major was British Chancellor of the Exchequer when Reynolds became Minister for Finance in 1988. The two men had hit it off, to the extent that when newly elected American president Bill Clinton had offered to send a peace envoy to Ireland, Reynolds had not felt it necessary. Soon after this offer, both men signed the Downing Street Declaration, which helped lay the foundation for peace.

Reynolds's downfall began with his attempted elevation of Harry Whelehan, a controversial choice. The former incumbent, Mr Justice Liam Hamilton, was moving to his new role as Chief Justice. Dick Spring, Labour Party leader and Tánaiste, and a man described earlier by counsel as the 'Mr Clean of Irish politics', had initially objected to Whelehan's appointment. After some intense political horse-trading, including a secret midnight meeting between Reynolds and Spring at Baldonnel airport, an agreement of sorts was hammered out to resolve the matter. Spring felt that Whelehan had imposed unnecessary restrictions during the Beef Tribunal, therefore he had been championing Mr Justice Donal Barrington for Chief Justice and Ms Justice Susan Denham for High Court President. However, the undisclosed Baldonnel agreement held until revelations over the Smyth extradition became public knowledge after the broadcast of an UTV documentary and related newspaper articles.

Reynolds asked Whelehan to account for the seven-month delay on deciding the Smyth extradition request, going so far as to have him answer questions on the matter at a Cabinet meeting held on 11 November. The Cabinet was told that Whelehan had not seen the extradition file, had not dealt with it and that the file had been handled by another senior figure in the Attorney General's office, Matt Russell. When Whelehan's appointment was moved by Máire Geoghegan-Quinn, Spring and his Labour ministers stood up and silently left the room.

Despite Labour's opposition, Reynolds later telephoned Spring and announced that the appointment would be approved by the president, Mary Robinson, at 5.30 p.m. that evening at Áras an Uachtaráin. At no time during the phone call did Spring confirm that the coalition was over, Reynolds said, although he did refer to the situation as a grave one.

The following Monday, Reynolds held four meetings with the recently appointed Attorney General, Eoghan Fitzsimons. It was during the second of these meetings that Reynolds learned for the first time of a second extradition case, that of John Duggan. The issue was further clouded by a serious disagreement that had arisen between the new Attorney General and Matt Russell. Reynolds suggested that Whelehan's swearing in should be delayed for a few days, but was informed at the final meeting that day with Fitzsimmons that Whelehan had refused to agree to this.

This plea to Whelehan was the fulcrum point of the whole tangled affair. Reynolds would have to convince a jury that he had not appreciated the significance of the Duggan case, despite the fact that the revelation troubled him enough to lead him to ask Whelehan to hold fire. The whole complex mess seemed like a storyline from the BBC comedy *Yes, Minister*.

After his meetings with Fitzsimons, Reynolds had continued to make preparations for the Dáil debate the following day. He had no intention of misleading the chamber; indeed, he had post-poned other duties to allow for a prolonged debate. Two drafts of a speech were given to the Attorney General in the normal way so that he could approve them. The speech was intended to be conciliatory in tone, to ensure that the coalition was preserved. The drafts were duly returned with some comments, but with no reference to the Duggan case.

The next morning, Whelehan was sworn in as president of the High Court. Reynolds was due to give his speech shortly after the Dáil sat at around 2.30 p.m. After lunch, he left his office for the chamber. It was soon after this that Fitzsimons arrived in the Taoiseach's office with his definitive summary of the significance of the Duggan case. It was dynamite. The documents were copied and given to the Taoiseach's private secretary, Declan Ingoldsby, to be relayed to Reynolds. Incredibly, the documents passed through several hands until they reached a ministerial colleague sitting next to Reynolds in the Dáil chamber. The minister apparently did not pass the documents to his party leader. The minister in question was Bertie Ahern, who would be Reynolds's successor.

Reynolds described how he had been appalled when he discovered the contents of the documents, later that evening. The following morning, he asked for Fitzsimons's help in drafting another speech for the Dáil, in which he would correct what had been said the day before. Dick Spring also had some additions he wanted included in the speech if the coalition was to be saved. Reynolds would have to eat platefuls of humble pie to remain as Taoiseach. By the time he delivered that speech, he already knew his government was doomed. Spring had received fresh information, which suggested that Reynolds knew about the Duggan case before the debate and that there was no satisfactory reason for him not informing the Dáil. Later that day, Reynolds resigned as Taoiseach after losing a vote of confidence.

If *The Sunday Times* lost the case against Reynolds, it could face enormous damages. This was no minor celebrity it had allegedly defamed. Albert Reynolds's political contribution to Ireland was immense, as described by the man himself. Not only had he helped to shape a framework for peace, his government had brought down the level of unemployment and drastically improved the economy, which at the time of the hearing was enjoying a growth rate three times the EU average. Surely, as one journalist pundit put it, canonisation for Reynolds could not be far away.

During the trial, Reynolds addressed the jury with an easy, relaxed manner gained from years on the campaign trail. At one point he held up the two editions of *The Sunday Times*, with their different stories. He pulled faces and waved his hands around to emphasise the wrong that had been done to him. He told the court how his lecture tours across Britain constantly brought back the pain and indignity he had suffered. Did his audiences, he wondered, see him as the 'gombeen man'?

James Price QC, opening for the defence, was quick to suggest a limit of £3,000 should the newspaper lose. *The Sunday Times* and other defendants based their defence on the twin arguments of justification and privilege, and that the article was true and based on events that had occurred in the Dáil. Price was known to have a very sharp mind and was equally razor-like in his cross-examinations; Reynolds would be in for a rough ride.

Price suggested that Reynolds had executed a U-turn on the suitability of Whelehan as president of the High Court.

'I most certainly did not involve myself in any U-turn,' Reynolds replied.

To jog his memory, Price read out extracts of Reynolds's speech to the Dáil on Wednesday, 16 November, saying that if he had known the previous Friday what he then knew, Whelehan would not have been appointed. Reynolds told the court that the Cabinet had questioned Whelehan closely on the Friday and that his ministerial colleagues had accepted Whelehan's good faith.

Price zoomed in on this apparent Cabinet harmony. Had Spring not written to the then Taoiseach to express his misgivings over the extradition explanation offered by Whelehan? Had this not led to Spring and his Labour ministers walking out of the Cabinet meeting?

Reynolds claimed that he thought Spring was simply absenting himself and his Labour colleagues from the decision to appoint Whelehan. He did not fully appreciate at the time that Spring was walking out of the coalition. This misapprehension was later reinforced by Spring's phone call, during which he did not mention a split. It was on the Sunday evening, after a press conference called by Dick Spring, that the full implications of the walk-out had finally struck Reynolds.

James Price addressed the court in a languid, Eton-educated voice, which at times he used to great effect to pour scorn on the plaintiff's answers. Although he would mock Reynolds's long-winded replies, he, too, had a propensity for verbosity.

Under further cross-examination, the reason for the newly appointed Attorney General's delay in informing Reynolds about the Duggan case was drawn out. Apparently the Attorney General had at first thought there was a case that provided a precedent, but could not recall the name of that case. The Minister for Justice, Máire Geoghegan-Quinn, had supplied the name. However, a serious altercation had arisen between the Attorney General and a senior member of his department over the exact details of the Duggan case. This was why the Attorney General was asked to look into the matter and report back to Reynolds.

Fitzsimons, according to Reynolds, had an 'on the one hand and on the other hand view' about citing the Duggan case as a precedent. What was required was a definite written view, which was what Reynolds requested. When he addressed the Dáil on

Tuesday, 15 November, his aim had been to dispel rumour and innuendo. He denied that he had deliberately misled the Dáil to save his job and his administration. He insisted that he would have thrown Whelehan to the wolves if he had seriously believed the coalition was going to crash. He told the Dáil the full facts as he knew them at the time. 'I don't tell lies,' Reynolds stated firmly.

Reynolds also denied that he had anticipated an unsatisfactory report from the Attorney General. He had no way of knowing what Fitzsimons would find. The plaintiff scored a point against the defence when he pointed out that Price's client had printed two opposing stories: 'Your own people, *The Sunday Times*, in the Irish edition, say quite the opposite. That is where the truth lies.'

The cross-examination then moved on to what actions Reynolds had taken when he did finally read the report from the Attorney General. Reynolds stated that he had asked the then Minister for Social Affairs, Dr Michael Woods, to tell the Attorney General to visit Whelehan at his home and instruct him to resign.

Price asked Reynolds to examine Dr Woods's contemporaneous notes on this task, which the minister had been given by the plaintiff. The defence QC pointed out that under a quirk of English law, the jury would not be able to see a copy of the notes and other documents unless the plaintiff agreed. Counsel for the plaintiff requested an immediate adjournment so that legal argument could take place in the absence of the jury. After ten minutes the jury was called back and Price posed several questions relating to Woods's notes, but the jury was forbidden from viewing a copy.

Reynolds refused to concede that Harry Whelehan was the only person who could have saved the government; he pointed out that Spring also had that ability. The former Taoiseach claimed to have no memory of promising Whelehan the first judge's position that became available if he resigned as president of the High Court.

'Are you saying that the man is a liar?' Price asked, referring to Woods's notes.

'I don't call Michael Woods a liar. I want to hear the evidence,' Reynolds replied. 'I don't have any recollection. If somebody there that night heard me say that, then I would have to accept it, yes.'

Price pointed out that it was beyond the court's authority to subpoena witnesses from Ireland. Reynolds brought smiles to the faces of the journalists present when he quickly replied that he had to operate under the same restraints. The jury would have been disappointed to hear this, no doubt, hoping that the testimony of one or other of the central figures would have made its job easier.

Price put it to Reynolds that if the notes had been correct, then the offer would have been an astonishing action to ask a man to resign because he had misled the government and then appoint him to the next judgeship that came along. Reynolds argued that it was hypothetical and he wanted the whole truth to come out, again making reference to the printing of opposing versions of the events.

Reynolds was questioned further over his motive in asking for Whelehan's resignation. Price hypothesised that it was part of a political plot to save Reynolds's government, that the answers Whelehan had given the Cabinet were technically correct but that the Labour Party had to be appeased. Reynolds shook his head repeatedly as Price continued on the same premise, and strenuously denied this: 'I will never accept that theory, even if you keep at it until the cows come home, as they say in Ireland.'

Price then pointed out that it had since been made clear in the Dáil that Whelehan had been right and that the Smyth case had indeed been the first to be considered under the 1987 Extradition Act. It also followed that if Eoghan Fitzsimons had cited the Duggan case, he would have been forced to resign if his report had reached Reynolds in the Dáil and been quoted by the Taoiseach. Price posited that the Duggan case had been a red herring all along.

'That's the tragedy of what happened,' Reynolds agreed.

The jury then heard of a speech made by Reynolds to the Dáil on 6 December 1994. This was testimony that had been awaited keenly by the Irish journalists in the court, as they knew it might help to clarify the role the speech had played in Spring's refusal to enter a coalition government with Bertie Ahern. This refusal had led to the unique circumstance of a change of government without a general election. Ahern had been just twenty-four hours away from becoming Taoiseach, only to see the prize cruelly snatched from him at the last moment. Spring went on to form a coalition government with John Bruton and his Fine Gael party.

The preparation of the speech was of most interest to the defence counsel. It emerged that Spring had asked the new leader of Fianna Fáil, Bertie Ahern, for clarification from Fitzsimons of events surrounding the collapse of the coalition. A draft of the Attorney General's recollections was faxed to Reynolds in Budapest. Reynolds made some alterations before relaying it on to Ahern. However, Price alleged that this was actually the second draft and that Reynolds had requested Fitzsimons to shred the first draft.

Reynolds could not be certain that the fax he had received had been from the Attorney General, but he did claim that the one he had read previously had been full of inaccuracies. Price asked him if the court was to believe that Fitzsimons was an idiot and a clown. Reynolds replied that he resented such a description being made by senior counsel, adding that Fitzsimons presumably had a faulty recollection. The gusto that had characterised many of Reynolds's earlier replies seemed to dissipate a little as Price pressed on.

The senior counsel made little effort to hide his exasperation at Reynolds's failure to accept his interpretation of events.

'You're an intelligent man,' Price was driven to point out. 'Please answer the question.'

'That's not what *The Sunday Times* called me. They called me a gombeen man. That's not an intelligent man,' Reynolds replied defensively.

The plaintiff's confident manner faded still further as Price explored the deletions Reynolds had made in the draft of his speech, deletions which concerned Whelehan's good character. Reynolds first explained this by claiming that Fianna Fáil advisor Martin Mansergh may have had something to do with the changes. Price seemed to know differently and managed to force Reynolds to retract that name and replace it with that of Noel Dempsey.

At this point the judge interrupted to ask Reynolds's daughter, Miriam Fogarty, not to keep bobbing her head. It could be construed as coaching of the witness, Mr Justice French explained.

Price continued to bait Reynolds into admitting that Spring had withdrawn from government because the Taoiseach had misled him and the Dáil. Spring had accused Reynolds of lying and *The Sunday Times* was doing no more than reporting that accusation.

Reynolds was having none of it, however. He referred defence counsel to the text of Spring's speech on 16 November, arguing that at no time had Spring called him a liar. Price was far from finished with the point. He returned to it time and again. Reynolds retreated into verbose and irrelevant answers, sorely trying Price's patience. Several times, counsel for the defence tried in vain to have Reynolds admit that Spring was an honourable man. It was a tense battle of wits, which kept everyone in court enthralled.

Unfortunately for the non-combatants, the verbal jousting was brought to a premature end over the question of sleaze.

'Is it true to state that a tribunal was sitting at Dublin Castle investigating sleaze allegations against Mr Haughey, you and the Fianna Fáil party?' Price said to Reynolds. The judge ruled the question inadmissible on the grounds that it contained comment. Price apologised and withdrew the question. He then asked if it was true that a tribunal had been sitting at Dublin Castle until July 1994.

Reynolds corrected counsel by saying that the tribunal had sat until July 1993 and published its findings in July 1994.

When Price started to ask probing questions about Michael Noonan, Reynolds's predecessor as Minister for Industry and Commerce, Lord Williams interrupted to request an adjournment. Mr Justice French granted an overnight adjournment, thus ending the Price–Reynolds showdown for that day.

When the hearing resumed the next morning, the jury had lost one of its number, who had suffered a diabetic attack and been excused from further duty. Both senior counsels agreed to allow the hearing to continue with eleven jurors.

Price went straight back on the offensive in his cross-examination of the former Taoiseach. Was not Reynolds, Price suggested, a little selective in hailing the success of his government? Naturally Reynolds disagreed, countering that the peace process had saved hundreds of lives.

Price pointed out that as Taoiseach, Reynolds had led his party to one of the worst general election results in 1992, that two coalition partners had pulled out of government with him and that he had grossly inflated the amount of EU structural funds his government had negotiated. Price quoted the Beef Tribunal report, saying that Reynolds had been criticised heavily by its author, Mr Justice Hamilton. Reynolds claimed that the report was critical of the government, not of him personally. Counsel suggested that this was open to interpretation: had not Reynolds's triumphal manner at the time deeply upset Spring?

Price went on to explore the controversy that arose over export credit insurance for Iraq. This had occurred against a background of Iraq using chemical weapons against its own people, a method that appalled many Irish citizens. Reynolds replied that he had wanted to kick-start the Irish economy. Price reminded Reynolds that when he had introduced in the Dáil the Bill to increase the export cover, no mention had been made of the fact that half the sum was to cover exports to Iraq. It was evident that Price's intention was to show the jury that Reynolds had previously misled the Dáil.

The 'Longford Slasher' was having none of it: 'This was considered a very minor piece of legislation. Officials prepared the script. I delivered it as I was handed it.'

'It might have become a major piece of legislation if the Dáil knew it was to licence exports to the Iraqi regime,' Price suggested.

'The script was prepared by officials,' Reynolds insisted.

'I understand you to be blaming your officials.'

Reynolds bristled with rage: 'That's a cheap shot, and I don't like it every time I hear it. I don't like that and I don't think it's nice.'

Price explained that he was not questioning the credibility of the Irish civil service, but that he was questioning Reynolds's own credibility. He maintained that Reynolds's claim to have been totally vindicated by the Beef Tribunal was misleading.

Mr Justice French brought an end to further questioning on the matter of the tribunal by asking the defence counsel to move on. Several of the numbed jurors nodded gratefully.

'Your Lordship has taken the very words out of my mouth,' Price responded.

The next barrage of criticism Reynolds faced concerned the 'passports for investment' scandal. He conceded that Irish passports had been granted to the Masri family, who had lent his pet food firm £1 million at favourable rates.

'That loan was negotiated by my son,' the plaintiff explained. 'There's been a scheme there since 1988. There are about thirty companies who are the beneficiaries.'

Price referred to an article in *The Irish Times*, which said that Dick Spring's reputation had been damaged, perhaps irrevocably, by his apparent zeal to find nothing wrong in the Masri passport case. The article, written by Vincent Browne, claimed that it was difficult to believe that the Taoiseach knew nothing about the soft loan.

'He attacks your integrity,' Price said. 'Did you sue Mr Browne?'

'I don't regard Mr Browne as calling me a liar in this article. He puts the two sides.'

'Are we to understand that it is all right to say it is difficult to believe, but not all right to say you tell a lie?' Price asked.

'I'm interested in the truth. As Shakespeare said: "To thine own self be true and you won't be false to others",' Reynolds replied, misquoting Shakespeare.

Another adjournment was granted, after which Price embarked on a line of questioning regarding the newspapers that had carried unfavourable articles about Reynolds's resignation, but had not been sued. The plaintiff admitted to having purchased several Irish papers on the Sunday after his resignation, but had not read them because the week had been 'too traumatic'. Price drew his attention to one particular article, in the *Sunday Independent*. Reynolds said that he had first read the article only four days previously and had consulted with his lawyer at that time.

Price exhibited astonishment at Reynolds's answer and requested that any legal correspondence relating to the article be brought into court. Lord Williams immediately objected to this and Price attempted to justify his request by saying, 'The jury have been told that *The Sunday Times* is the only paper in the whole world that have made accusations against Mr Reynolds. I seek to correct that impression.'

The jury was then asked to retire and to refrain from reading the article while legal arguments were being heard. Mr Justice French ruled that Price could continue his cross-examination on the point of the articles, in order to give the plaintiff the opportunity to explain why he had not objected to them. The jury was recalled.

Price held up the article from the *Sunday Independent,* written by Gene Kerrigan, which was headed: 'No dignity in the Dáil of deception'.

'In the first paragraph,' Price quoted, 'he says that your claim to be a man of integrity is a piece of nonsense.'

'I am a man of integrity,' Reynolds insisted.

The judge intervened to say that all Price was seeking to establish was that the plaintiff disagreed with what had been written.

Price continued quoting from the article, which alleged that many of the Fianna Fáil ministers had also known about the Duggan case before Reynolds rose to give his speech in the Dáil that Tuesday. 'Yet,' Price asked incredulously, 'none of them drew your attention to the article? One million people in Ireland read that article and the plaintiff has made no complaint about it,' he told the court.

Price quoted a second article, from the *Irish Independent*: 'Spring wins the long and tortuous battle for integrity'. Price reminded the jury that Reynolds had stated in court that he would pursue anyone who attacked his integrity. But, once again, no complaint had been made. The *Sunday Tribune* had published a story describing Reynolds's version of the Whelehan affair as 'arrant nonsense'. Again, the plaintiff had made no complaint. Nor had he commenced litigation for an article in *The Irish Times* that referred to 'a saga of deceit'.

Price summarised his point: 'Generally in the Irish press you were seriously libelled all that week. For an Irishman whose business is in Ireland, whose family is in Ireland, to choose to sue in England when all that is in the Irish papers is bizarre, isn't it?'

Price landed another blow on the reeling Reynolds: 'Were you at all concerned that if you sued in Ireland, your accusers, Mr Spring and Mr Fitzsimons, would have given evidence?'

'How did I know that that they would not give evidence here?' Reynolds parried.

When asked why it had taken him four months to complain about *The Sunday Times* article, Reynolds replied that his wife had been very much against him taking an action. He had thought that the newspaper would print a correction, as other papers had done in the past. It had failed to do so.

Price sat down, his cross-examination of Reynolds concluded.

Lord Williams took Reynolds back over some of the points Price had raised. Before starting, he urged his client to keep his answers short and to avoid Shakespeare, leading some of the spectators to believe that Reynolds would have been better served by quoting Yeats.

To counter the accusations regarding articles in the Irish newspapers, Williams asked if Reynolds would have been willing for evidence to have been heard under oath in Ireland before a judge, or for evidence to have been given by video-link. Reynolds said that he would have been happy to assent to those arrangements if *The Sunday Times* had requested it.

Referring to the Masri soft loan, Williams asked if Spring had examined the files and found nothing out of place. The plaintiff agreed that this was true. Lord Williams also quoted from a section in the Beef Tribunal report that stated that there was no suggestion that Reynolds believed he was acting outside the national interest. 'So you felt justified in saying that you had been vindicated?' Williams suggested. Reynolds agreed.

To add to the earlier, glowing account of his political triumphs, Williams asked Reynolds about his lecture duties in Britain and his continued contact with senior British politicians. The court heard that Reynolds was to receive an honorary Doctor of Law degree from Aberdeen University the following month.

This brought an end to Reynolds's testimony from the witness-box. His legal team had a number of further witnesses to call. The first was Miriam Fogarty, Reynolds's daughter, who lives in Edinburgh and works as a tax consultant.

Fogarty told the court that the libel action against *The Sunday Times* had been a nightmare for the family. In a voice trembling with emotion, she gave detailed testimony as to the effects on the family and the stress her father had felt during his six days giving evidence. He was not a man comfortable with discussing his inner feelings of hurt, his daughter averred; usually such feelings could be better judged by the things he did not say. In her opinion, her father would not have put his family through the ordeal of a trial if he had not considered it truly necessary.

She had been the first member of the family to see the article in the British edition of *The Sunday Times*. It had made her furious. She told Williams that she had first seen the other newspaper articles mentioned in court on the day the hearing commenced. She recalled reading the Gene Kerrigan article and saying something like, 'Jesus, that's worse!'

After Fogarty had finished giving evidence, Williams announced that that was the end of the plaintiff's case. Price was clearly surprised by this and got to his feet to tell the court that it was his understanding that other witnesses were to be called by the plaintiff's side. The journalists looked dismayed; many had expected to see several former Fianna Fáil ministers giving evidence. It took a few moments for the defence to prepare to open.

When all was ready, Price called Alan Ruddock, who was a co-defendant as one of the journalists who had written the contentious article in *The Sunday Times*. Ruddock was asked to give the court a brief résumé of his career: he had been born and educated in Dublin and had been appointed Irish editor of the newspaper a little over a year before the controversial publication.

Ruddock said that when he took over there was a weakness in the newspaper, in that it was perceived as being too anglicised. He had been instrumental in introducing an Irish-slanted edition. It was a good decision: within two-and-a-half years, sales had doubled. In reply to a question from Price, Ruddock confirmed that it was a frequent and regular practice to treat a story differently in the two editions. British readers had little appetite for heavyweight Irish stories, unless they concerned matters of common interest on both sides of the Irish Sea.

Albert Reynolds was a very tough political opponent, Ruddock said, but he was also a key player in the peace process. He admitted that his recollection was that Dick Spring had stated quite clearly that he had been lied to and that the House had been lied to. Although Spring did not say that explicitly in the Dáil, Ruddock said that that was his impression. It was perceived the same way by the media covering Spring's Dáil speech. As Irish editor, it fell on him to explain the background behind the rift and how one partner in government believed he could not trust the other.

What was of more interest to the plaintiff's side was Ruddock's admission that he had kept no notes from his preparation of the article. This was not that surprising given that Reynolds's initial complaint had not been made for some time after the publication of the article. Ruddock confirmed that Fergus Finlay had been his main source for the story. Williams described Finlay as Spring's 'spin doctor'. As the journalists in the court listened avidly to what was being said, a certain *schadenfreude* may have been unavoidable.

Lord Williams criticised the newspaper's decision not to print the defamatory allegations in its Irish edition. The people of Ireland, North and South, would, he argued, have been the ones most concerned to hear the truth, as *The Sunday Times* saw it.

Ruddock was surprised to learn that Reynolds had been upset by the phrase, 'Mr Spring had done a deal with the devil'. Spring had stated that no party could coalesce with Fianna Fáil unless it underwent radical transformation.

The next witness for the defence was John Burns, another of the co-defendants named in Albert Reynolds's action. In his testimony, Burns said that although his by-line had appeared on the article, his contribution was minimal. In fact, Lord Williams would later agree to have the action against Burns struck out because he had written none of the allegedly defamatory words.

The editor of *The Sunday Times*, John Moore Witherow, was called to the witness-box. Witherow told the court of a Friday editorial conference, at which it was decided to cover the Taoiseach's resignation and also the angle the newspaper would take on this. Ruddock had been asked not only to outline the background, but to explain how the government had fallen. Witherow considered that the article had achieved that brief very successfully.

Witherow admitted that he had not read the copy for the Irish edition, but had seen the headlines and photographs. He had been aware that Irish journalist Vincent Browne had been asked to write a 'different and softer version' for that edition. Price asked him if he had been happy with that.

'We're not a newspaper which tells journalists what to write. We ask them to go out and find out the facts and form a conclusion,' Witherow replied.

Price then asked the editor how he had learned that Reynolds had made a complaint. Witherow said that he had received a letter from Reynolds's solicitor, requesting an apology. He had referred the letter to the newspaper's solicitors, and together they had decided that no apology was warranted.

Towards the conclusion of the witness's testimony it emerged that the newspaper had tried to have Spring and Fitzsimons appear as witnesses, but had failed.

Lord Williams started his cross-examination by asking Witherow if he had been aware at that Friday editorial meeting that Reynolds's version of events would not be included in the article. Witherow agreed that he had been aware of this. He added that Ruddock had tried to contact Reynolds, but had been unsuccessful. If they had spoken, then it was probable that Reynolds's version would have been included.

Counsel reminded the witness that Reynolds's version had been delivered in the Dáil and was therefore freely available. It therefore followed that a decision had been made not to include it in the English edition. Witherow disagreed with Williams's assumption, saying he had not made a conscious decision to omit anything. Ruddock's story was the truth as he saw it.

Lord Williams asked the witness how he felt about different articles being published in Ireland and in the UK. Witherow told the court he would have preferred if both editions had carried Ruddock's article, but Vincent Browne had been asked to write a story and he had come to a different conclusion from Ruddock.

'Why didn't you spike Browne's story and run Ruddock's?' Williams asked.

Witherow replied that Browne's article had contained much more detail and was therefore appropriate for an Irish audience. Under further pressure from counsel, Witherow said that the English article had a more definite conclusion, while the Irish one remained on the fence. He added that he had not spoken to Browne about the article, and the journalist had not been called as a witness.

There was a shock in store for the court when Price announced that he would be calling no further witnesses. It had been thought that Fergus Finlay would give evidence, as he had been seen earlier in discussion with the defence's legal team. Price gave no reason for his decision, other than to point out that the plaintiff's side had not called any supporting witnesses either.

When Witherow stepped down from the witness-box, it brought an end to live evidence and signalled the commencement of recorded testimony. Price apologised to the jury for having to read to them 'indigestible' evidence from the Dáil's Select Committee report on the downfall of the coalition government. Happily, he added, he would not have to read the entire contents.

The first extract concerned Máire Geoghegan-Quinn's speech to the Dáil on 16 November 1994. The Minister for Justice apologised to the house for misleading it over whether or not the Smyth extradition had been the first to be considered under a new section in the Extradition Act. Price then read from a second speech of Geoghegan-Quinn's in the Dáil, on 6 December, when she stated that she could not recall telling Attorney General Fitzsimons that the government had decided not to refer to the Duggan case in the Taoiseach's speech outlining the delays in Smyth's extradition. The minister added that she could not remember making that statement, 'but I accept [Fitzsimons's] word.'

The plaintiff's legal team requested that Bertie Ahern's evidence to the Select Committee also be read out. The passage was read wherein Ahern recounted Fitzsimons's attempt, on 14 November, to explain the complexities of the Duggan case to ministers. Ahern explained that they were content to wait for clarification. A further passage was read out concerning Ahern's denial that there was any formal agreement to withhold information on the Duggan case.

After hearing ninety minutes of extracts, the jury was spared further suffering when the judge called an adjournment, saying that the extracts were difficult to absorb. The jury members would have a weekend to prepare themselves for a four-hour video-recording of evidence from the Select Committee.

On Monday, the start of the third week of the hearing, Price read a further twenty passages from the committee's report, pointing out that the evidence recorded had not been given under oath. For a while the jury was permitted to follow the extracts on written copies, but these were later withdrawn after legal submissions. Price asked the jury to bear with him with regard to the significance of the extracts, that he and opposing counsel would put them in context during their closing addresses.

After lunch, the videotape was played for the jury. It showed Fitzsimons giving evidence to the effect that on the Monday evening, he was certain that Reynolds was 'crystal clear' on the implications of the Duggan case and would refer to it during his Dáil speech of 15 November. The Attorney General had made notes of his recollections and referred to them. In answer to a question posed by Derek McDowell, a Labour deputy, Fitzsimons said that he had 'a firm understanding' that the case was going to be mentioned. In reply to a further question, Fitzsimons said that Geoghegan-Quinn had phoned him at noon on 15 November to inform him that it had been decided that the Duggan case would not be mentioned that afternoon in the Dáil.

Further videotape evidence from Fitzsimons suggested that there had been a reluctance to take his report to Reynolds into the Dáil chamber. Fitzsimmons would not confirm that he believed there was a conspiracy, but he felt a decision had been made that the Duggan case would not be disclosed.

At this point there was a break in proceedings as one jury member, an elderly man, fell ill with an acute stomach upset. There was a further one-day delay as another jury member suffered a bereavement and had to leave to attend the funeral.

While the hearing was in adjournment, Price issued an apology, via his solicitors, for a quip he had made two days previously when some of the jury members were having difficulty with Deputy Willie O'Dea's accent. The judge also had trouble making out O'Dea's words and had asked what was to be done. Price had made a light-hearted response that perhaps elocution lessons could be arranged for O'Dea. In his apology, Price said that he now accepted that his comment might have caused offence.

The videotape evidence finally resumed at the start of the fourth week. Without a doubt, the most eagerly anticipated video evidence was that of Harry Whelehan. In his evidence to the committee, Whelehan had said he was not surprised that the Duggan case had not been mentioned in Reynolds's speech because it had no relevance. In reference to having refused to reconsider his appointment after Fitzsimons had asked him to do so, Whelehan had told the committee that he did not think it appropriate that members of a government should bring pressure on a judge to resolve a political problem.

The jury also watched Dick Spring's evidence to the committee. He recalled writing a note in preparation for a meeting with Fianna Fáil ministers. In the note he said that the tenor of Reynolds's speech to the Dáil was misleading, untrue and concealed the facts. The jury watched evidence in a similar vein from Brendan Howlin, a Labour shadow spokesman. By midafternoon, Price had concluded the case for the defence. The court would begin to hear closing addresses the following day.

Price commenced his closing summary by telling the jury that the case was a simple one: Reynolds had told a fib too far. He had known enough on the Monday evening to form the view that

Whelehan should not proceed with being sworn in, yet in his speech he had said of Whelehan: 'there is nothing to say he is not as suitable today for high office as he was a few weeks ago'.

The plaintiff's excuse for this, Price continued, was that he was not prepared to impugn Whelehan's integrity on incomplete information. This could not justify his failure to inform his Tánaiste of the circumstances.

Price accused Reynolds of giving false evidence under oath. He described the former Taoiseach as a reckless gambler who had rashly risked all on one last turn of the card. Fitzsimons was described as an honest and distinguished man going about his job in difficult circumstances. He report had been viewed by Reynolds as a life-raft he could cling to in order to save his government. Counsel continued: 'Was there any justification for Mr Reynolds to drive a stake through Harry's heart on Wednesday? No, everybody accepts that now, including Mr Reynolds, that there was no need.'

Ruddock, Price suggested, had got as close to the truth as anyone could on the basis of the information available at the time. He had not acted maliciously. Reynolds claimed that Ruddock had acted dishonestly, but in truth Ruddock was of the same opinion as the majority of Irish journalists reporting on the matter. The plaintiff had suggested that Ruddock was unfair and wrong in his failure to contact Reynolds for his version, yet Reynolds himself had told the court that he had been so traumatised by events that he could not bear to read a newspaper, let alone talk to journalists.

Price told the court that Reynolds had been a 'lonely man' during the hearing; none of his former colleagues had given evidence in his support. Notable by their absence were Charlie McCreevy, Noel Dempsey, Martin Mansergh and Máire Geoghegan-Quinn. Had they become shy, did they not wish to step on board a sinking ship, 'or was the problem that they could have told the truth when cross-examined by me?' Price asked the jury.

Counsel pointed out that livelihoods were at risk. Ruddock was currently seeking a job, but there was no evidence that Reynolds's demand as a guest speaker had diminished. In an attempt to further reduce damages if the jury found against his clients, defence counsel reminded the jury members that the article had not been published in Ireland, where Reynolds's business interests were located. He also asked how many of them, before the hearing started, could even remember who Albert Reynolds was.

It was a scathing closing address. Price referred to four flashes of light that had burst forth during the hearing, calling them defining moments of the trial. He took the jury back through each one: Eoghan Fitzsimons's notes; the way the Attorney General's letter had been covered up; the removal of passages of support for Whelehan from Reynolds's speech of 16 November; and Dr Michael Woods's notes in his diary, which seemed to suggest that Reynolds had promised Whelehan the first High Court position that came up if he resigned as president of the High Court.

Lord Williams then rose to begin his closing address to the court. He pointed out that it was up to *The Sunday Times* to prove that Reynolds had lied and it had not done so:

> They thought Albert Reynolds's back was broken. They were wrong. They thought, he's not Taoiseach any more, we can have some sport and let's give Albert a kicking … Take a smear, add a pinch of tittle-tattle, stir it all up and what do you get? A mess.

Counsel asked how the defence could sneer at Albert Reynolds's achievements, claiming there were a lot of people in Ireland who no longer had to worry about their fathers coming home safely, thanks to the dedicated work of the brokers of the peace process.

Williams gave the court a lesson in good journalism, quoting a list of tasks that a reputable journalist must fulfil: go to the best sources; research all sides; talk to those directly involved; check facts; publish all across the British Isles; make careful notes; put it right if he got it wrong. None of these things, Lord Williams pointed out, was done by the journalists working for *The Sunday Times*.

Taking Price's points one by one, Williams attempted to discredit them. Reynolds's decision to sue in Britain was a legal one, based on the fact that not a single copy of the defamatory article had been published in Ireland. The defence had not called journalist Vincent Browne because they knew he would have destroyed them by relating the story he had written. Lord Williams queried why Spring and Reynolds's other accusers had not been called as witnesses: 'Is it because somewhere inside them they think Mr Reynolds was indeed wronged?'

Reynolds had done all he could to appease his coalition partners: he had asked the Attorney General to make an immediate report on the Duggan case and, when he eventually read it, had brought the matter to the Dáil's attention.

If Albert Reynolds had wanted to deceive the Dáil, why send a copy of his speech to his own Attorney General to comment on? It is as stupid as a burglar ringing up a bank manager and saying 'I am coming around, will you be there?'

Williams conceded that, with hindsight, mistakes may have been made. Government ministers were tired because they were working long, demanding hours, which may have led to some confusion. There was a 'gombeen man' in this case, Lord Williams asserted, and his name was Fergus Finlay. He then launched a vitriolic attack on Labour's political advisor, accusing Finlay of having brought down the coalition government. As Lord Williams saw it, Alan Ruddock's was the hand, but Fergus Finlay's was the knife *The Sunday Times* had stuck into Reynolds's back: 'He is a programme manager, he is a fixer, he is an anonymous figure, he hides, he skulks in the dark. He wouldn't even put his name in the paper. If he is accusing someone of lying, should he not at least be upfront about it?' Referring to Finlay's appearance at the hearing, Williams said: 'He came, he saw, he ran away.'

Williams told the court: 'There are two possibilities: Fergus Finlay was afraid to give evidence in case the truth came out; or *The Sunday Times* was afraid to call him because they were afraid the truth would be got out of him. Or both were afraid. You would not use the word chicken because that would be unfair to chickens. They think they can play with people's lives and then not call one source.'

In conclusion, Williams suggested an award of £125,000 in damages. Pre-empting an instruction from the judge that that amount might be excessive, Williams said he would not argue against that, but pointed out that £45,000 should be an absolute base minimum. He referred the jury to a recent libel case *The Sunday Times* had lost against American businessman Victor Khiam. Although the newspaper had apologised within three weeks of publication, Mr Khiam still received an award of £45,000. When deciding the amount in this particular, Lord Williams asked the jury to bear in mind how *The Sunday Times*'s *defence* had exacerbated the hurt inflicted on Albert Reynolds, the former Taoiseach.

Williams sat down. While his concluding address was brief compared to Price's, it did not lack punch.

Not surprisingly, Fergus Finlay issued a statement in protest at his unflattering portrayal during the closing addresses. The Irish Minister for Equality and Law Reform, Mervyn Taylor, also commented on the matter, saying he had been deeply offended and angry about the impression the court had been given about Finlay. Taylor described Finlay as 'among the finest and most decent people ever to work in the public service in this country'.

A spokesman from Lord Williams's chambers stated that the QC was prohibited from responding to Finlay's statement while Reynolds's case was still in progress.

Mr Justice French commenced his summing up on the seventeenth day of the hearing. He reminded the jury that the trial turned on what Albert Reynolds had known on Monday night, 14 November 1994. On that date, did he know the relevance of the Duggan case, or did he not appreciate that until the following night? The judge noted that in a civil case the burden of proof was on the balance of probabilities and not, as in a criminal case, beyond reasonable doubt. The jury would also have to consider if the defendants' actions had been led by malice:

The use of the word is more complex than you might have thought. The plaintiff has to prove malice because he alleges it. In law malice does not just mean 'spite or ill-will', though it includes spite and ill-will. Malice is inferred from what the author had said and what he knew. Evidence of his state of mind lay in what was written. Carelessness does not amount to indifference to the truth.

Commenting on the video evidence, the judge remarked that it was unusual, but permitted. Unfortunately the witnesses could not be cross-examined, so it was up to the jury members to decide on the accuracy of such evidence. He also warned them against paying heed to hearsay evidence, of which there had been a great deal in the case. Statements made by Fitzsimons and Whelehan to the Select Committee were read aloud by the judge, as were Dáil speeches made by Geoghegan-Quinn.

There was a further two-day delay because the mother of one of the jurors was hospitalised. The judge's summing up was expected to last for a further two or three days after that.

When the case resumed, Reynolds was absent for the first time. He had hurt himself in a fall, but in light of the previous delays, it was agreed to press on in his absence. Most of the remaining closing address from the judge comprised the reading aloud of the transcripts taken from the videotape and his summarisation of relevant evidence. He then turned his attention to a number of legal points that had been raised during the jury's absence – the main one being that the plaintiff's case was not whether he knew of the Duggan case on the Monday but whether he had understood its importance before receiving Fitzsimons's report.

French told the jury that in considering damages, the members should bear in mind awards made to people who had suffered personal injury: a quadriplegic would be awarded in the region of £110,000–£130,000, which did not include loss of earnings; a person who had lost an arm at the shoulder could expect an award of £50,000. The judge concluded his charge to the jury by reading through the issue paper on which the jury had to reach verdicts:

1. Is the allegation complained of by the plaintiff in substance true? If yes, the remaining questions do not arise.
2. Was Mr Alan Ruddock acting maliciously in publishing the words complained of?
3. Was John Witherow acting maliciously in publishing the words complained of?
4. How much do you award the plaintiff by way of damages?
5. Do the words complained of correctly report Mr Dick Spring's stated reason for withdrawing from the coalition government?

During the hearing, the defence council told the jury that it had to answer question five because it might be the subject of legal argument at a later date. The judge explained that question five had two parts: (i) what were the stated reasons for Dick Spring withdrawing his support? (ii) were the words complained of correct in reporting those stated reasons?

Before the jury was sequestered, Lord Williams asked leave to raise some legal points. The jury was removed after receiving a warning not to start any discussion until formally instructed to do so. The jury was eventually allowed to retire to consider its verdicts at 12.55 p.m. on the twenty-fourth day of the hearing.

Following three days of deliberation, the jury announced its verdict in the Albert Reynolds libel case against *The Sunday Times*: a 10-1 majority (one jury member had fallen ill) held that Reynolds had not lied and the article was not true, but that Ruddock and Witherow had no malicious intent. The jury found that the correct reason had been given for Dick Spring's withdrawal from the coalition government.

The jury stunned the courtroom by awarding zero damages, clarifying that this meant zero pounds and zero pence. Mr Justice French increased this to 1p to reflect its finding on the issue of truth. Reynolds had been vindicated, but at a cost: he would have to bear his own legal costs and those of the newspaper, a sum estimated at about £800,000.

Legal experts blamed the judge's summing up for the extraordinary result. His address to the jury had lasted for two days and would have filled an average paperback. He had thus failed in his primary objective, i.e. to clearly identify the main arguments for both the plaintiff and the defence. This had left the jury with a muddled version of the case.

The appeal hearings, which took place in the Appeal Court in October 1998 and the House of Lords in October 1999, would help to clarify the right to free speech in British law. The crucial point to be examined was whether the media could claim qualified privilege in that it had a duty to provide a healthy flow of information to the public, and also to examine and discuss a matter of public interest for the benefit of those who had an interest in knowing it – what the tabloids like to call 'the public's right to know'. If this were accepted, Reynolds would fail in his appeal, even if the defendants could not prove the validity of what they had written. There could, however, be an exception if the plaintiff proved a malicious element.

The collapse of the Irish coalition government was obviously of importance at a time of faltering peace talks in Northern Ireland. On the other hand, there were legal precedents that had to be factored into the equation. In 1958, Mr Justice Diplock ruled in *Silkin v Beaverbrook*: 'Every man, whether he is in public life or not, is entitled not to have lies told about him.' Further to this, in 1982 the courts had shied away from allowing qualified privilege when upholding an award of £45,000 to a civil servant plaintiff working for a Department of Energy committee, whose reputation had been damaged by a newspaper's claim of incompetence.

Lord Lester of Herne Hill QC, counsel for *The Sunday Times*, asked the Court of Appeal to take a fresh look at the thorny subject of qualified privilege, citing Article 10 of the European Convention of Human Rights and rulings in preliminary cases brought by the former New Zealand prime minister, David Lange. Lange had been vilified while in office and had embarked on what would become an odyssey through the courts. Early rulings suggested that qualified privilege would be allowed as a defence in political or government matters.

For its part, the media would have been keen for the British courts to adopt the American model of qualified privilege, where a public figure plaintiff has to prove that what was published was false, or at least reckless with the truth – an almost impossible task. Fortunately for Reynolds, the Court of Appeal did not go down that road. Instead, it sided with a 1986 decision in a case before the European Court of Human Rights, where the right of qualified privilege had been upheld when Peter Lingens, a magazine journalist, had successfully brought a case against the Austrian state. Lingens had earlier been fined for comments he had written about Bruno Kreisky, the Austrian chancellor, whom he alleged had protected former members of the Nazi ss for political motive.

It was a ringing endorsement of freedom of speech and a major victory for *The Sunday Times* on a point of principle. The ruling had a sting in its tail, however. The Court of Appeal was willing to allow a defence of qualified privilege only if the media could prove it had acted reasonably in the circumstances. In the *Reynolds* case, *The Sunday Times* was judged not to have done so because it had failed to identify its political source, had been selective in its reporting and had failed to offer the allegations to Reynolds for comment. In the ordered retrial, *The Sunday Times* would therefore be prevented from using a defence of qualified privilege.

The Sunday Times had taken a hard punch, but it was no knock-out. The newspaper took its case to the highest court in the land, and Albert Reynolds was present in the balcony of the House of Lords when its decision was handed down on 28 October 1999. The Lords upheld the Appeal Court's ruling by the narrowest of margins: a 3 to 2 vote. While lauding the Appeal Court's judgment for being 'forward-looking and imaginative', the House of Lords expressed reservations about the constraints of reasonable care. If investigative journalism was a duty of the media, then an unwillingness to disclose the identity of its sources should not be allowed to weigh unduly against it.

DEFAMED!

The retrial was listed for the High Court in October 2000, but was settled out of court, on undisclosed terms, three weeks before it was due to commence. While both sides could claim a victory of sorts, undoubtedly the freedom of the press emerged the real winner.

04 | THIRD TIME LUCKY:

PROINSIAS DE ROSSA v SUNDAY INDEPENDENT & ANOR [1997]

When Eamon Dunphy sat down in early December 1992 to write an article for the *Sunday Independent,* he sparked a seven-year litigation saga that would encompass three High Court hearings and an appeal to the Supreme Court. Dunphy's target was Proinsias De Rossa, the leader of the Democratic Left political party. The libel case that resulted from the article would set a barrage of records in Ireland – not all of them desirable – and add to the clamour for reform of the libel law. At times, the story that unfolded in court resembled a movie based on a John le Carré novel – not quite *The Spy Who Came in from the Cold*, but there were plenty of mysterious armed men, trips to the Soviet Union and even a forged letter to contend with.

The lengthy process would try the most dedicated observers and commentators. The first two hearings attracted a large press corps, but their enthusiasm had waned somewhat by the time the third one got underway. Like many Hollywood sequels, the plot became repetitive and the characters had lost much of their pulling power over time. For the third hearing, Proinsias De Rossa would not be drawing up outside the Four Courts in a government limousine because he and his political allies were now sitting on the opposition seats in the Dáil. On top of that, a new blockbuster had opened across town and was attracting large crowds: former Taoiseach Charles Haughey was giving evidence at the McCracken Tribunal, an inquiry into reports about secret payments allegedly made by Ben Dunne to Charles Haughey and Michael Lowry. On top of that, most were of the belief that De Rossa III would be a bit of a damp squib. As a result, not one of the jaded hacks was expecting the shock ending the story delivered as a final twist.

Eamon Dunphy was a former professional footballer, now better known for his blunt manner as a pundit on sports and current affairs programmes, often making the headlines for his outspokenness and errant behaviour. Even his admirers considered him a bit of a loose cannon, but few could deny that he had genuine talent as a chronicler of modern Irish life. The controversial article he wrote that day in 1992 contained observations about Proinsias De Rossa in his capacity as leader of the Democratic Left. It was published in the *Sunday Independent* on 13 December 1992, at a time when attempts were being made by a number of political parties to form a coalition government. The main thrust of Dunphy's story was that Irish society was divided and, as the various political parties manoeuvred to seize power, the nature of those differences was emerging. The alleged offending passages read:

> On one side of the argument are those who would find the idea of Democratic Left in cabinet acceptable. These people are prepared to ignore Democratic Left leader Proinsias De Rossa's reference to the 'special activities' which served to fund the Workers' Party in the very recent past.
>
> The 'special activities' concerned were criminal. Among the crimes committed were armed robberies and forgery of currency.
>
> The people engaged in this business occupied that twilight world where the line blurs between those who are common criminals and others of that ilk who would claim to be engaged in political activity.
>
> The world is inhabited by myriad groups, some dealing in drugs, prostitution, prostitution rackets, crimes of which the weakest members of society are invariably the victims.

It is therefore ironic, wickedly so, that a political party claiming to 'care' for the workers should accept funding from 'special activities' of a particularly nasty kind.

There is no doubt that elements of De Rossa's Workers' Party were involved in 'special activities'. What remains unproven is whether De Rossa knew about the source of his party's funds. There is evidence, strengthened by revelations in *The Irish Times* this week, that De Rossa was aware of what was going on.

If one is to allow him the benefit of the doubt, and why not, one must nevertheless have misgivings about those with whom he so recently associated.

Justice demands that we welcome Democratic Left's recent conversion to decency and, indeed, acknowledge that their Dáil deputies are exemplary in the conduct of their work they engage in on behalf of their constituents.

Still, questions remain unanswered about the Workers' Party's 'special activities' phase, not to mention their willingness to embrace the Soviet Communist Party long after the brutal oppression that this and other communist regimes visited on workers, intellectuals and others who would think and speak freely.

Proinsias De Rossa's political friends in the Soviet Union were no better than gangsters. The communists ran labour camps. They were anti-Semitic. Men like André Sakharov and Vaclav Havel were persecuted. Citizens who attempted to flee this terror were murdered. In Berlin, the bodies were left to rot in no man's land between tyranny and liberty. Is it really necessary to remind ourselves of those 'special activities'?

Let us just say that some of those with whom Dick Spring has conducted a pact for government have kept bad company in the recent past. Ireland divides between those who would choose to forget and those of us who do not.

De Rossa was outraged by what he considered a slur on his good name and he immediately sought an apology for the article. When that was not forthcoming, he instituted legal proceedings.

The first hearing commenced in November 1996, but Mr Justice McCracken called a halt to it after eight days subsequent to the *Sunday Independent* publishing an article relevant to the hearing. The second hearing started in February 1997 and lasted fourteen days. Mr Justice Moriarty discharged the jury after it deliberated for nine hours without reaching a verdict.

The third hearing was listed in the High Court for 3 July 1997, but at the request of the defence counsel was postponed until 15 July, to allow affidavits to be taken in Moscow. Mr Justice Carney was to preside; the selected jury consisted of eleven women and one man.

Paul O'Higgins SC made the opening submission for the plaintiff. He told the court that the *Sunday Independent* was a powerful newspaper in Ireland, with a readership of over one million, and that it had published material that could effectively have ended a politician's career. It was asserted that the article had been written with a political agenda. There had just been a general election with no overall winning party, so negotiations had commenced to see if a coalition government could be formed. Any defamatory attack on the leader of one of the parties at such a crucial moment could have had a serious effect on those negotiations.

The court heard De Rossa being described as a decent man who had spent all his political life fighting the very evils mentioned in the article. The plaintiff did not want compensation for himself; he would have been content with an apology and a contribution to charity. Neither had been offered.

De Rossa's personal and political backgrounds were outlined for the court. He was born in the middle of a family of twelve siblings in Dublin's inner city. His father was a farm labourer and produce delivery man, while his mother ran a small greengrocers under their flat on Parnell Street. He attended school at the all-Irish Scoil Colmcille on Marlborough Street. The family were committed republicans: his father was a Michael Collins man; his mother leaned more towards Eamon de Valera. After leaving primary school, Proinsias De Rossa had some engineering training at technical colleges, but failed to get an apprenticeship with the ESB. His prospects were bleak – unemployment was rampant and the commercial outlook was unpromising. An uncertain future and his nationalist background helped to shape his political ideology.

He was first elected to the Dáil in 1982 and became leader of the Workers' Party in 1989. In early 1992 he resigned as leader after failing to win approval for a new party constitution. In March that same year he and approximately 80 per cent of his former party colleagues formed the Democratic Left Party. Within four months the new party was in negotiations to be minority partners in a coalition government.

The Irish Times published a letter on 26 October 1992, allegedly signed by De Rossa and Seán Garland, who was general secretary of the Workers' Party. The letter, dated 15 September 1986, was purportedly a request on behalf of the Workers' Party for funds of £1 million from the Communist Party of the Soviet Union. The letter set out the financial difficulties of the Irish party and how in the past any shortfall had been met by 'special activities'.

De Rossa had been quick to deny authorship of the letter or any knowledge of it. His emphatic denial was accepted by most people at the time. O'Higgins told the jury that not even the *Sunday Independent* now asserted that De Rossa had written the letter, yet De Rossa could never again hold up his head in politics, or privately, if he left unchallenged the association implied by the offending article.

It was claimed that the damage inflicted by Dunphy had been immediate and terrible. However, De Rossa had continued to plot a successful political course as a career politician, confident that he had no connection with the 'Moscow letter'. He had been a Minister for Social Welfare in a coalition government, although the earlier court hearings may have had a negative effect on his poll in the recent general election.

The case for the *Sunday Independent* was then outlined. It admitted to publishing the article, but denied that it had done so falsely or maliciously. The thrust of the story was that De Rossa had been leader of a party that had previously accepted funds raised by criminal activity and that there had been public comment on a letter, signed, but not knowingly, by De Rossa that appeared to refer to this activity. In short, the words complained of were true and accurate.

Justification can be a tricky defence, and should it fail, can result in a higher award of damages. The newspaper was confident it could prove a link between De Rossa and Seán Garland, other than the two having been members of the same political party.

When De Rossa took the witness stand, he described his early days in the republican movement. He had joined Na Fianna, a junior wing of the republican movement, around the time he left primary school. By the age of sixteen he was an IRA volunteer, trained in the use of the Lee Enfield rifle. In May 1957 he was arrested during a training march in the Wicklow Mountains. He served a two-month prison sentence before being transferred to the Curragh internment camp for a further two years. He was arrested again in 1960 and jailed for a few months. When he came out of jail on the second occasion, he refused an offer to take part in active service in Northern Ireland and, disillusioned, resigned from the IRA. He did not believe any cause was worth the spilling of blood.

Seven years later he joined Sinn Féin, taking a special interest in social issues. Sinn Féin split in 1970 and De Rossa remained with the Official branch. In 1977 Official Sinn Féin changed its name to Sinn Féin, the Workers' Party; in 1982 the 'Sinn Féin' was dropped.

The Workers' Party had often been in dire financial straits and when De Rossa was elected as a deputy, he signed loan guarantees to help fund the party. Subsequent to setting up the Democratic Left, he was asked by several banks to clear the outstanding balances and he had done this by instalment, finally clearing them the previous year, 1996. By De Rossa's calculations, some £500,000 had been donated to the Workers' Party from his salaries as a deputy and MEP. During his time with the Workers' Party, De Rossa had made several trips abroad, visiting the United States in 1984 and North Korea in 1986; both legs of the Korean trip were via Moscow. He returned to the Soviet Union in 1987 and again in 1989.

De Rossa had first learned of the 'Moscow letter' when he received a call from the London *Independent* in October 1992, asking him to confirm if he had been in Moscow in 1986. He told the newspaper that he might have been. He was asked about a letter, but could not recall any such document. When an article about the letter duly appeared in the London *Independent*, Irish journalists contacted him for comment. He declined to make a statement, but his opinion that he knew of no letter remained unaltered. De Rossa added: 'As far as I was concerned, I had nothing whatever to do with the letter. It had nothing to do with me.'

When the letter was published by *The Irish Times*, De Rossa realised at once the damage it could do to him. He told anyone who cared to listen that he had had no hand, act or part in the writing of the letter. When requested to do so by *The Irish Times*, he provided a sample of his signature for analysis.

De Rossa first learned of the *Sunday Independent* article when a friend telephoned to advise him of it. He bought the newspaper and read it for himself and was deeply shocked at the contents of Dunphy's article. In it, he was accused of being a crook, and the worst kind of criminal at that. His reputation as a decent man had been attacked in the foulest way. His thoughts then went to his family, who would have to walk the streets, meeting friends who would be speculating whether he was a criminal.

When De Rossa was asked to elaborate on his feelings at the time, he described the countless times he had raised funds for the Workers' Party by box collections, in all kinds of weather. The article had accused him of virtual oppression of the people; it went against everything he had ever believed in and for which he had fought.

Liz McManus, a Democratic Left Party colleague and a Dáil deputy for Wicklow, was called to give evidence and she described the effect the article had on her party leader: 'Proinsias has a kind of sparkle about him, especially when he smiles or laughs. I think that sparkle went out of him. The man was shattered by it.' She added that it was a scurrilous attack and a hatchet job on a decent man.

Liz McManus had first met De Rossa in the mid/late 1970s, but did not know him well at that point. She resigned from the Labour Party in protest over a possible coalition with Fine Gael and joined the Workers' Party. She was surprised when De Rossa was elected to the Dáil in 1982 because although she considered him a good and capable man, she did not think he would win a seat at that time. From that point on she got to know him better, especially when he was elected party leader in 1988. He was a breath of fresh air, in her opinion, forward-looking and a reformist and she considered him a man who truly believed in what he was doing and who would fight for social justice.

At the time Dunphy's article was published, McManus explained, the Democratic Left was negotiating with Labour with a view to a possible coalition. Everyone in the party was exhilarated at the prospect of entering government. Her husband drew her attention to the article, and she was shocked by its viciousness. She appreciated that anyone in politics had to grow a thick skin and learn to suffer a certain amount of stick, but this was an attempt to take away a man's character.

When asked how long it was before her party leader got over the article, McManus replied: 'He doesn't express his feelings publicly. I felt he was hurting and did not get over it quickly.'

Another Democratic Left colleague who gave evidence, Pat Rabbitte, recalled what his thoughts were upon reading the article. His primary concern was that it meant 'curtains' for the Democratic Left's efforts at entering a coalition government. He had been at the heart of negotiations and felt that the article had been a body blow to all the hard work.

De Rossa himself imagined that in the ordinary sense any reader of the article would assume he was a person who had benefited from crime. He was particularly critical of Eamon Dunphy for talking about evidence when he had failed to produce it. Reference was made to the letter appearing in *The Irish Times*, but Dunphy had produced no evidence to substantiate his defamatory allegations. 'I don't think,' De Rossa said, 'Eamon

Dunphy is entitled to treat me that way and take my good name that way.'

Furthermore, Dunphy had attempted to link De Rossa's name to inhuman crimes in Eastern Europe and the Soviet Union. His claims, De Rossa insisted, were a total subversion of the truth: 'There was an attempt made to destroy me personally and prevent me from being part of a government. The newspaper was reckless with my reputation and would not apologise.'

The newspaper had offered De Rossa a right to reply in the newspaper, but he felt this was far from good enough. He wanted vindication. He wanted his name cleared, even if it took three High Court hearings to achieve that. For De Rossa, he needed his family and friends to be able to go on with their lives without this shadow hanging over all of them.

Counsel for the defence rose to begin his cross-examination of De Rossa. For this hearing, Independent Newspapers plc had retained the services of Michael McDowell SC. This was a change of counsel from the first two hearings, when the defence had been led by Patrick MacEntee SC. McDowell was a Progressive Democrat TD who would later became Minister for Justice and Tánaiste in a Fianna Fáil/PD coalition government. The verbal sparring between the defence counsel and De Rossa would be lengthy and, at times, brutal.

McDowell immediately went on the attack. He wanted to know what had happened to all the letters and correspondence De Rossa had collected during his years with the Workers' Party, both as member and leader. De Rossa told the court that he had destroyed all the material relating to his former party. He had collected up all the documents, lit a bonfire in his garden and burned all the paperwork, which comprised a mixture of accumulated election literature, policy documents and constituency files.

McDowell expressed incredulity that anyone should want to destroy the memories of a political lifetime. De Rossa explained that the break from his former party had been traumatic for him and he wanted to be rid of old documents. As leader of a new party, he wanted to look forward, not keep glancing over his shoulder at the past.

Was it true, McDowell wanted to know, that the bonfire had been set just days after De Rossa had asked his solicitors to write a letter of complaint to the *Sunday Independent*? The letter had been dated 18 December 1992, McDowell reminded him. De Rossa could not recall the exact date of the bonfire, but he narrowed it down to between Christmas Day and the New Year.

Next, the political ethos of the Workers' Party was put under the spotlight. Wasn't it, McDowell asked, a hardline Marxist party? De Rossa denied this. He said that in 1983 the Workers' Party had established links with the Communist Party of the Soviet Union (CPSU), but the relationship had frequently been an uneasy one. The Workers' Party did not approve of the CPSU's support for the Provisional IRA.

McDowell then asked the plaintiff for his views on the labour camps in the Soviet Union. De Rossa said it was probable that back in 1983 he did not believe the reports circulating about these camps, that he thought the claims were Western propaganda. Soviet Union visitors to Ireland had assured the Workers' Party that labour camps did not exist. De Rossa admitted that the Workers' Party had been somewhat uncritical and naive at the time, although he pointed out that the Irish government had also had a political relationship with the former Soviet Union. He now accepted that the Soviet Union had been ruled by an oppressive and brutal regime.

De Rossa then endured a detailed and potentially damaging line of questioning regarding a former Workers' Party member, Brian Lynch. It emerged that a print shop had operated from premises at the rear of the party's headquarters on Gardiner Place, Dublin. Repsol was the name of the company running the print shop, and Lynch had been a director. Other directors were confirmed to be Cathal Goulding, Tomás MacGiolla, Séamus Lynch and Seán Garland, who at one time been general secretary of the Workers' Party. It was further confirmed that the directors had held the company in trust for the Workers' Party. Repsol printed most of the Workers' Party's literature, but also imported books from the Soviet Union.

In response to a volley of questions, De Rossa admitted that in November 1983 the gardaí had raided Repsol's premises in connection with an investigation into the counterfeiting of £5 notes. De Rossa pointed out that the premises was just one of a number searched by the investigating team of gardaí. McDowell enquired if Brian Lynch had 'disappeared off the face of the earth' at around this time. De Rossa denied being aware of it then; he heard it through gossip at a later date. De Rossa rebuked McDowell for mentioning in court the name of a person who had not been charged with any offence.

Repsol, it emerged, also owned a number of properties in Dublin and Mornington, Co. Meath. De Rossa was not surprised to learn that the properties had been mortgaged in March 1987 to secure a debt because the Workers' Party had been constantly short of funds. It had come as a revelation, however, to learn that Repsol was the beneficial owner of the property.

Counsel's attention now moved to the 'Moscow letter'. Seven months after De Rossa's split from the Workers' Party, Alan Murdoch of the London *Independent* rang the politician to confirm that he had been in Moscow in 1986. De Rossa told the court that he replied that he might have been. His answer was vague because the journalist was talking about events six years earlier and his recollections could not be exact. In reply to a further question from McDowell, De Rossa said that the letter had not rung any bells with him and that he had not contacted Garland to see if it meant anything to him.

McDowell explored the relationship between the two men. De Rossa said that as far as Garland and others in the party were concerned, he was a traitor and they would not speak to him. 'They would not walk on the same side of the street as me and they would not speak to anyone belonging to me,' De Rossa explained.

Returning once more to the letter, McDowell asked if Murdoch had asked about the 'special activities' referred to therein. Again, De Rossa denied any recollection of such an enquiry, nor could he recall telling the journalist that he had had no role in the party's finances at that time. De Rossa refused to look at the *Independent*'s article. He said that defence counsel was there to destroy his character and he was not going to assist him.

'You are being paid by the *Sunday Independent*, are you not?' De Rossa said in justification.

'Of course I am. At least I hope I am,' McDowell replied.

Murdoch had drawn De Rossa's attention to an accusation made at a Workers' Party conference over a secret army operated by Garland. Further to this was Murdoch's claim that Soviet experts had trained five party members. De Rossa had found the suggestions alarming, though he did tell Murdoch that some party members in Northern Ireland had special authority to carry personal handguns for self-defence. This was because anyone who opposed the Provisional IRA was at risk; the son of a leading party member had been shot dead in one incident.

There had been a huge difference of opinion between Garland and De Rossa regarding the role of weapons. Garland believed that any revolutionary party should have arms at its disposal in order to defend itself. McDowell asked whether Garland would have told De Rossa if party members had retained the capacity to use weapons. De Rossa answered that Garland would not have told him this, pointing out the contradiction in the fact that Garland had often been highly critical of the use of arms.

McDowell pushed on, suggesting that it was entirely plausible that there existed an armed group linked to the Workers' Party, and, considering the danger to their lives, it would have been madness not to have taken some defensive measures. De Rossa said he would not draw that conclusion.

The possibility of the existence of such a group was critical to the newspaper's case. If these 'heavies' existed to defend Workers' Party members, then the press could well speculate over links between the party and men of violence. Again, De Rossa denied counsel's conjecture. When McDowell pressed further, De Rossa agreed that any party that was linked to violence was on the slippery slope to undemocratic politics. He denied emphatically that the Workers' Party had been such a party.

In his evidence, Pat Rabbitte also insisted he had known nothing of illegal fund-raising on behalf of the Workers' Party. When questioned about the phrase 'special activities' mentioned in the 'Moscow letter', he testified that he had never heard or seen such a phrase until the publication of the letter in *The Irish Times*.

Rabbitte was grilled over a report on the draft budget for 1988/89, which was prepared for the *ard comhairle* (central executive committee) of the Workers' Party. Included in this report were details of a subscription of £28,000 and a noted reference to a 'verbal explanation from Seán Garland'. Rabbitte was asked why the source of this money had not been put in writing. He replied that many contributors did not want their identity to be known; there was nothing unusual about such a request.

He was then asked if, after the collapse of the Soviet Union, he had seen reports claiming that the Workers' Party had received funds from the Communist Party in Moscow. Rabbitte recalled an article in the London *Independent* before Christmas 1992 or 1993, but denied seeing a report claiming that the Workers' Party had received £28,000 from the Communist Party. His only knowledge of the Workers' Party's financial affairs was when he had acted as guarantor for a £100,000 bank loan.

Rabbitte insisted that the figure of £28,000 had not 'rung a bell' with him. He would not have connected it with Garland's note in the draft budget. It was his belief that the Workers' Party had never received a single rouble from the Communist Party, and his conviction remained the same to this day.

De Rossa was asked if Garland had lied to him regarding a request to the Soviet Union for funds. Quotes were read from an interview De Rossa gave, which was published in *The Irish Times* on 4 January 1991. In it, he denied recent reports that the Workers' Party had received funds from the CPSU. Yet, one week later, Garland told a Workers' Party *ard comhairle* meeting that requests had been made, but that no funds had been received to date.

De Rossa admitted that the news had come as a shock to him. He remembered thinking that Garland had sought funds without the *ard comhairle*'s authorisation. It had earlier been decided not to approach Moscow for financial aid, but to make tentative approaches to the Russian embassy in Dublin instead. The former leader of the Workers' Party insisted that the main thrust of the *ard comhairle* meeting was a reconstitution of the party.

When asked, De Rossa agreed that Garland's action had represented serious misbehaviour. He further admitted that Garland had lied to him. Put under pressure from defence counsel, he added that he was there to defend himself, not to defend or denigrate Garland. There had been a certain amount of ill-feeling between the two men in the early 1990s, which had been exacerbated when the party spilt.

The jury heard of a Workers' Party meeting held in De Rossa's constituency, to which he was not invited. Garland would speak to him of a need to maintain party unity, De Rossa said, while simultaneously expressing a different view to others. Seemingly exasperated with this line of questioning, De Rossa tried to sum up his working relationship with Garland by saying that it was usually cordial and friendly, but they were not bosom buddies or drinking pals.

Garland had been shot and seriously wounded in the 1970s. De Rossa was asked if the shooting had been a result of a feud between the Irish Republican Socialist Party/Irish National Liberation Army and the Sinn Féin Workers' Party/Official IRA. De Rossa denied there was any feud between Official Sinn Féin and any other party or organisation. McDowell then asked if Seamus Costello had split with Official Sinn Féin to form the Irish Republican Socialist Party (IRSP). De Rossa agreed, but could not confirm if the IRSP had an armed wing known as the INLA.

To observers in the well of the court, it seemed the plaintiff had learned much from debate with his fellow Leinster House politicians, who, when it suits them, are adept at metamorphosing into the monkeys who see no evil, hear no evil and speak no evil. What is common knowledge to the man in the street can, apparently, fail to reach the ears of Ireland's political representatives. Ignorance can indeed be bliss.

McDowell then returned to the question of the signature on the 'Moscow letter', telling the plaintiff that he would be calling a handwriting expert who would testify that the signature was De Rossa's. Conflicting evidence from experts called by the defence and the prosecution had been a feature of the second hearing.

'I am putting it to you,' McDowell said, 'that it was written in your hand and by you.'

De Rossa was having none of it. He denied time and time again having anything to do with the letter. He had not signed it; the letter had not been authorised by the party; the party had not discussed the issues in the letter. 'As far as I was concerned, the letter was a forgery,' De Rossa insisted.

Next on the agenda was an interview the plaintiff gave to the *Evening Herald* on 5 March 1992, about two weeks after his resignation from the Workers' Party and roughly the same time length before the founding of Democratic Left. De Rossa attempted to clarify, at some length, the pre-break-up situation within the Workers' Party. He felt there had been a lot of groundless speculation that the party had links with a paramilitary organisation. He did not accept that there was such a thing as the Official IRA, but that if it had existed, it would not have been satisfactory for the Workers' Party to have links to it.

McDowell made special reference to one sentence in the printed summary of the interview: 'If those of us who should have known better can be accused of anything, it's that we were too trusting.' De Rossa explained that in saying that he had been referring to the changes he had been planning to make to the Workers' Party, and that people opposed to them were secretly organising against those changes, people whom he thought would have been more 'upfront'.

Defence counsel quoted a further newspaper article in which it was alleged that Pat McCartan TD had accused senior figures in the Workers' Party of trying to recruit for the IRA in 1991. De Rossa admitted that he had read the article, which had been published nine months after his split with the Workers' Party. He spoke to McCartan and was assured that the article was inaccurate – an opinion that tallied with his own belief that there was no substance to the story.

The printing company Repsol was reintroduced when McDowell asked the plaintiff about a pamphlet it had printed in the 1970s. The pamphlet was entitled *The IRA Speaks Out,* and on the back featured a message prompting interested readers to call or write to 30 Gardiner Place – the shared premises of the Workers' Party and Repsol. De Rossa denied ever having seen the pamphlet. McDowell appeared surprised by this and asked De Rossa if he was sure he had not seen it in the discovery of documents (a pre-hearing legal formality during which both sides provide each other with copies of all documents relevant to their cases).

'As I have said, I do not recall seeing it, no,' De Rossa replied.

McDowell continued to put questions concerning the pamphlet until Seán Ryan, for the plaintiff, rose and objected: 'He said he has not seen it before. This is trial by ambush.' The judge allowed defence counsel to carry on with his line of questioning.

De Rossa continued to deny that he had seen the pamphlet before and added that it did not have any reference to Official Sinn Féin on the cover. But as counsel was quick to point out, the pamphlet did have '30 Gardiner Place' printed on it. 'Where could that be except the Workers' Party's premises?' McDowell asked. De Rossa did not budge. He replied that the pamphlet was undated and bore no reference to Official Sinn Féin. There was nothing more he could say.

McDowell's cross-examination drew to a close. There had been little evidence that had not been heard at greater length in the first two hearings. The jury, of course, would be instructed by the judge to refrain from letting that interfere with its objectivity.

On day seven of the hearing, the defence got the opportunity to put its case. McDowell opened by reading the article and reminding the jury how, when under pressure, De Rossa would repeat his 'mantra' that he had been called a pimp, a drug-pusher and a criminal: 'It was never and is not now the *Sunday Independent*'s position that Mr De Rossa is or was a criminal or participated in any criminal activities. That is not our case.'

The jury was taken through the article and Dunphy's motivation in writing the contentious statements was explained. The journalist had genuinely believed the 'special activities' referred to meant criminal activity. McDowell also reminded the jury that Dunphy had stated in the article that it 'remained unproven' that De Rossa had known the source of a portion of the Workers' Party's funds. He had even gone so far as to say that De Rossa should be given the benefit of the doubt. Most people would have found this fair and balanced, yet De Rossa had complained bitterly about it. At no point, McDowell said, had Dunphy accused De Rossa of being involved in or condoning criminal activity. What he did say, however, was that the regime with which the Workers' Party had established fraternal relations was one that ran labour camps and operated like gangsters. This fact was something the plaintiff now accepted, though at the time he believed it was Western propaganda. It was Dunphy's view that the recently founded Democratic Left had severed links with a very unsavoury party.

McDowell then went on to counteract opposing counsel's assertion that the Independent Group was all-powerful and could afford to pay heavy costs and damages. The assets of his client should not matter, McDowell argued. What the jury had to decide was whether the article was defamatory. He championed the need for a free and campaigning press by citing the crusading journalists in the Group, Sam Smyth and Veronica Guerin. McDowell pointed out that more than a million people read the *Sunday Independent* because it was a responsible and respected newspaper. Its content ranged from the trivial, such as 'The Keane Edge', to serious political analysis.

McDowell asked the jury members to consider the evolution of the Workers' Party. They had been presented with a sanitised version of the truth, but they should bear in mind that the party had been born out of the republican movement. IRA training camps in the 1960s served the same purpose as those in the 1990s. McDowell concluded his hour-long opening address by saying: 'It is not good enough for Mr De Rossa to say "I'm a forward-looking person. Don't ask me about the past".'

Eamon Dunphy was the first, and most vital, witness to be called by the defence. He described himself as having a keen interest in politics. When he had lived in Britain, he had been an active member of the Labour Party; in Ireland, he had advised Fine Gael and was a supporter of the Progressive Democrats. He varied his voting, having voted for Labour in 1992 because of the criticism of Fianna Fáil. There was a ripple of laughter around the court when Dunphy added that he had given his second-preference vote to counsel Michael McDowell.

Dunphy explained, in some detail, how he had observed the negotiations to form a coalition government after the 1992 general election had failed to produce an outright winner. He was dumbfounded at the apparent willingness of Dick Spring and the Labour Party to partner Fianna Fáil so soon after they had been instrumental in bringing down Albert Reynolds's government. Having said that the character of Fianna Fáil rendered the party unfit for government, Spring was now proposing to put it back in power. Labour was considering taking in the Democratic Left to make up the numbers.

The *Sunday Independent* of 6 December 1992 published an article by Dunphy commenting on political alliances. On Monday he had read an interview De Rossa had given to *The Irish Times*, which contained a reference to the character of the party he had left nine months earlier. Dunphy believed that the clarification provided by De Rossa fell short of the mark, especially regarding the authenticity of the signature on the 'Moscow letter' and the reference to 'special activities'.

The next few days had seen frantic political activity and intense speculation over the formation of a coalition. By Thursday, Dunphy had probably decided on the main thrust of his article for the next edition of the Sunday newspaper. He spent some time in the Independent Newspapers' library, looking for other references to the letter that had turned up in the Moscow archives.

Seán Ryan, for the plaintiff, cross-examined Dunphy. He started by asking him if there were standards in his profession which ought to be applied and to which practitioners ought to adhere. The witness agreed that there were. Ryan then asked if it was a journalist's duty to be fair and moderate. Dunphy agreed that fairness was necessary, but did not think that moderation was necessarily a virtue. He considered passion to be a valuable commodity in a journalist, alongside care and diligence. Dunphy could not agree with Ryan that reasonableness was an asset – it would not be the first quality he would look for in a journalist, or possibly in a human being.

When asked if an article read by a great number of people had the capacity to do harm, Dunphy qualified his agreement on the basis of the supposed article being unfair. He told the jury that a journalist should be careful not to hurt people. By this point it was evident that Dunphy was cautious enough to avoid shooting himself in the foot.

Ryan asked whether an article that had indeed hurt someone could also have the capacity to hurt the friends and family of the injured person. Dunphy agreed, saying that he had been repeatedly hurt and defamed and it was not something that could be put right easily. However, he went on, people do forget and go on about their business.

Counsel began to examine the witness's working routine. Dunphy explained that the *Sunday Independent* had no role in deciding what he wrote. He usually worked from home, visiting the office mid-week to pick up mail. He wrote a soccer column and some articles for the back page – one of the most important pages of the paper. He did not type and normally got someone to transcribe his longhand into type copy, which was then telephoned or e-mailed into the office. Often he would not decide on an article's content until Friday, and would then discuss it with features editor Campbell Spray, or with news editor Willie Kealy. Once it had been submitted, Spray would sub-edit the article and put a headline on it, before setting it on a page mock-up. Dunphy had not known specifically of the cartoon of De Rossa that accompanied his article, but it was a common practice for one to be included. Since it was election time, the cartoon may have been part of a stock set of party leaders commissioned by the newspaper.

Ryan probed deeper into the nature of Dunphy's journalism. He asked the witness if he had ever described himself as the

'*Sunday Independent*'s highly paid boot boy'? Dunphy admitted that he had done so in response to a question during an interview for *Hotpress* magazine. The term was a derogatory one, which had subsequently been used in the *Phoenix* magazine and possibly once in *The Irish Times*. It had become a stick that was used regularly to beat him. Dunphy insisted that it was not a description that he could accept because it referred condescendingly to his career as a footballer and his working-class roots.

Ryan drew the court's attention to an article Dunphy had written on 28 November 1993. In the article, he had used the phrase to describe himself. The witness explained that he was being ironic in using the description, that it was a self-deprecating irony. 'I am not a boot boy, Mr Ryan. I am a journalist and a conscientious journalist,' Dunphy argued.

Dunphy went on to agree with counsel that if anyone felt he/she had been libelled, then he/she had the right to seek redress in court. He added that many people threatened and intimidated journalists all the time and that these people should 'put up or shut up'.

No one could have accused Dunphy of grandstanding during his time in the witness-box – in fact, it was quite the opposite. The jury was told how he had spent years castigating Jack Charlton, who went on to achieve an immortality of sorts as a national icon. He had also been heavily critical of Mary Robinson, who became the most popular person in the country. He had been derisive of Roddy Doyle's novels; the northsider later won the Booker Prize. Dunphy pointed out that his record had led Fianna Fáil to beg him not to endorse Bertie Ahern.

Next on counsel's agenda was a series of questions concerning the editorial in the same edition of the *Sunday Independent* that featured Dunphy's contentious article. The editorial was headed: 'The 'Jobs' Chimera' and Ryan suggested that the tone of the piece was aligned to Dunphy's article. The witness agreed that this was the case. The editorial suggested that Labour had wasted a lot of time in discussions with the Democratic Left and that any promise of solving unemployment by throwing large sums of money at the problem was disingenuous. Dunphy felt that some politicians were dishonestly claiming to care for the unemployed: that was why the word 'Jobs' was placed in inverted commas.

James Nash, a handwriting expert, was called to the witness-box. Nash had just returned from Moscow and was somewhat persuaded that the De Rossa signature on the 'Moscow letter' was genuine. He had first seen the letter in 1992, when a copy had been given to him by *The Irish Times*. He had not seen the original at the time, but had expressed the opinion that, on the balance of probability, both Garland's and De Rossa's signatures were genuine.

Nash's first opportunity to examine the original letter was on 16 November 1996, on which date he travelled to the Centre for the Preservation of Contemporary Documents in Moscow; a second visit had been made just before the hearing. Two documents had been shown to him there: the seven-page 'Moscow letter' and another, two-page letter signed solely by Garland. He had not been allowed to photograph the letters, but several photocopies had been made for him. He had examined the signatures and compared them with several sample signatures with which he had been provided.

Nash considered that the De Rossa signature on the 'Moscow letter' had been fluent, written freely and signed with speed. There was no evidence of hesitation nor tremor of pen-lift. Both letters were typed on the same typewriter. The 'Moscow letter' was on the headed notepaper of the Workers' Party and bore a watermark.

There was further document-related evidence when the next witness was called. Bill O'Brien had been a contemporary of De Rossa's in the Wolfe Tone *cumann* in Ballymun. He had joined Clann na Éireann, an Irish republican group in Britain, while working in England. Upon his return to Ireland, in 1971, O'Brien had joined Official Sinn Féin. Following the Aldershot bombing, a ceasefire was declared in May 1972. After the annual *ard fheis* (party conference), Tony Hefferman, the PRO and chairman of the *comhairle ceanntair* (executive committee), had passed him a secret document.

(There was some dispute as to whether Hefferman was the PR officer of the *comhairle ceanntair* or its 1970–71 chairman. Hefferman later served as the assistant government press secretary in the Rainbow coalition government in which De Rossa was Minister for Social Welfare. He was now press officer for the Democratic Left.)

The secret document was a proposal for a restructuring of the IRA, with the military and political wings combining into one revolutionary-type organisation. The proposal was discussed at some length and eventually provoked a split, leading to the formation of the IRSP in 1974. O'Brien had left the organisation at that time to seek employment in the Isle of Man. On his return to Ireland, he joined the Communist Party of Ireland (CPI) and remained a member for eighteen months.

Paul O'Higgins, in cross-examination, asked O'Brien if it was correct that the Communist Party of Ireland had supported the Provisional IRA's (PIRA) campaign of violence. O'Brien replied that it had not supported the PIRA, although it was in favour of a thirty-two-county Ireland. O'Higgins suggested to the witness that the Workers' Party had perhaps tried to convince the Communist Party not to back the Provisional IRA because the party did not advocate such a position. O'Brien denied having any knowledge of that political scenario, repeating that he had never been a member of any military wing. He admitted having taken part in H-block marches, but strenuously denied having anything to do with the sacking of four workers who did not take a day off in support of the H-block march.

O'Brien told the court that he had sold *The United Irishman*, but denied ever selling *An Phoblacht*. O'Higgins put it to the witness that his purpose in giving evidence to the court was to damage De Rossa and the Workers' Party because he did not approve of their stance on Northern Ireland.

The next witness, Detective Chief Superintendent Joseph Egan, a member of the Garda Síochána since 1964, told the jury that he had spent eighteen years investigating terrorist activity. Under the

Offences Against the State Act 1939, the IRA was an illegal organisation and membership was a criminal offence. The law did not differentiate between the Provisionals and the Officials: subsections were purely semantics as far as the Garda Síochána was concerned. Egan confirmed that Official IRA operations had not ceased entirely after its 1972 ceasefire.

Detective Superintendent Ted Murphy, now based at the National Bureau of Investigation in Harcourt Square, Dublin, gave evidence relating to a time when he was the head of a section of the Fraud Squad. A search warrant had been granted for premises on Green Street East, Hanover Quay, Dublin. A raid was mounted at 11.00 p.m. on the night of 16 November 1983.

Inside the premises, the gardaí had found two printing machines, 110 reams of white opaque paper and a number of wastepaper bags. Inside the bags were hundreds of trial sheets of £5 notes. The witness held up an exhibit sheet of forged notes. The detectives had also found a quantity of white opaque ink, which could be used to forge watermarks on the notes. Inside cardboard cartons, the detectives found serial numbers and a collection of printing plates. Some of the printing plates were for documents used in the building trade and for Custom and Excise vehicle importation forms.

Following on from the garda investigation, a search warrant under the Forgery Act was obtained for the Repsol premises in Gardiner Place, Dublin. A search was conducted on 25 November 1983 and the same serial numbers were found, as well as other Custom and Excise forms and plates for an AIB account of the Irish Life Assurance Company. A number of Repsol employees were detained for questioning, but one suspect, Brian Lynch, had not been traced.

Detective Murphy was asked how he could be so precise as to what had been found at the respective premises some fourteen years earlier. He replied that he had personally drawn up the original report, which had greatly assisted his recollection.

The court was now given a chance to hear from a Russian witness. Vladimar Bukovsky told how he had found the 'Moscow letter' during preparation for a court challenge to Boris Yeltsin's banning of the Communist Party of the Soviet Union. The archives of the central committee of the Communist Party had been taken over by Russia's new government in 1991, and Bukovsky had found the Workers' Party's letters in June 1992. The witness outlined the manner in which the documents had been stored: each one had a title, date, code and sequence number. There were thousands of documents relating to the finances of revolutionary parties.

Judge Carney interrupted the witness during a discussion on the provenance of the Workers' Party's letters to remind him that he should say 'appeared to him' when referring to the authenticity of the signatures.

Before adjourning on the ninth day of the hearing, the judge told counsels that they would be delivering their closing statements the following day. He would then make his address to the jury. The judge warned the jury members that they should not allow anyone to 'winkle' information out of them regarding the discussions in the jury room. Once a verdict had been decided, they would be free to discuss aspects of the case if they so desired, but discussions that had taken place in the jury room had to remain confidential.

This caution was no doubt provoked by a radio broadcast Dunphy had made on the preceding evening. The journalist had been brought in front of the judge to account for his actions. Although the broadcast had not referred to the trial directly, Dunphy, according to Judge Carney, had eulogised the *Sunday Independent* while speaking to political advisor Fergus Finlay and journalist Kevin Myers. Counsels for the plaintiff were allowed to listen to a half-hour recording before deciding what, if any, submission to make. Senior Counsel Ryan told the judge that the trial could proceed because he had no wish to subject his client to a fourth hearing. Judge Carney told Dunphy that if a mistrial had been ordered, the journalist would have been liable for costs. As it was, the judge was adding Dunphy to a conditional order for the sequestration of assets of Independent Newspapers, which had been put in place following a complaint from De Rossa concerning articles published in the wake of the aborted first hearing.

On the tenth day of the hearing, John MacMenamin made the closing address for the defence. He told the jury that De Rossa's litigation was an attempt to escape from his past. If it was indeed De Rossa's signature on the 'Moscow letter', then in all likelihood Seán Garland had tricked him into signing it. Garland had the motive, the means and the opportunity to do so. It was the newspaper's case that certain elements close to Garland were indeed involved in 'special activities', but it had never been the paper's intention to accuse De Rossa of criminal activity. No reasonable person reading the article would have drawn that conclusion.

De Rossa had provided the court with a storybook version of reality, counsel said. The plaintiff had tried to reinvent history and wanted the jury to come to a verdict on his selectivity. MacMenamin sympathised with the jury for having to endure long periods of mind-numbing testimony, including a discourse on Marxist-Leninist history. Perhaps, he suggested, this was a case where the jury should pay more attention to what De Rossa had *not* said. De Rossa had not talked about Garland and the role he had played. He had not mentioned Repsol in direct evidence. He had been vague in his account of the history of the Official IRA. Had the plaintiff treated the jury members in a way that insulted their intelligence, or had he told the whole truth?

MacMenamin told the jury that the handwriting expert who gave evidence had been approached by De Rossa's legal team in a bid to get him to assist on their side. Counsel reminded the jury that both of the letters were written at a time when De Rossa and Garland were in Moscow. He asked them to consider how the letters could have ended up in a Moscow archive if they were forgeries.

Dramatically holding aloft one of the sheets of forged £5 notes, MacMenamin said that this was evidence that was not hearsay. He referred the jury to the other hard evidence that the gardaí had discovered.

Turning to the complaint itself, counsel said that De Rossa had instructed his solicitor to write to the newspaper on 18 December 1992. Then, some time between Christmas Day and the New Year, the plaintiff had lit a bonfire in his garden and burnt all documentation connected to his time with the Workers' Party. The jury was free to deduce what it would from that action.

The jury was urged to look at Dunphy's entire article in context and not to cherry-pick certain sentences or phrases from it. There was a high probability that elements of the Workers' Party had been involved in unsavoury activities and it was not unreasonable to suggest that De Rossa, the party leader, may have known about them. As to the article having harmed De Rossa's reputation, counsel suggested that the jury should consider that up to a few months before he had been a minister, one of the most powerful people in the country.

In conclusion, MacMenamin said that De Rossa had repeatedly asserted that he always tried not to be a prisoner of his past. The jury might think that De Rossa was trying to break out of the prison of his past and eliminate all past events and embarrassments. This reincarnation, he concluded, should not be at his client's expense.

Seán Ryan stood to make the closing submission for the plaintiff. He said that the *Sunday Independent* had created a smokescreen and a cloud of prejudice instead of focusing on whether or not his client had been defamed. The learned counsel for the defence had spoken for ninety minutes before mentioning Dunphy's article. Indeed, such was the irrelevance of the closing submission for the defence that Ryan had considered asking for a mistrial. MacMenamin had cast doubt on the plaintiff's veracity. 'How dare he make that suggestion!' thundered Ryan.

He also attacked the defence counsel for elevating the 'Moscow letter' to hard fact. There was no evidence that De Rossa had known about it. As for the other 'evidence' of which the defence had spoken, it had no relevance to what the jury was being asked to decide.

The hearing had taken ten days, but the plaintiff's ordeal had lasted for almost five years. It was time for it to be ended. His client had been vilified and was justified in seeking redress. An apology and a contribution would have sufficed, but the newspaper did not take that option. Now the only way left for De Rossa to be vindicated was by an award of damages. Counsel asked the jury to find for his client and award him a large sum of money, since anything else would be a victory for the *Sunday Independent*.

In his summing up, Mr Justice Carney told the jury that the case had been one of the hardest fought in the history of Irish jurisprudence. There had been an enormous barrage of publicity surrounding the three hearings, and there was no point trying to suppress this. However, the jury should confine its deliberations to what had been said within the courtroom.

The judge then dealt a rap across the knuckles to both legal teams. He admonished MacMenamin for holding apparently contradictory stances with regard to accepting De Rossa's word that he was not a criminal. He castigated Ryan for telling the jury that he had considered calling for a mistrial; that was, Carney said, a grossly improper thing to say to jurors.

The judge referred to several other High Court cases that might indicate the amount of any damages awarded. He mentioned an action brought against a journalist who had written that a politician had 'tweaked his beard' outside Leinster House. If the injury incurred in that case were compared to allegations that De Rossa was involved in or tolerated serious crime, then the awards should probably be at opposite ends of the scale. The judge reminded the jury that he was not allowed to suggest a figure for damages, though De Rossa's position as head of a political party that at the time was trying to enter government could not be ignored.

After reading aloud the evidence given by the witnesses and charging the jury with directions arising therefrom, the judge told the jurors that their job was to decide the issues of fact. Their decision would be virtually immune from challenge. Judge Carney reminded them that, unlike criminal law, where the case must be proved beyond reasonable doubt, in a civil case the standard rested on the balance of probability. He recognised that the members of the jury had a Herculean task before them, but advised that it would be desirable if they could reach an unanimous verdict. De Rossa's side had argued that the article was defamatory, while the defence had argued that the case had been brought on an incorrect interpretation of the article. It was now up to the jury to decide who was right.

The jury was asked to decide on two issues:

1. Do the words complained of mean: (a) that the plaintiff was involved in or tolerated serious crime? (b) that the plaintiff personally supported anti-Semitism and violent communist suppression?
2. If the answer to question 1 or any part thereof is 'yes', assess damages.

The jury retired to consider its verdict. Two hours later, the members trooped back into the courtroom and its chairperson handed a note to the judge. The jury had unanimously answered 'yes' to 1. (a) and (b). Damages were awarded under 2. at £300,000.

The courtroom erupted when the verdicts were read out. An enigmatic smile spread across Proinsias De Rossa's face, then one of delight as family and friends rushed to congratulate him. The amount was a record award for an Irish libel trial. Up until now, the record had been £90,000 damages awarded to barrister Donagh McDonagh [see Chapter 1].

When the courtroom had settled down again, Ryan asked for costs in the second and third hearings of the libel action. The judge said he would give him costs and all reserved costs. McDowell, for the defence, said there would be substantial argument over costs on the second, hung hearing. The judge replied that costs for the third hearing would be given now and he would reserve the question of costs on the second hearing for a later date, to be fixed by the court office. Counsel for the defence also asked for a stay on the award, pending an appeal. The judge agreed on a stay on the damages award as long as £100,000 was paid immediately. However, the judge refused to order a stay on costs. The costs of defending the libel action were expected to be in the region of £1.5 million. Costs of about £400,000 for the first hearing had already been awarded against the newspaper.

The judge told the jury members that they would have life exemption from further jury duty owing to the protracted nature of the case they had just heard, then discharged them.

Outside the Four Courts, De Rossa spoke briefly about his delight at the verdict before he and his entourage went off to celebrate a hard-won victory. The excessive length of his ordeal had made him the iron man of litigation, but it was a case he could not have given up on.

David Palmer, managing director of Independent Newspapers (Ireland), said the verdict would have profound implications for Irish journalism. Dunphy gave a short statement thanking his supporters and his legal team.

Independent Newspapers (Ireland) lodged an appeal against the decision. It was heard in the Supreme Court in December 1998. Independent Newspapers submitted that a jury in a libel trial should be given guidelines on awards by reference to appropriate levels of damages for pain and suffering awarded in personal injury cases and previous libel awards. For example, a victim of an accident that left him a quadriplegic could be awarded only £250,000 in damages. Hopes were dashed across the publishing world when the appeal was dismissed in July 1999 by a 4–1 majority. The opportunity to set new guidelines for libel damages had been ignored by the Supreme Court. It was another costly loss for the newspaper as De Rossa, by this time a MEP and president of the Labour Party, was awarded the costs of the appeal hearing.

Prior to the hearing there had been considerable speculation that the Supreme Court would heed an obligation to the

European Convention on Human Rights, which states that all awards must be proportionate to the damage suffered. There was also a precedent for the Supreme Court to reduce awards: *Barrett v Independent Newspapers* [1986]. This optimism for the possibility of a successful appeal had been reinforced by the Law Reform Commission's assertion, in 1991, that it was time for change, and by expressions of intent in some political circles.

It must be borne in mind that the drive for legislative change may be slowed when almost a quarter of libel plaintiffs are politicians, as is the case in Ireland. A result like that achieved in the *De Rossa* case would have done little to encourage reform. While there is no dispute that Proinsias De Rossa was defamed, much disquiet remains over the level of damages awarded.

In the wake of the *De Rossa* case, Independent News and Media and Independent Newspapers (Ireland) Limited took a case against the Irish State to the European Court of Human Rights. In what was seen as a bold move, it was hoped that the European Court would force the Irish government to expedite libel reform. Unfortunately, in June 2005 the court dismissed the claim that the limited guidance given to Irish juries in determining libel awards was in breach of the rights to freedom of expression as provided in Article 10 of the European Convention on Human Rights. With that final hope extinguished, it is certain that jury awards in Ireland will continue to be unpredictable until a new Defamation Act, with suitable guidelines, is passed.

In October 2005, on the eve of the Workers' Party's annual conference, Seán Garland was arrested in Belfast. At Belfast Recorder's Court it was revealed that a US grand jury had indicted Garland for the transportation and distribution of counterfeit US currency, namely $100 bills. It is believed that the counterfeit currency was printed in North Korea. The US authorities had applied for Garland's extradition.

Despite opposition from the Crown, Garland was freed on a bail of £27,000. The terms of his bail included that he reside at an address in Northern Ireland, but this restriction was subsequently lifted to allow him to travel to the Republic for medical treatment. In December 2005, Garland failed to reappear in court and a warrant was issued for his arrest. He remains on the run.

05 | WORTH A PUNT:
KIEREN FALLON & ORS v MGN & ORS [1998]

When flat-race jockey Kieren Fallon and his former trainers, Lynda and Jack Ramsden, took *The Sporting Life* (a MGN paper) to court, there was a very real sentiment that the Sport of Kings itself was on trial. Every punter suspects that, from time to time, a trainer or a jockey pulls a fast one, yet they also know that proving such an abuse would be close to impossible. After it pointed the finger of suspicion at the Ramsdens and at Fallon, *The Sporting Life* would have to do just that in a libel court.

It was not the first time a jockey had taken part in a libel case: Lester Piggott recovered £250 from the *Mirror* in 1955, the award having to be approved by a judge because the prodigy Piggott was technically a minor; Scobie Breasley and Michael Dickinson had also won libel actions. By the late 1990s, racing was under attack on a number of fronts: allegations about doping, race-fixing and betting coups organised from the Far East. The last thing the sport needed was to see the reputation of a champion jockey dragged through the mud.

Kieren Fallon had come late to racing. He did not learn to ride until he was eighteen. He rode his first winner at Navan in 1984, but few race-goers at the Meath track that day could have imagined the heights the young jockey would attain in just over a decade. Riding for Jimmy Fitzgerald when he first moved to England, Fallon quickly established himself by guiding Evichstar to a win at Thirsk. He moved to Lynda Ramsden's yard as stable jockey for a number of years, before joining Henry Cecil in 1997 to form one of the most successful partnerships in turf history. He rode 202 winners, including two classics that first year, to claim the crown of champion jockey. Yet this was only the first step in a career that reached new highs with each passing season.

Despite his success, Fallon was dogged by controversy. In 1994, he was banned from riding for six months when he attempted to pull a fellow jockey from his horse after a race. He was also penalised a number of times for excessive use of the whip.

The worst criticism came in 1995. After a poor showing in the Swaffham Handicap at Newmarket, Fallon was accused of short-changing the punters by holding back his ride, Top Cees. When the horse went on to win its next race, the Chester Cup, there was some adverse comment by television pundits. The next day *The Sporting Life* published an editorial accusing Fallon and Lynda and Jack Ramsden of cheating. It was an extremely serious accusation to level – one that could ruin a jockey's and a trainer's reputation.

Writs began to fly until eventually, two-and-half years later, a London High Court was asked to decide the matter. The hearing was awaited with great anticipation, not only because the champion jockey would be giving evidence and the Ramsdens would add glamour to the proceedings, but also for the chance to see a television personality squirming in the full glare of publicity.

Lynda Ramsden, her husband and business partner, Jack, and champion jockey Kieren Fallon were in court for the start of the libel hearing. The case was listed for 3 February 1998, in court 13 – not the most auspicious number for people as superstitious as race-goers. That first day saw considerably more country tweed and Barbour jackets than is usually worn by observers in the public gallery.

The Ramsdens were one of racing's more colourful couples. Lynda first took out a licence to train in 1987 in the Isle of Man, and had gained a reputation as a shrewd judge of horseflesh and jockeys of talent. Her method of training horses was somewhat unorthodox, including the use of extensive blood-testing and an oval training track, rather than the more conventional straight gallop. An animal lover, she had four dogs and five hedgehogs as pets. She was an elegant and well-groomed woman, who would not wear the same outfit twice during the hearing.

Jack Ramsden had once been a successful stockbroker, but now preferred the adrenaline rush of gambling; he considered it more of a business than a hobby. He had helped finance the couple's move to Breckenborough House, near Thirsk. While many of their horses' owners are senior figures from racing's establishment, the couple had provoked some comment from race stewards regarding their racing style. Lynda Ramsden preferred her horses to keep their distance in the hurly-burly of the early stages of a race, then, as others tired, to take up the running.

Patrick Milmo QC, for the plaintiffs, opened the case by condemning outright the contentious articles. The first story had been published on the front page of *The Sporting Life* the day after the Newmarket race, and appeared under the heading: '*Punters fume over Fallon*'. A later editorial, headed '*Contempt for the Punter*', contained a description of the angry reactions of the race-goers after Top Cees romped home by five lengths to win the £40,000 Chester Cup over 2.25 miles on 10 May 1995 at odds of 8–1.

Counsel told Mr Justice Morland and a jury of seven men and five women that Lynda Ramsden had been the champion woman trainer for the last three flat seasons, and that Kieren Fallon's success in securing the jockey's championship in 1997 owed much to experience gained on Ramsden rides. Each year, Lynda Ramsden saddled between forty and fifty winners. She and her husband had paid £15,000 for Top Cees in October 1994 on behalf of owner Alan Leonard, who was still the horse's owner at the time of the Swaffham Handicap.

During the 1995 flat season, Top Cees had run at Doncaster, finishing a disappointing sixth. The horse's next race was the

1.75-mile Swaffham Handicap at Newmarket in April, where it was posted as favourite but trailed in fifth. Before that race, the Ramsdens had instructed Fallon, who was partnering the horse for the first time, to hold it back for the early part of the race and give it its head as late as possible. Jack Ramsden had suggested to Fallon that the horse might not make the distance, but to do his best. Fallon freely admitted that he had waited too long and had been blocked by other horses. The race stewards launched an inquiry on a possible breach of Rule 151, under which it is an offence to instruct the jockey not to win or to give him inadequate instruction to do so. The investigating stewards accepted Fallon's explanation, and after a blood test proved negative the Jockey Club saw no reason to re-open the inquiry.

Lynda Ramsden chose to run Top Cees three weeks later at Chester, in what was considered 'a stayer's race'. There, Fallon rode the horse to a convincing but unanticipated victory. While the Chester stewards did not consider the result exceptional enough to justify staging an inquiry, others took a different view. The renowned Channel 4 racing pundit John McCririck took deep exception to the result and expressed his outrage very forcibly. The editorial that followed the next day in *The Sporting Life* was a 'savage verbal onslaught' on the plaintiffs. Lynda Ramsden was accused of putting two fingers up at the Jockey Club.

It was claimed that the accusations of cheating were wholly false and the product of the writer's 'overworked imagination'. Associate editor Alastair Down had denounced the 'seedy and deeply unpopular victory' and referred to the 'damning patter of perhaps three sets of hands clapping – all hands presumably attached to relations by blood or marriage to Jack and Lynda Ramsden'.

Lynda Ramsden described to the court how she ran her successful yard at Sand Hutton, Thirsk, in north Yorkshire. She had been the top woman trainer for the previous three years, accumulating about £400,000 in prize money annually. Some of her charges were well known in the racing world as quality runners, such as Chilly Billy, Rafferty's Rules, Island Magic and

Travelling Light. Currently she had fifty-two horses attached to her stable. She said that Top Cees had only won on the Flat over a mile, before going hurdling during the 1994–95 winter. The horse was a bit of a monkey and cunning at times, often unseating its rider and reluctant to work on the gallops. She had given serious consideration to gelding Top Cees, now owned by racing magnate Robert Sangster.

When asked about the horse's chances at Newmarket, Lynda Ramsden replied: 'We felt that the past history of the horse's running over that trip was that he faded and did not look like getting that trip. So I told the jockey to hold the horse up for as long as you can to give him every opportunity to get the trip.'

Ramsden was asked if, by doing so, she had put two fingers up at the Jockey Club.

'Certainly not,' she replied defensively. 'They could take my licence away if they thought I was doing that.' She went on to say that she had been amazed when MGN said it would defend the action and maintained that it would prove she had cheated in three other races.

Richard Hartley QC cross-examined Lynda Ramsden for the defence. Footage from the three races in question was shown to the court. Special attention was paid to the Swaffham Handicap, a race the jury would see time and time again as the case progressed. It was pointed out that Fallon had not been blocked and could have pushed on the horse. Ramsden disagreed strongly with that interpretation of how the race had been run.

Jack Ramsden was a gambler of some repute, though Lynda Ramsden insisted that she generally had no idea on which horses he had placed bets: 'He does his thing in his office and I'm out in the yard and, to be honest, I'm not interested in betting. We always discuss the well-being of the horses over breakfast and he will have a look at the form book. But I don't say every day, "What are you having a bet on?"'

Ramsden strongly objected to the repeated suggestion that there was a 'lethal conflict' between the gambling success of her husband and her side in the operation of running a training yard.

She insisted that all her horses were trying to win and her husband did not back them all.

When he took the witness-box, Jack Ramsden told the court that when Top Cees had won the Chester Cup, it had not run under the burden of any bet of his. He had instead backed the runner-up, Harlestone Brook, a proven stayer. He had wagered £250 to win and £100 to place, and a further £70 bet on an outsider that finished seventh. 'As a man who makes calculations on the evidence of the form book, I thought he represented better value,' Ramsden stated.

Ramsden's betting prowess was well known in the racing world. He gambled on a system that could earn him as much as £100,000 a year. Studying the Time Form guide daily, Ramsden had devised a unique rating system that he kept updated by computer. He had been an astute and successful gambler over the previous twenty-five years. Three major book-making chains – Ladbrokes, William Hill and Coral – had closed his accounts because they had shareholders to whom they were answerable. As a result, he now placed his bets with on-course bookmakers Colin Webster and Leslie Steel, occasionally asking his son, friends or owners to lay wagers on his behalf.

Ramsden had had sixty-five good days of 'winning bets' the previous year, ten of which were on horses trained by his wife. On one day he had staked £5,000 on a single losing gamble. He had not enjoyed that and did not think he had made a bet of a similar size since then. He usually preferred smaller bets, sometimes as part of a combination, although the swimming pool at their yard had been paid for by a £1,500 bet at 14–1 on one of his wife's runners. He mentioned that it was now known as the Arbory Street pool in honour of the winner of the 1989 race.

The admission that bookmaker Colin Webster was also an owner and that he paid Ramsden a £5,000-per-year retainer for information on horses was a dangerous one for Ramsden. He was sailing close to the wind of the 'lethal conflict' his wife had explicitly denied. Ramsden was a punter who had a trainer for a wife and a bookmaker who was also an owner – the perfect ingredients for a coup. In an attempt to extricate himself, Ramsden suggested that that scenario was based on the assumption that Webster wanted to wager, but in fact a lot of bookmakers did not wish to place bets. Ramsden was pressed further until he finally conceded, 'If you get it right and you have a bet, then I suppose yes.'

Ramsden was in the paddock before the Newmarket race. He was with his wife, Kieren Fallon, Top Cees's owner Alan Leonard and his daughter. His instructions to the jockey were the same as usual for Top Cees: hold the horse up as long as possible to give him every chance of getting the trip, and for Fallon to do his best. That was the last time he had spoken to Fallon before the race; it had been his wife who had given the jockey a leg-up.

Leonard had had a bet riding on the horse that day, but Ramsden did not know how much it was for. It would emerge later that it was £400 each-way.

Ramsden described how he had been appalled that someone as honest as his wife could have been labelled a cheat. He accepted that trainers could expect protests, but when breeders and owners read about it in the trade press, then it is bad news. There were people around today, Ramsden said, who still thought that the published accusations were the truth. There had been times when he had considered dropping his legal action, but his belief in his wife had made him continue. People could call him anything they liked, but they could not be allowed to do that to Lynda. Ramsden felt that many of the stewards bore a grudge against him and his wife.

It was then the turn of Kieren Fallon to give evidence. It was obvious to anyone who had observed Fallon's unease over the early days of the hearing that the jockey would have preferred to be anywhere else but the courtroom. However, his deep respect for the Ramsdens meant he had never once considered not testifying. His slight figure and an air of being overwhelmed by the occasion lent him a touch of vulnerability, but that would have been a mistake: no jockey can make it to champion without a rock-hard physique and steely determination.

In his evidence, Fallon said that he thought Top Cees had started so well in the Swaffham Handicap that the race was his for the taking. However, the early part of the race had been fast and when he looked for a gap at the later stages, there was none. By the time a gap had opened up, the horse failed to quicken. As a result, he did not ride a proper race, the race he wanted to ride. 'You do your best to win and when you get not-nice articles written about you, you read them and very nearly believe it,' Fallon said.

After the race he explained his poor ride to the race stewards and they were content to accept his clarification. It was the sort of thing that can happen in any race, Fallon argued. Later, Nigel McFarlane, secretary of the Jockey Club disciplinary committee, wrote to Fallon explaining that the governing body had reviewed the running of the race and decided not to instruct the committee to hold an inquiry. A relevant section of the letter was read out in court: 'However, you should not assume from this decision that the stewards were satisfied with your riding.' This was a startling revelation: the Jockey Club was willing to exonerate a jockey in public while showing him a yellow card in private. It was exactly this lack of transparency that had done so much to tarnish the sport's image over the previous decade.

Fallon described how he had felt when he received the letter and read the criticism it contained. 'I wasn't satisfied with my riding either. I went for the wrong gap. [The Jockey Club] have every right to say that.'

Fallon consistently denied that he had not made sufficient effort. Rather, he had simply made an error of judgment. His readiness to accept criticism did much to win over many of the public in the court. He did not try to portray his disciplinary record as anyone's fault but his own. Fallon accepted that early in his career he had probably had the worst record of any jockey.

In its defence, *The Sporting Life* claimed that the article was true in substance and in fact, or was in fair comment on a matter of public interest or was protected by qualified privilege. Always a difficult defence to prove, it was further handicapped by the many accepted variables in racing: the going, the weight, the horse and trainer's form are all factors that affect the outcome of any given race. This was going to be a tricky one.

The defence opened its case by calling Alastair Down, the writer of the contentious editorial and a former Racing Journalist of the Year. Down related how he had watched the Newmarket race on a television in the press room. Some of his fellow journalists had expressed reservations about Fallon's performance. Down had spoken to Steve Taylor, a fellow journalist with *The Sporting Life*, and together they had reviewed the race on television. Down was certain the stewards would have to look at it again. He was positive that the horse had been 'not off' – a turf term for a horse not trying to win – and therefore was surprised when the stewards accepted Fallon's explanation.

When Top Cees won at Chester a little over three weeks later, Down watched the race in the company of Tom Clarke, editor of *The Sporting Life*. Down was struck by a post-race comment from Lord Oaksey, who said that Top Cees's victory that day rendered the Newmarket result not satisfactory for racing. Down admitted that when Fallon had won at Chester, he had been performing at his very best, which made his showing at Newmarket all the more remarkable. Both Down and Clarke believed that the trainers had been cheating and that this needed to be brought to the notice of the public. Shortly thereafter, he wrote his piece, which contained the disputed opinions.

Throughout the hearing Down stuck to his belief that Top Cees was 'not off' at Newmarket. He did admit, however, that he should not have written that the Chester Racecourse switchboard had been jammed by calls from irate race-lovers because there was no evidence to show that such a thing had occurred.

Jim McGrath, Channel 4's racing commentator, and Alan Amies, senior race-reader for Raceform, were called as expert witnesses for the newspaper. McGrath was particularly scathing of Fallon's performance at Newmarket: 'At the time of his likely challenge, he twirled the whip and it would have been easy to go round other horses if he seriously considered winning the race.' McGrath conceded that Fallon was a splendid rider who had ridden a copybook race in the Chester Cup. However, under cross-examination he admitted that he did not like Jack Ramsden.

There was never any doubt that the key witness in the hearing would be Derek Thompson, or 'Tommo', the popular Channel 4 racing presenter. As well as being a television celebrity, Thompson also ran a phone-in tipping service. He was an unenthusiastic witness, who had been compelled to appear on behalf of *The Sporting Life*. The subpoena had been served on Thompson just four days earlier, after he returned from a business trip to Dubai. This late contact and the fact that he was testifying against his wishes would play a major part in the jury's final verdict.

Thompson said he believed that Top Cees should have finished an awful lot closer in the Swaffham Handicap, and probably should have won. On the night of the Newmarket race meeting, Thompson had dined with jockey Richard Fox and his wife at The Old Plough, not far from the racecourse. He had met Fallon there at around 10.00 p.m. and briefly discussed the race with him. Fallon had been having a drink with weighing-room colleague, Michael Wigham. This was when the reason behind Thompson's reluctance to appear at the hearing emerged. He told the judge and jury: 'I don't want to repeat this in open court, which is why I've tried to stop it coming to open court, because it was said to me in confidence.'

The judge told Thompson that he would have to give evidence. Many of the court observers had sympathy for Tommo's predicament. Nobody likes to tell tales, after all, especially when your career is based partly on a carefully nurtured friendship and trust with jockeys. Nonetheless, upon the judge's insitence, Thompson continued:

> I was asking, 'What happened with Top Cees this afternoon as I thought he would win?' and Kieren's words were, 'Yes, I thought the horse would win as well, but when I got into the paddock, Jack told me to stop it.'

If true, Fallon's statement was dynamite. Thompson had raised the matter with two people at a Channel 4 production meeting the following morning. He suggested to them that it might be worthwhile interviewing the jockey because the horse's failure was a story in the racing world. Fallon was reluctant to be interviewed, however, even though Thompson gave him an assurance that what they had talked about at The Old Plough would not come out. As the press was hounding Fallon, Thompson suggested that a television interview might do him good by helping to put a lid on the frenzied speculation.

If Thompson felt umbrage at being questioned by the defence, it was about to get much worse for him as he was subjected to a very aggressive cross-examination.

'What you have just told the court about Kieren Fallon is an outrageous lie – that's right, is it not?' demanded Milmo.

'If you think so, that's up to you. But no, it's not,' Thompson replied.

Milmo suggested that Thompson had lied or embellished the truth to Channel 4 and that telling the truth now, i.e. that Fallon had said nothing of consequence, would show him up as a liar to his employers. Rather than let Channel 4 know the truth, Milmo said, Thompson was prepared to ruin the career of one of the best jockeys in England.

Thompson strenuously denied the supposition, stating that it was utterly ridiculous: 'I have the greatest respect for Kieren Fallon as one of the finest horsemen in the world and the last thing I want to do is to be sitting here.' But sit he had to, while he was accused of deceiving people on a day-to-day basis. This accusation was a reference to the fact that Thompson continued to supply racing tips on his premium line number even when he was out of the country. Milmo also made much of discrepancies between notice of evidence supplied by *The Sporting Life* before the hearing and the oral evidence given by Thompson in court. Faced with an uncooperative witness, who was also out of the country, much of the gist of the evidence supplied by the newspaper had been assumption. The key passage in Thompson's written version about the conversation in the pub had Jack Ramsden saying to Fallon: 'We have missed the price. Today is not the day.' This had not been repeated in oral evidence.

Thompson denied the suggestion that it was his duty as racing presenter to bring misdemeanours of which he had become aware to the attention of the racing authorities. He insisted that what he had heard in the pub was man-to-man and he had no way of substantiating it. He had heard a lot of things in the racing world that he had no wish to repeat.

Jack Ramsden was recalled to the witness-box when the court resumed after the weekend adjournment. He told the court that it was totally untrue to suggest that he had told Kieren Fallon to stop a horse and that he had been horrified by Thompson's evidence: 'The first thing I did was ring Mr Fallon to see if there was the remotest truth in it, I couldn't believe it … I was pretty appalled at someone suggesting anything like that.'

Thompson's evidence had clearly upset Jack Ramsden. He and his wife had had dinner with Thompson just four months previously and the court case had not been mentioned. At no time had Thompson ever queried what Fallon's riding orders were on that day.

Ramsden admitted that there was no evidence at all that the owner had backed the horse at Newmarket. He objected to the suggestion that it would not have stopped him from ordering the jockey to hold back the horse. 'I wouldn't have any owners left in the yard if they didn't trust me,' he protested.

It was put to Ramsden that the reason he had not backed the horse himself was because the 6–1 odds were not good enough. The odds had shortened considerably after a newspaper had tipped the horse. Counsel said in accusation: 'That's why you decided the horse shouldn't be allowed to run on its merits.'

Ramsden found the idea incredible: 'With the owner standing beside me and knowing he'd backed it!' Lynda Ramsden confirmed that her husband had definitely not taken Fallon aside to speak to him before the race.

On the fifteenth day of the hearing, Fallon was given a chance to challenge Thompson's evidence. Once again, the jockey strongly denied stopping the horse:

It would be a terrible thing for any jockey to even think about stopping a horse, let alone doing it, and jeopardise your [sic] career. Mr Thompson has invented it and he is a liar.

It was put to him that Thompson had told the court that the witness had said: 'Yes, I thought the horse would win as well, but when I got into the paddock, Jack told me to stop it.'

Fallon denied this and told the jury that he would never have called his employer 'Jack': 'I don't know Mr Thompson other than that he was a television presenter. I wouldn't discuss with someone like that instructions I had been given by the trainer of the horse I was riding. I have never been told to stop any horse by Mr or Mrs Ramsden.'

Fallon was asked if he would stop a horse if he were asked to do so. He replied that no, he would not risk losing his licence by doing so. Counsel suggested that for a rider of Fallon's ability, it would be an easy thing to do without drawing attention to himself: 'Find trouble. Don't take gaps. Don't urge the horse on. It's the easiest thing in the world for someone as competent and excellent a rider as you.

Fallon replied: 'Riding along at 30 mph, three inches from the heels of the horse in front of you, you don't look for trouble, you try to avoid it. Different things happen in the race. It's always moving. You make decisions – sometimes it's the wrong one.'

Having heard all the evidence, it was time for counsel to make their closing addresses. Milmo began his concluding speech with a warning to the jury that people do not act dishonestly just for the hell of it, rather 'they do it for a reason and the usual reason is some sort of enrichment, either directly or indirectly'. The jury would have to ask itself why, if they had been at the heart of some form of betting coup, neither Ramsden nor his wife had a bet on

Top Cees when it won at Chester. Indeed, the jury had heard
evidence that Jack Ramsden had preferred to wager on two other
competing horses in that race. Perhaps, Milmo conjectured, the
Ramsdens had run Top Cees at Newmarket so the handicapper
would favour it with a lower weight? Not so, as its outing that day
had resulted in the weight being raised. Neither did the horse need
the run-out because it had been racing over the winter and was
race fit. In fact, he went on, there was not a shred of evidence that
the Ramsdens had ordered the horse to be held back because the
price was not right. The court had heard that Alan Leonard, the
owner, had £400 on it that day: how long would trainers stay in
business if they allowed that to happen?

Milmo reminded the jury that about 250,000 people read *The
Sporting Life* each day, including those in authority in racing. The
litigation had been an ordeal for his clients and any award given
should be at the top end of the scale, approaching six figures.

In closing for the plaintiff, Hartley told the jury that it was
grotesque to think Thompson had come to court to lie. He had
been reluctant to give evidence because he had no wish to damage
the careers of the plaintiffs. When he did come, however, it had
been to tell the truth – even if it meant damaging his own career –
because he could not stand back and watch an injustice being
perpetrated. Thompson had no possible motive to lie in the
witness-box, but could the same be said of the plaintiffs? Hartley
continued:

> People love racing for all sorts of different reasons and they
> want it to prosper. But it can only do so if its integrity stays
> intact and if sordid, squalid and seedy stains like the Swaffham
> are scrubbed clean. The plaintiffs have told so many lies and
> half-truths and contradicted themselves so many times that
> you may think Walter Scott had them in mind when he wrote,
> 'Oh, what a tangled web we weave, when first we practise to
> deceive'.

The judge, Mr Justice Morland, made his charge to the jury the following day. He had already ruled that qualified privilege would not run as a defence, so it was incumbent upon the newspaper to prove that what had been written was true. The jury heard the judge outline the evidence given during the hearing, but he gave it a warning on the Thompson evidence: 'You must treat the evidence of Derek Thompson with caution. Only after very careful consideration should you act on his evidence. You have to be satisfied that his account of the conversation is truthful and accurate and that what he said Fallon said amounted to a confession.'

The jury returned its verdict after six hours of deliberation. The jury foreman announced that it had found by a majority of 10–2 that the newspaper had not established that the words complained of were substantially true in relation to Kieren Fallon and Jack Ramsden. Its finding in favour of Lynda Ramsden on this basis was unanimous. The jury had also found against the newspaper on the defence of fair comment by the same majority. The plaintiffs had not established that editor Tom Clarke or writer Alastair Down were malicious in publishing the words complained of, therefore costs were awarded against the newspaper, estimated to be £500,000.

Outside the court, Alastair Down said to the assembled media: 'We fought a good fight. We got beaten and there's no point whingeing about it. It's not been a good day for the press or the punters, but I hope we will continue to look after our punters' interest.'

Down's words may have come back to haunt him. A short time later, *The Sporting Life* ceased publication. The MGN group talked of a relaunch later in the year, but it never happened.

Fallon was not in court to hear the verdict, as he had one runner at Lingfield that day. The jockey assistants had run a book on the verdict and when the news came through, there was much celebration in the changing rooms. The jockey had been awarded

£70,000, Lynda Ramsden £75,000 and Jack Ramsden £50,000. After hearing the news, Fallon picked up his whip and went out to the parade ring to mount his ride of the afternoon. To nobody's great surprise, he guided the horse home in first place. He would go on to win another four jockey championships in the next five years, although trouble had a way of following him: a bad fall at Royal Ascot almost finished his career; Henry Cecil axed him after tabloid stories appeared over the jockey's relationship with Cecil's wife; and in 2003, Fallon had to have treatment for alcohol problems. In spite of it all, he bounced back to win the Epsom Derby in 2003.

Fallon was embroiled in further controversy in subsequent years. There was another claim of race-fixing in March 2004, when an undercover *News of the World* journalist secretly taped Fallon predicting the winner of a race at Lingfield Park. Shortly before the start of the race, the Jockey Club was alerted to internet betting irregularities. Fallon's mount, Ballinger Ridge, led for most of the race, but seemed to slow towards the post, allowing the odds-on favourite, Rye, to snatch the race by a short head. Perhaps equally damaging to Fallon's career was the newspaper's claim that Fallon had been drinking again.

The now six-times champion jockey was arrested in September 2004 by the City of London police along with trainers Alan Berry and Karl Burke. Lengthy investigations into possible irregularities in eighty races continued until July 2006, when Fallon and ten others were charged in relation to corruption in racing. Fallon was also charged with conspiracy to defraud customers of Betfair. Banned from racing in the UK, Fallon continued to ride in other countries, but in November 2006 was given a six-month ban in France after failing a drugs test at Chantilly. The French racing authorities requested that other jurisdictions recognise the ruling.

Fallon returned to the libel courts in March 2006 and accepted undisclosed damages from *News of the World*. In February 2004, the newspaper had repeated an allegation previously made by jockey Stuart Webster that in September 1994 Fallon had launched a violent locker-room assault against him. The assault – in which Fallon was alleged to have head-butted Webster and thrown punches – occurred as a follow-up to the incident when Fallon had pulled Webster from his horse at the end of a race at Beverley, Yorkshire. It transpired that there had indeed been an assault, during which Webster's nose was broken, but that Fallon had been acting in self-defence. The newspaper was willing to acknowledge that the story was false and apologised for the distress caused to Fallon.

His licence to ride in the UK was restored in December 2007 when, two months into the headline-grabbing trial, the judge ruled that Fallon and his fellow defendants had no case to answer and the jury was instructed to return not guilty verdicts.

06 | THE TROUBLES I'VE SEEN:
THOMAS MURPHY v THE SUNDAY TIMES & ORS [1998]

The rehearing of the Thomas Murphy action against *The Sunday Times* was one of the most sensational libel trials ever held in Ireland. It was never going to be one of those dry-as-dust legal cases in which bewigged learned counsel endlessly trade dull points of law in front of a judge while the jury and press struggle to stay awake. Nonetheless, very few would have expected the ensuing drama to be quite as high-octane. There were some clues, however, not least the assembled cast.

Rarely had such a diverse collection of people crowded into the same courtroom: terrorists mingled with Special Branch detectives, intelligence operatives mixed uneasily with their targets, IRA gunmen stared ominously at former comrades turned informers. It must have been a nightmare for those in charge of security in the Four Courts. Most ominous for Murphy and his supporters, however, was the presence of Adrian Hopkins, the skipper of the failed gun-running ship, *Eksund*. The atmosphere was electric, intimidating and charged with menace; everyone there knew that it would take only a spark to set off a conflagration. They were to be disappointed if they hoped to see a mass brawl, as had happened in Crumlin Road courthouse in Belfast during some of the supergrass trials during the 1980s.

However, the repercussions of this case would prove quite extraordinary, being swift, bloody and far-reaching.

Thomas 'Slab' Murphy, a Co. Louth farmer, had a notorious reputation long before *The Sunday Times* 'outed' him as a leading member of the IRA on 30 June 1985. The stories told about the smuggler and crime godfather were legendary: how the border bisected his mother's small farm and the manner in which he would make fools of the RUC and the Garda Síochána by simply walking across the yard, leaving one jurisdiction and entering another. Goods of all description were smuggled through the vast shed he had built straddling the border, with much of the profit finding its way into IRA coffers. Customs and Excise men knew well enough what was going on, but they had families and loved ones to protect. IRA volunteers working on Murphy's farm provided cheap labour and ensured that for over twenty years, nobody challenged his right to live like a medieval warlord.

The British Army erected an observation tower on a south Armagh hilltop a mile away so it could keep an eye on the comings and goings at the Murphy farm. 'Slab' outwitted the Army by building an even larger sheet-metal fence in direct eyeline between the tower and his yard. However, smuggling was not the only illegal activity in which Murphy was involved. He was also the driving force for the IRA's south Armagh active service unit, perhaps the most bloodthirsty faction within the Provisionals.

It was no secret that both the Northern Ireland Chief Constable and the Garda Commissioner would dearly have loved to gather enough evidence to convict Murphy. It was one of his men who had planted the bomb that killed Lord Mountbatten in 1979 – a great tragedy and a great embarrassment to the Irish government. In mid-1985, John Hermon, RUC Chief Constable, suggested in a radio interview that the prime suspect for the murder of four of his constables was a pig farmer from Co. Louth. It was this allegation that led to *The Sunday Times* unmasking 'Slab' Murphy and provoking his retaliatory defamation suit.

Murphy may have enjoyed playing the 'culchie' – he certainly looked the part with his stocky build, ruddy face and balding, unkempt hair – but he was a shrewd man who had others do his dirty work; a modern-day outlaw who was not beyond using the law to his advantage. Twice he had brought successful libel actions against those who had dared to print accusations about him. The *Daily Mail* had paid him £15,000 and costs in an out-of-court settlement, while the New English Library, publisher of *Financing the Terror*, settled an action at the cost of a £60,000 payout. The author of that book was James Adams, a journalist with *The Sunday Times*.

Indeed, *The Sunday Times* had come within minutes of settling Murphy's litigation at a secret negotiation meeting on 27 October 1987 at the Mourne Country Hotel in Newry, Co. Down. Murphy wanted £500,000 and costs to date to drop the joint suit he and his brother Patrick had initiated, but the newspaper's lawyers had bargained the sum down to £480,000. The proposed settlement was aborted when the newspaper's editor, Andrew Neil, baulked at paying out such a large sum, which could conceivably end up in the hands of the IRA. Neil threatened to resign if any payment was made. The newspaper courageously opted to fight the Murphy brothers in court.

The case was to have been heard just days later, in early November, but was put back until February 1988 at the request of Murphy's legal team. Despite having little co-operation from the security forces, the newspaper won the case, primarily by proving that Thomas Murphy was reputedly a member of the IRA. The brothers made a successful appeal to the Supreme Court, which ordered a retrial in 1996. The appeal judgment said that the presiding High Court judge, Mr Justice Lynch, had not fully explained to the jury how it should view opinion evidence.

The brothers made a number of other applications to the High Court and eventually made another successful appeal to the Supreme Court to have their cases heard separately at a retrial, each with their own legal representation. To the newspaper's consternation, the courts had raised the bar for the retrial: this time *The Sunday Times* could not rely on evidence of reputation, it would have to prove with hard evidence that Murphy was in the IRA – a much tougher prospect.

Thomas Murphy's case was listed for courtroom 4 of Dublin's High Court on 30 April 1998, some thirteen years after the alleged defamatory article had been published. By this time, there was a very different political background in Ireland. The IRA had declared a ceasefire and the security forces of several countries were now more willing to assist the newspaper, which hadn't been the case at the original hearing. The IRA would have preferred Murphy to drop the case, since it was likely to prove an embarrassment to the organisation's newly avowed aim of progress through peaceful political means. Eamon Leahy SC represented Murphy, while the defence solicitors, A&L Goodbody, had retained Paul Gallagher SC and Kevin Feeney SC. The defendants were *The Sunday Times*, its former editor Andrew Neil and journalists Andrew Hogg, Barrie Penrose, Chris Ryder and Rowena Webster. Mrs Justice Catherine McGuinness was the presiding judge and a jury of eight women and four men was sworn in.

The case would be fought along relatively simple lines. Murphy's legal team would have the easier task. If the newspaper could not back up with proof what it had published about Murphy, it would lose. It therefore had a much more difficult mountain to climb. With little physical evidence to present, the newspaper would have to rely on its witnesses convincing the jury that Murphy was a criminal. Unfortunately, two of the newspaper's key witnesses weren't exactly candidates for beatification. Who would the jury believe?

Opening the case for Murphy, Leahy told the jury that after hearing the evidence it would be satisfied that the damage done to his client was the grossest done by any newspaper to any person in Ireland. The article, he said, fell squarely in the context of being outrageous.

The article was read in full to the court. It had been published in *The Sunday Times* on 30 June 1985 under the heading, 'Portrait of a Check-in Terrorist'. A subheading in bold read:

Last week, the police announced that they had discovered an IRA plan to plant bombs in 12 seaside resorts. They detained over a score of people and appeared to have destroyed one of the Provisional IRA's active service units. But the triumph has a dark side; there are more of these units. How are they created and how are they destroyed? A report by Andrew Hogg, Barrie Penrose and Chris Ryder.

Extracts read:

In Ireland itself the planning of mainland campaigns is surrounded now by a more tightly-knit security. The IRA's army council last February appointed a farmer in the Republic, called 'Slab' Murphy (which is not his real name) to be its operations commander for the whole of Northern Ireland. He has no convictions for terrorist activities and this, plus the fact that he is on the other side of the border, makes him a security headache hard to cure.

Murphy is likely to have sanctioned certain key Provisionals travelling to Britain to take part in this summer's planned bombing campaign. It would have been a task made easier to keep secret by the fact that his farm is close to the small town of Dundalk where IRA men on the run can gain sanctuary in 'safe' houses.

Thomas Murphy had been born in north Co. Louth, adjacent to the border, and now lived close to his childhood home at Ballybinaby in Hackballscross. Murphy was a common enough name in the area, where there is a local custom of using nicknames to differentiate families. His father had been known as 'Slab' Murphy, and the name had been passed to all of his sons. Since the publication of the article, it was alleged, the name 'Slab' Murphy had become notorious in north Louth and south Armagh.

The newspaper could not hide behind the excuse of the words in the article not meaning what the plaintiff took them to mean. There was no doubt what the words meant and were intended to mean: that Thomas Murphy was a prominent figure in the IRA and that he had sought, planned, sanctioned and aimed to cause indiscriminate slaughter. Murphy would give evidence that there was no truth to the article and would describe the devastating effect it had on him. Driving his point home, counsel told the jury that his client had never been charged with membership of the IRA. The skulking character assassins who had written the article had not cared about the plaintiff's good reputation, his counsel stated, but now that they had been challenged and brought to court, they would have to adduce evidence and proof to support their claims.

Thomas Murphy was called to give his evidence. It would be one of the shortest appearances in a witness-box by any libel plaintiff in living memory. Murphy told the court that he had been shown the article on the day of publication and upon reading it had felt extremely distressed. He understood it to refer to him, as did numerous other people who made a point of mentioning it to him in subsequent days. A caustic remark made to him by Bernard Finnegan, a milkman, had stuck in his memory the most.

To the majority of observers in the court, Murphy did not come across as a man who would have sleepless nights over what a delivery man thought of him. Most felt that the brooding Murphy would revel in being regarded as a figure of fear.

Paul Gallagher cross-examined Murphy for the defence. He asked the plaintiff why it had taken him two years to issue a writ against *The Sunday Times*. Murphy explained that he could not be sure how long it was. It could well have been June 1987 by the time his solicitor's letter reached the newspaper, but he had consulted with them immediately after the article had been published. It was the start of an evasiveness that would colour much of Murphy's testimony.

Murphy was asked what had made him believe that the article referred to him. Was it not true that there were a great many other Murphy families living in that area? Murphy agreed that there were other families, and a number of Thomas Murphys amongst them. Most of them also bore a nickname of one sort or another, but when he read the article, he did not think it referred to anyone other than himself. In 1985, he would not have been known as anything other than Thomas or 'Slab'. His house was about 250 m from his parents' house, which was right at the border.

When asked if he had ever been called 'The General', Murphy smiled enigmatically and denied it. That was the end of the cross-examination and Murphy was allowed to step down from the witness stand. The court would hear from him again later.

Kevin Feeney opened for the defence. It had been agreed before the case that the normal running order of the hearing would be altered. Keen to avoid a recurrence of the evidence problem that had provided grounds for the retrial, Mrs Justice McGuinness had ruled that evidence of fact and reputation should be separated.

Justification was the basis of the newspaper's defence. *The Sunday Times* was certain that the article was true, and that was the issue upon which the jury would have to decide. The defence planned to call witnesses who would give evidence that Thomas Murphy was a prominent member of the IRA. There would be further evidence about a false passport Murphy was holding, one of a batch stolen from the Department of Foreign Affairs in 1984. Other passports from this batch had turned up in the possession of people convicted of IRA-related activity. The two principal witnesses for the newspaper were both former IRA volunteers who had turned informer: Seán O'Callaghan, who had turned Queen's evidence before his 1989 conviction in Britain, and Eamon Collins, also a former member of the Provisionals.

Seán O'Callaghan was called first. The last time he had been in the Four Courts had been to stash a gun so that an IRA man could escape. A slight, dapper man with a haunted face, O'Callaghan had flown in that morning from a secret address in England. He blew a kiss at Thomas Murphy as he entered the courtroom. Murphy responded with a guffaw, before his face quickly slipped back into the inscrutable mask it would wear for most of the proceedings.

O'Callaghan was born in Tralee, Co. Kerry in 1954 and had grown up in a republican home; his father had once been interned in the Curragh. Seán O'Callaghan had joined the Provisional IRA in 1970, when he was just fifteen years old. He was jailed for six months after causing an accidental detonation with home-made explosives he was working on at the rear of his parents' house. After his release, he became a full-time member of the IRA. In 1975 he grew disillusioned with the cause: the motives for fighting the British were not as clear-cut as he had first envisaged and he felt that many of his fellow Provos in the North were fighting for a different cause. After witnessing the delight some of his comrades took in the murder of a young Protestant woman, he decided he could not continue to be part of the movement. He resigned from active duty and moved to England. It took him four years to decide that merely leaving the IRA was not enough; he wanted to help defeat them.

He returned to Co. Kerry in August 1979 and rejoined the Provisionals so that he could secretly pass information to the Garda Síochána. At first he was mainly involved in training, but as the years passed and he became more trusted, he rose through the ranks, eventually becoming head of the IRA's Southern Command in 1984. He left the IRA again in 1985.

Back in England, O'Callaghan talked to the British police and, with the Garda Síochána's permission, attended a lengthy debriefing in Europe. In November 1988 he walked into Tunbridge Wells police station and said he wanted to confess to the murder of RUC Detective Inspector Peter Flanagan in Omagh, Co. Tyrone on 23 August 1974. In May 1990 he pleaded guilty to two charges of murder at Belfast Crown Court. Fifty-four other charges, ranging from attempted murder, possession of explosives and the hijacking of cars, were taken into consideration. The court handed down two life sentences and 549 years in prison. O'Callaghan was released in December 1996, after eight years in custody. He had been granted the Queen's prerogative and his sentence was subsequently reduced to sixteen years. He was then granted a 50 per cent remission for good behaviour.

As a garda mole, O'Callaghan had relayed information that led to the capture of the Co. Kerry gun-running ship *Marita Ann* in 1984. Future Sinn Féin TD Martin Ferris was arrested on board the ship after a cargo of weapons was transferred from the Boston-based *Valhalla*. Intelligence supplied by O'Callaghan had foiled a kidnap bid on retail magnate Galen Weston in 1983 and led to the release of an alternative victim, supermarket executive Don Tidey. O'Callaghan also passed information to British intelligence and is credited with preventing numerous killings and bombings in Northern Ireland.

There was no doubt that O'Callaghan's life was still at risk and he had deep reservations about giving evidence in the present libel case. Despite this very real fear, he pointed out Murphy, who was sitting in the crowded public gallery: 'He is sitting there. The man with the leather jacket and blue tie.'

O'Callaghan had met Murphy on several occasions. Their first meeting was at an IRA Revolutionary Council assembly in 1983 in Charlestown, Co. Mayo. Senior figures present were Gerry Adams, Sinn Féin president, Pat Doherty, vice-president, and Martin McGuinness. Others in attendance included Danny Morrison, Joe Keohane, Martin Ferris, John Noonan, Tommy Devereaux and J.P. McDonald. Murphy had also been present at two meetings of the IRA GHQ staff, in 1984 and 1985, which O'Callaghan had chaired as Officer Commanding the IRA in Southern Ireland – a position he had been given in the wake of Martin Ferris's arrest on board the *Marita Ann*. These meetings had taken place at Heath House, a Georgian mansion in Co. Kildare owned by veteran republican Uinseann MacEoin. Only high-ranking IRA members could secure a position on GHQ staff. Amongst those attending the meetings were Kevin McKenna, IRA Chief of Staff, Pat Doherty, Adjutant General, Kieran Conway, Director of Research, and Danny Morrison, Director of Publicity. Security had been so tight at Heath House that the participants had been more or less locked up together for thirty-six hours.

Thomas Murphy had been at Heath House as the Officer Commanding the IRA in Northern Ireland. O'Callaghan recalled a conversation he had overheard at one of the meetings in early

1985. Doherty had asked Murphy how the IRA was going to win the war against the British. Murphy had replied: 'Bomb them to the conference table, and then booby-trap the table.'

'What about the Sinn Féin delegation?' Doherty asked.

'We never tell people where we're putting our booby-traps,' Murphy said.

It was a quip that had chilled O'Callaghan to the bone and brought back memories of why he had first left the IRA. The lust for blood amongst some of the members was beyond his comprehension.

The first day of the libel hearing ended sensationally. At 4.00 p.m. the court was adjourned until the following morning and the parties made their way from the Four Courts building. Murphy had gone to great lengths to avoid being photographed by the waiting press, exiting with a coat held firmly over his head and shoulders. But it was O'Callaghan's departure that caused a scuffle inside the corridors of the Four Courts. *The Sunday Times*, at O'Callaghan's insistence, had asked that he be given a garda escort, but some of Murphy's supporters quickly surrounded them, shouting abuse and jostling them. It took twenty minutes for order to be restored and a shaken O'Callaghan to be ushered safely away. Even then, their exit was a bit of a scramble and one of Murphy's men managed to tag along, having been mistaken for a plain-clothes officer.

It would have been a simple task to harm O'Callaghan there and then, if that had been the intention. O'Callaghan's troubles were far from over, however. Garda detectives arrested him on the front steps of the Four Courts and swiftly bundled him into a waiting squad car. The news of the arrest was a body blow to the newspaper's hopes of winning the case: what hope was there of maintaining O'Callaghan's credibility now? Murphy no doubt appreciated the irony that it was the Garda Síochána who had seriously undermined the principal witness against him.

O'Callaghan was driven to Naas garda station for questioning under Section 30 of the Offences Against the State Act. Detectives wished to interview him in connection with the murder of a fellow IRA man and informer, Seán Corcoran, in 1985. Corcoran's body had been found dumped in a Co. Kerry field. Gerard Colleran, editor of *The Kerryman* newspaper, said that O'Callaghan had admitted to him during a phone conversation that he had killed Corcoran, who was a fellow garda mole.

O'Callaghan had stated publicly that he had killed Corcoran and in 1997 John O'Donoghue, then Minister for Justice, had ordered an inquiry into the admission. It had always been O'Callaghan's assertion that he had done all he could to save Corcoran's life after suspicion had fallen on him and felt others had decided that Corcoran's death was a sacrifice worth making. He claimed that his fake admission that he had killed Corcoran had been an attempt to focus attention on the man's death and expose those he considered to be culpable.

The detectives were granted a twenty-four-hour extension to O'Callaghan's detention. The former double-agent was eventually released two days after his arrest, without being charged. Despite being provided with a safe house in Dublin, O'Callaghan felt he could trust nobody and flew back to England. The libel hearing sat again on the following Tuesday and O'Callaghan returned in time to resume his evidence.

If the credibility of their witness was to be preserved, the first hurdle *The Sunday Times* legal team had to get over was to explain to the court why he had been arrested. O'Callaghan admitted that he had indeed once confessed to killing Seán Corcoran. He had hoped that his false confession might prompt the RUC into inadvertently supplying him with any details it had about the murder. O'Callaghan had suspected for some eighteen months that Corcoran's life was in danger and he had done his best to prevent his death. Mrs Justice McGuinness interrupted the witness to say that if he felt he was being asked to incriminate himself, he could ask her for guidance.

While the life of an informer may undoubtedly depend on his potential for duplicity, O'Callaghan's use of misinformation was regarded as a weakness and one that would come back to haunt him in cross-examination. The impact of his evidence seemed diminished after his arrest, reducing the 'star' quality of his second-act performance.

O'Callaghan described a 1983 meeting in Sinn Féin's office in Parnell Street, Dublin. Murphy had been present at that meeting and had spoken briefly with O'Callaghan afterwards. Murphy had requested that O'Callaghan supply him with rifles suitable for killing deer. Arrangements were made via a third party, Dickie O'Neil, for the stolen rifles to be delivered to Dundalk, Co. Louth.

In 1983, O'Callaghan had been ordered to England as a bomber. It was this campaign to bomb seaside towns that *The Sunday Times* had referred to in the article. In order to save lives, O'Callaghan had ensured that the bombs did not go off and also that a plot to kill the Prince and Princess of Wales at the Dominion Theatre, London was aborted. The revulsion felt by the British people at the IRA's bombing of Brighton's Grand Hotel during the 1984 Conservative Party conference, in an attempt to kill Prime Minister Margaret Thatcher, was part of the motivation for *The Sunday Times* article.

The witness finished his evidence for the defence by telling the court how the IRA had tried to discredit him. He repeated that his life was in danger and would probably remain so, ceasefire or no.

Murphy's legal team was quick to seize the golden opportunity presented to it by O'Callaghan's arrest. It was important to show O'Callaghan as someone who was a stranger to the truth and an opportunist, a man who had decided to give evidence not to see justice done, but to drum up publicity for his book, *The Informer*, due to be on the bookshelves in less than a fortnight.

Leahy started his cross-examination by asking O'Callaghan if he had always been truthful with journalists. O'Callaghan agreed that that had not always been the case, although sometimes the inaccuracies that found their way into print were not his fault. The witness also conceded that providing the occasional false statement to the RUC and to *The Sunday Times* had not helped his credibility in public perception.

O'Callaghan was asked to describe Murphy as he was at the time of their alleged first meeting in 1983. He remembered him as having more hair, not quite as grey. He was not so fat as he currently was and was about 5' 10" or 5' 11" in height. He recalled that his nose was rather a funny shape and he had a dour expression.

O'Callaghan was then required to explain the nature of his relationship with *The Sunday Times*. Liam Clarke, its Northern Ireland correspondent, had first interviewed him in 1992. After that contact was fairly often, but not on any regular basis. He wrote articles for *The Sunday Times* and for other newspapers. He was now writing his autobiography, in co-operation with Cathy Johnson, Liam Clarke's wife.

Extracts from O'Callaghan's articles were read to the court and he was asked if he considered them to have an anti-Irish sentiment. O'Callaghan agreed and said there was some 'black humour' included. He was then asked to explain payments he had received from *The Sunday Times*. He answered patiently with a detailed account of the monies he had been paid. A trip he had made to the United States had been partly funded by *The Sunday Times*. The purpose of the trip was to tell Irish-Americans about the dangers of supporting violent Irish nationalism. He stated that he had also received money from the British authorities.

The spotlight was kept firmly fixed on O'Callaghan's financial dealings as he told the court about the £175,000 advance he had received for his book. He denied that his financial future and the book's success were linked to the libel hearing. O'Callaghan insisted he had not come to Dublin to promote his book; he was there to tell the truth. He would not agree that testifying at the hearing would enhance the book's sales; Murphy was not mentioned in the book. (A postscript was added in a later edition covering the libel trial.) When asked if he had sent Corcoran's widow a bank draft from the book's advance, O'Callaghan said he did not believe he had ever said he would. He hoped to speak to Mrs Corcoran before his book came out, and had declined to speak about her husband's death on Pat Kenny's radio show on RTÉ.

O'Callaghan was forced to admit his history of deceitfulness once again when asked to name one person in the last ten years to whom he had consistently told the truth.

'It's extremely difficult to give you that answer,' he replied.

Before O'Callaghan was allowed to step down, Paul Gallagher re-examined for the defence, eager to repair some of the damage that had been done. O'Callaghan said that he had told the truth to the court. He had recounted the facts about meetings where he had met Murphy. He denied that his appearance in court was a publicity stunt. Indeed, his publisher had advised him against appearing. Liam Clarke had asked him to give evidence and he had agreed because he did not think Murphy should get one penny from any court or from any individual.

Having heard from its principal witness, the defence now decided to present what little physical evidence it had.

Retired Garda Detective Inspector Dan Prenty had been stationed in Dundalk for a number of years, during which he had encountered Murphy on many occasions. During a search of the house of Elizabeth Murphy, Thomas Murphy's mother, Prenty had discovered a forged passport bearing Murphy's photograph, but issued under a different name. The gardaí had planned the search for 27 June 1989. When he saw the gardaí approaching the house, 'Slab' had leapt out of a window and run across the yard into Northern Ireland. Three passports were found during the search, two of which appeared to be legitimate, while the third had been issued in 1983 and was in the name of Jim Faughey, a neighbour of Murphy's. The given day and month of birth was the same as the other passports, though the birth year was 1951. Height and weight details were also a match for Murphy.

Some days after the search, Murphy had presented himself at Dundalk garda station for questioning with regard to the murder of two high-ranking RUC officers. No charges were brought. Prenty also told of an earlier search of Murphy's land and the discovery of a buried oil tank in a nearby field. Inside the tank, the gardaí had found a number of bullets and metal fins similar to those used on home-made mortars. As anyone could have had access to the hidden oil tank, no charges had been brought against Murphy in connection with the discovery.

As the prosecution continued with the strategy that the defence witnesses were being paid in one way or another, Prenty was obliged to admit that he had carried out work as a private investigator and had delivered some of the summonses in relation to the hearing for solicitors A&L Goodbody. He had also helped track down some of the garda witnesses.

Patrick Scullion, head of the Passport Office, gave evidence that he could find no trace of a passport ever having been issued to a Jim Faughey. A batch of 100 passports had gone missing in 1984; the Faughey passport was one of the missing batch. Some others had been found in Holland and were returned by the Dutch authorities.

Adding credence to the suggestion that the missing passports were in IRA hands, Inspector Edward Aerkhon of the Dutch police told the court that a number of known IRA men – Gerard Kelly, William Kelly and Brendan 'Bik' McFarlane – had been arrested following a raid on a house in Amsterdam in January 1996. A number of forged passports were found during that raid, some of which were from that missing batch. Gerard Kelly and 'Bik' McFarlane, IRA escapees from the Maze prison, were returned to Britain, while William Kelly was deported to Belgium to face charges there.

Document expert David Jones had compared the writing on the Faughey passport with two of the Amsterdam passports and found them to be identical. While he could not exclude the possibility of another person having been involved, on the balance of probabilities the same person had written on all three passports.

Detective Constable Alan Nash of the Metropolitan Police in London gave evidence that he was the exhibits officer at the Old Bailey trial of those persons charged with the bomb in the Grand Hotel, Brighton in 1984. Among the exhibits were a number of false passports linked to the Faughey one. Nash had interviewed Thomas Murphy at Dundalk garda station in June 1989, but he had remained tight-lipped. Once again, no charges had been brought against him.

The passport evidence was vital to the newspaper's case, but it also exposed a crack that was going to be hard to paper over. In Ireland, it is possible to convict a person of being a member of the IRA simply by the assertion of a Chief Superintendent that he believes it to be true. If the gardaí considered Murphy to be a top IRA figure, then why had no such charge ever been levelled against him?

When you are telling a story and the pace begins to flag, author Raymond Chandler advises writers to bring on a man with a gun. Defence counsel did something similar when they called the next witness: former IRA volunteer Eamon Collins.

Collins spoke about his childhood in Newry, Co. Down. He had attended St Colman's school before going on to Queen's University, Belfast to read law. He left university after just two years, found work as a customs clearance agent, then drifted into the Provisional IRA. Over time he was involved in setting up bombings, murders and other operations.

Collins's direct evidence relating to the plaintiff arose from the attempted murder of a Newry RUC detective in October 1983. Collins had the job of identifying the target, but had bungled his part and an innocent Catholic civilian, Seán McShane, had been killed. A month later Collins had attended a social function in Dundalk, which had been laid on by his officer commanding, Len Hardy. Hardy told Collins that the purpose of the evening was to impress the IRA generals, and he later pointed out Murphy as one of the most significant men in the IRA. Brendan Burns, a senior IRA south Armagh operative, also identified Murphy to Collins.

Collins's next meeting with Murphy was under more sinister conditions. The IRA Army Council was subjecting him to a three-month investigation for his part in the accidental murder of the Newry civilian. Murphy had identified himself to Collins and interviewed him at considerable length about the failed operation. There was a great deal of nervous laughter in the well of the court as Collins described a farcical incident that had taken place during the investigation. The owner of the house where he was being questioned had thrown a rubber boot onto the fire, which immediately started to spew out a pall of thick, acrid smoke, forcing a quick exit for the 'nutting' (punishment) squad and their suspect. Weeks later, Murphy told Collins that he had been exonerated for the mistaken shooting and had been reinstated for operational duty. Collins had thought Murphy an impressive man, professional and diplomatic.

Collins had been allowed to return to active duty and had continued to mount operations until he was arrested in the wake of a 1985 mortar attack on Newry RUC station, which had killed nine officers inside a makeshift canteen. Special Branch had broken him after an intensive five-day grilling at Gough Barracks, Armagh. Although not involved in the mortar attack, he confessed to his IRA activities between 1978 and 1985. Collins was charged with five murders and a number of other crimes, but the court ruled his statement of admission to be inadmissible because he had been subjected to inhuman and degrading treatment in Gough Barracks. The prosecution withdrew its case and Collins was released from jail in 1986.

Although he was a free man, some forty former IRA colleagues had been arrested on Collins's information; a few of them were later convicted. Collins decided he wanted to turn his life around and do some good for a change. He worked with homeless children in Dublin until he developed health problems and underwent a triple heart bypass operation. He was now back in Newry with his wife and four children. A television documentary had been screened about his time in the IRA and he had written an acclaimed autobiography, *Killing Rage*.

Collins said it had been a difficult decision for him to give evidence against Murphy. He fully realised that he was going head-to-head with a very powerful man in the IRA hierarchy, and was therefore apprehensive about his own safety.

'If Tom Murphy decided I should be killed, I would be killed. And that's the power he has at his fingertips,' Collins told a hushed court.

Leahy again attempted to diminish a witness's credibility by linking him to a financial motive. Collins admitted that *The*

Sunday Times had paid £15,000 to improve security at his home and had offered to pay him £10,000 in living expenses if he had to leave home for a period of time. Furthermore, an advance of £18,000 had been paid for his book; the publishers were expecting good sales.

It is impossible to estimate how much weight the jury gave to revelations about financial benefits witnesses may have accrued for speaking out against Murphy. O'Callaghan and Collins were both men living on the edge. Their lives and the lives of their families had been disrupted beyond comprehension. They would spend the rest of their years looking over their shoulders, never really being able to trust anyone, waiting for a bullet to the back of the head. No monetary reward could compensate for such an intolerable existence. On the other hand, the Irish psyche harbours a natural distrust of informers. A retired garda may be seen in the same light as a doctor or engineer giving evidence: someone worthy of compensation for his/her professional input. Not so a tout.

Murphy was recalled to the witness-box under the case's revised running order. He winked sinisterly at a couple of the jury members, who blanched visibly. His performance in the witness-box in this, the final act of an enthralling courtroom drama, was perhaps the turning point for the majority of the jurors.

Murphy denied being, or ever having been, a member of the IRA. He said he abhorred violence and described how the newspaper article had affected him. He claimed that he had been distraught, had to stop going to cattle markets in the North and rarely attended those in the Republic. His social life had more or less been curtailed for a long time afterwards. He had stopped going to football matches or to the pub because people had come up to him and made embarrassing remarks. All in all, it had been a very bad time in his life.

Murphy gained little sympathy in the courtroom with his protestations of having been shamed as a man of disrepute. He went on to suggest that O'Callaghan's and Collins's testimonies were recompense for money that had been paid to them. He said their evidence was all lies because he had not met either man until the hearing had started.

Murphy stuck to his story about getting the passport from a Peter Murray, whom he believed worked in the Passport Office in Dublin's Molesworth Street, even though it had been proven that no such person worked there. A man he met in a pub had made the introduction to Murray. Murphy then exhibited difficulty remembering his date of birth. After changing his mind a few times, he finally plumped for 26 August 1947 – the date on the legitimate passports.

He had made a number of trips to Athens, staying for just twenty-four hours on each occasion – not the typical behaviour of a tourist, counsel suggested. Murphy explained the immigration stamps by saying that he had made trips to various Greek islands. He shrugged and said he could not give any reason why his passport had been stamped as though he was leaving Greece – something that would not have been done on trips between islands. Murphy was adamant that he had not travelled to Greece to buy arms. His attention was drawn to Yugoslavian immigration stamps on the forged passport. Had he visited Yugoslavia to buy arms for the IRA?

'No way,' Murphy insisted.

'Would you agree that the IRA sourced or did source some of their arms in Yugoslavia?'

'I would know nothing about that.'

'Would you agree or do you know anything about the fact that Libyan arms sometimes came through Greece?'

'I don't know anything about that.'

The focus then turned to the oil business run by the plaintiff's brother, Patrick. An aerial photograph of the Murphy farm was examined; a number of oil tanks and tankers were clearly visible in the picture. Murphy was asked if it was possible for tanks on the Northern side of the border to be filled from the Southern side. He did not know because that was his brother's business.

The case was adjourned for the weekend, but there was a surprise in store when the court resumed on Tuesday morning. In open court, Murphy alleged that over the weekend another brother of his, Frank, had received a death threat from the Loyalist Volunteer Force (LVF). He emphasised that neither Frank nor his family had anything to do with the hearing. The defence objected to Murphy's allegation, saying it was not an appropriate matter to be raised in front of the jury. Mrs Justice McGuinness agreed and instructed the jury members to put the allegation from their minds. One male jury member had been excused because of a family bereavement, but both parties in the case agreed to continue with eleven jurors.

Towards the end of the hearing Murphy made a feeble attempt to account for having been stopped by the gardaí a number of times and for being arrested under the Offences Against the State Act. The first confrontation with the Garda Síochána had been in 1983. Murphy disagreed with the reason stated for his arrest, telling the jury that he had been charged with a motoring offence. There was laughter in the court when Murphy suggested that the Offences Against the State Act included motoring offences. Counsel assured him that the Act did not; Murphy obdurately insisted that it did. It was the start of a series of absurd denials that drifted further and further into the farcical.

In February 1984, Murphy was arrested near Tallanstown, Co. Louth after he had been found to have convicted IRA leader Kieran Conway in his car; he was held overnight at Ardee garda station. Murphy had initially given the gardaí a false name and claimed that Conway was a hitch-hiker whom he had never met before. He stuck to this story even when told that Conway's car had been found only yards from Murphy's.

Monaghan gardaí had arrested Murphy in June 1985, when Michael McKevitt and Kevin Martin were found to be in his car. (McKevitt would later lead a breakaway IRA group, the Real IRA, before being jailed in 2003 for directing terrorism and for membership of an unlawful organisation. The Real IRA was behind the Omagh bombing on 15 August 1997, in which twenty-nine people were killed.) Murphy replied that he had been arrested on a drink-driving charge and that he had not known the two men, that he had simply offered them a lift from the pub.

Counsel sympathised with the plaintiff for his run of bad luck in being arrested with men he did not know in his car. Murphy said he had been arrested only once, on a drink-driving charge. When asked if he had been arrested a number of times under the Offences Against the State Act, Murphy replied that the gardaí might have mentioned it a few times, but he could not be sure.

Several further garda witnesses were able to clarify the technicalities of Murphy's various arrests, though it transpired that he had not been arrested in the last nine years. Superintendent Michael Staunton stated that he had been stationed near the border for most of his career. Gardaí at Dundalk believed Murphy to be a member of the IRA, while he personally considered him to be a senior member.

Murphy's counsel suggested it was nonsense that an alleged 'senior figure' in the IRA would not have been questioned in the past nine years.

'It's not nonsense, regrettably,' Staunton replied. He went on to say that a person charged with being an IRA member could possibly face conviction on the word of a Chief Superintendent, but that getting a conviction without further evidence was difficult.

Murphy denied attending the unveiling of a memorial in Crossmaglen to IRA man Séamus Harvey in January 1997. He also denied attending a similar memorial to IRA member Eugene Martin, though he almost certainly had been at Martin's funeral in June 1974. He admitted that the funeral had been a paramilitary one, though the men in black were not an IRA guard of honour. Murphy remembered several guards of honour from GAA and cycling clubs to which Martin had belonged.

Murphy was asked to explain how a false passport bearing his photograph could be matched to a false one in the possession of Maze-escaper Gerard Kelly. Murphy had some recollection of a man of that name having escaped from a prison in the North. Gallagher thought it unlikely that the witness had not heard of the Maze prison. The judge was of a like mind. 'Come on, Mr Murphy,' Mrs Justice McGuinness urged. 'You must have heard of the Maze.'

Murphy continued with his evasiveness, much to the exasperation of most of the observers in the court. He claimed that he thought the prison the men had escaped from was called Long Kesh. It was explained to the witness that the Maze prison was formerly known as Long Kesh.

The hearing was drawing to a close, but Murphy was once again given the opportunity to declare that he had not been a member of the IRA, that he had not been appointed Officer Commanding Northern Ireland in 1984, that he had not sanctioned the participation of any persons in a 1983 bombing campaign of British seaside towns. Murphy said that both O'Callaghan and Collins had stated that he was clean-shaven when they claimed to have met him, but that he had in fact had a thick, bushy beard from the late 1970s to about 1984. This was a major gaffe on Murphy's behalf, as his legitimate passport, issued in March 1979, showed him to be clean-shaven.

A number of character witnesses spoke on Murphy's behalf. Owen Kelly, a former SDLP councillor, said that he had known Tom Murphy since childhood and considered him to be an honest and hard-working man. When Kelly had read the article in *The Sunday Times*, he thought it was a joke. Bernard Finnegan, a milkman, had known Murphy for thirty years and had not known him to be involved in any business other than farming. Henry McIlroy, a farmer, told the court that he had kept his distance from the plaintiff after the article appeared because he thought Murphy might be assassinated. Owen O'Callaghan, owner of the bar at which Collins alleged he had met Murphy, told the court that no such function had taken place. Eamon Laverty, a neighbour of Murphy's, said that the plaintiff was a 'real gentleman'.

Paul Gallagher made his closing address for the defence. He told the jury that it had heard evidence of a false passport and a false driving licence. The plaintiff had failed to adequately explain his possession of these items, nor indeed his many short-term trips to Greece. The jury had heard from a number of witnesses who may have placed themselves in danger by testifying. Members of the

Garda Síochána had also given evidence about the plaintiff's alleged activities.

Leahy then closed for the plaintiff. He accused *The Sunday Times* of having put up 'a cowardly cocktail of defences'. The jury was cautioned to be wary of evidence from Seán O'Callaghan, a convicted murderer, and from Eamon Collins, who had admitted involvement in five murders. Both men had told lies when it suited them and had negotiated financial deals with *The Sunday Times*. The defence had been prepared to call paid witnesses to give evidence but not the four journalists who had written the article.

Mrs Justice McGuinness took the jury through a summary of the evidence and charged the members with what they had to decide. She told them that the evidence of Murphy being a member of the IRA was largely circumstantial, adding '… but it's open to you to look at it in the light of his general demeanour in the witness-box and his general responses.'

The first two questions on the issue paper read:

1. Did the words complained of mean and were they understood to mean:
   (a) Thomas Murphy was a prominent member of the Provisional IRA, an unlawful organisation and an organisation associated in the public mind with unlawful violence, brutality and murder?
   (b) Thomas Murphy planned murder and the bombing of property?

If the answer to 1(a) or 1(b) is yes, proceed to question 2.

2. Have the defendants proved that such words were true in substance and in fact, that is to say:
   (a) That Thomas Murphy was a prominent member of the Provisional IRA, an unlawful organisation and an organisation associated in the public mind with unlawful violence, brutality and murder?

(b) That Thomas Murphy planned murder and the
    bombing of property?

The jury returned its verdict within an hour. It answered Yes to
questions 1 and 2, therefore it did not have to consider three other
questions relating to injury to reputation and amount of damages.
Murphy was not present to hear the judge read out the verdict. He
was absent for the first time since the start of the trial. His
supporters left the court before the judge had finished speaking.

Mrs Justice McGuinness thanked the jury and discharged its
members from further duty for eight years. She awarded costs to
the defence, plus half the costs of the Murphy brothers' previous
unsuccessful hearing. Estimates of the total costs facing Murphy
were put between £1 and £1.5 million.

The court pundits considered that Murphy had done himself
no favours in the witness-box. He had been cagey and evasive in
his answers, appearing more like a defendant than the plaintiff.
His posse of 'heavies', who had exuded menace daily in the
courtroom, had undermined his assertion that he was a poor
and simple farmer. Nor had he been of any assistance to his
paramilitary peers at a time when reconciliation and disarmament
were the order of the day. He had also exposed the inner workings
of the IRA to unwanted publicity.

The verdict did not mean that the gardaí could move against
Murphy, however. A criminal prosecution, in which the case
would have to be proved beyond any reasonable doubt, was as far
away as ever.

The Sunday Times faced some criticism over its decision to pay
witnesses, but defended its strategy by arguing that it was similar
to the police placing key former criminals in witness-protection
schemes. When fighting a man like Murphy, with his resources,
extreme measures were necessary.

Murphy did lodge an appeal application against the decision,
but withdrew it in November 1999.

There was to be a tragic ending for one of the witnesses in the
Murphy libel hearing. Eamon Collins was murdered near his

home on 27 January 1999, less than a year after he had forecast it during his evidence. His brutalised body was found in a lane close to his house. He had been beaten and stabbed and his tongue had been cut out. No one has yet been charged with his murder. A few days before his death, he had removed graffiti not far from his home; someone had spray-painted his death notice on a roadside wall.

There has been no ending as yet for Murphy. In an attempt to recover its costs, *The Sunday Times* instituted an investigation into Murphy's financial standing. A lengthy and exhaustive probe uncovered a property empire allegedly linked to Murphy. In October 2005, the Police Service of Northern Ireland's Assets Recovery Agency and the Garda Síochána's Criminal Assets Bureau moved against suspected Murphy property holdings in Ireland and the north of England. The Manchester police assisted in this offensive, codenamed Operation Front Line, and it is thought that some 250 properties were involved, valued at €50 million. Although Thomas Murphy's name does not appear on any of the paperwork and deeds, it is thought that the documents seized will eventually allow for the confiscation of his apparently considerable assets. Some €900,000 in cash and cheques found in a sack on Murphy's farm was seized by the Criminal Assets Bureau. The money and the property have been frozen by the respective courts while investigation continues. Should Murphy's ill-fated trip to the Four Courts result in the IRA losing a sizable chunk of its investments portfolio, his future could prove bleak.

07 | MONEY, MONEY, MONEY:
LIAM NEESON AND NATASHA RICHARDSON v DAILY MIRROR & ORS [1998]

The subject of multiple awards for defamation is a bone of contention for most publishers. If a person is defamed, then certainly he/she deserves to be compensated in one form or another. If the same defamation is repeated by other publishers, is it not immoral and injudicious to award further damages?

A personal injury plaintiff can pursue one claim for damages and that is the end of it. If a woman is knocked down on a pelican-crossing by a car driven negligently and has her leg smashed, then, quite rightly, she can initiate a claim for damages. What she cannot do – except in extraordinary circumstances – is to pursue a second claim, say, twenty years later, should she develop arthritis in her injured leg. In libel litigation, on the other hand, it is quite common to have a second, third and even fourth bite at the cherry. These multiple claims may arise simultaneously, or over a longer period separated by significant lapses of time.

For example, in 1952 a British police officer serving in Palestine sued Menachem Begin for defamation. In his book *The Revolt*, Begin stated that the officer had shot and killed in cold blood the leader of the Stern gang, Abraham Stern. Twenty-one years later, Secker and Warburg paid the same officer £4,000 when the defamation was repeated in *The Terrorists* by Roland Gaultier.

Patrick (Paddy) McGrory. (PA Photos)

Albert Reynolds and his solicitor outside the High Court in London.
(PA Photos)

Albert Reynolds following the verdict
of his court case. (PA Photos)

Proinsias De Rossa (*centre*) with party member Joe Sherlock and
Liz McManus TD at the High Court. (Photocall Ireland)

Eamon Dunphy (*left*) with the managing director of
Independent Newspapers (Ireland) David Palmer after the
award to Proinsias De Rossa. (Photocall Ireland)

Jack and Lynda Ramsden with Kieren Fallon (*centre*) during
the case against *The Sporting Life*. (PA Photos)

Thomas 'Slab' Murphy being protected by two minders as he leaves the
High Court on the first day of his libel action. (Photocall Ireland)

Thomas 'Slab' Murphy leaving Ardee Court following his arrest in November 2007. (Pacemaker Press International)

The farm complex along the South Armagh border belonging to Thomas 'Slab' Murphy. (Pacemaker Press International)

Beverley Cooper Flynn leaving the High Court
after the jury returned in her libel trial
against RTÉ. (Photocall Ireland)

Charlie Bird gives a victory salute after RTÉ won costs against Beverley
Cooper-Flynn. Pictured also are Ed Mulhall, Head of News at RTÉ
(*left*) and Kevin Healy, Head of Public Affairs. (Collins Photo Agency)

Charlie Bird offering Beverley Cooper-Flynn a handshake
after she lost her appeal judgment. (Courtpix)

Liam Neeson and his wife Natasha Richardson. (PA Photos)

Seán Sherwin. (Collins Photo Agency)

Aengus Fanning and Jody Corcoran following the verdict
of the High Court. (Collins Photo Agency)

Tom Gilmartin. (Collins Photo Agency)

Judge Joseph Mangan. (Collins Photo Agency)

Ian Bailey leaving Cork Circuit Court. (PA Photos)

The media wait for Michael Douglas and Catherine Zeta-Jones at the High Court in London. (PA Photos)

Catherine Zeta-Jones and Michael Douglas leaving the
High Court in London. (PA Photos)

Piers Morgan arriving at the High Court in London. (PA Photos)

Weidenfeld & Nicolson paid a further award seven years after that, when the same mistake was made in *Ben Gurion* by Michael Bar Zohar.

While acknowledging that the real culprit was undoubtedly sloppy research and poor editing rather than malice, the police officer still engenders sympathy for having been defamed over three decades. This will not always be the case, however. Sonia Sutcliffe, wife of the 'Yorkshire Ripper', turned libel litigation into a production line process during the mid-1980s. Peter Sutcliffe, one of Britain's worst serial killers, was jailed in 1981 for multiple murder. By 1990 it was estimated that Sonia Sutcliffe was receiving £50,000 a year tax-free for libel and copyright claims. Damages awarded to Mrs Sutcliffe included:

1983: £5,000, *Bradford Telegraph and Argus*
1988: £25,000, *Yorkshire Post*
1989: £7,500, *Yorkshire Post*
       £800,000, *Private Eye* (reduced to £160,000 on appeal)
       £35,000, *Daily Star*
       £75,000, *Daily Express*
1990: £26,500, News Group Newspapers Ltd

These figures do not include £100,000 awarded in two subsequent actions or fees earned from interviews and photographs. Sonia Sutcliffe lost a second libel action and costs against News Group Newspapers after refusing to accept the £50,000 the group had paid into court. The jury agreed with the assertion of the legendary libel advocate George Carmen QC that Sutcliffe had perjured herself in an earlier libel action. Undaunted, Sutcliffe went on to win a further libel action over claims made about her in a book about her libel actions.

The average criminal injury compensation award made to surviving victims of the 'Yorkshire Ripper' was £7,000.

One of the dangers of the modern world's insatiable demand for news twenty-four hours a day, 365 days a year is that when a newspaper gets it wrong – as they all do from time to time – the error will be repeated a great number of times before it can be corrected. The greater the subject's celebrity, the faster the publications will multiply. No one cares less if Joe Bloggs of Notown has been seen in the arms of a mysterious blonde woman. But if it were David Beckham, for example, who was spotted in an amorous clinch, then the story would spread like wildfire. It is interesting to compare how newspapers handle a showbiz scoop that quickly sours into multiple defamation suits. In 1998, the *Daily Mirror* carried a story in the Matthew Wright column claiming that Natasha Richardson was planning to divorce her husband, Liam Neeson. The *Daily Telegraph* published a similar story, written by Alison Boshoff. The reports stated that Richardson was filing for divorce without her husband's knowledge and that the marriage was a sham, and inevitably set off an explosion of publicity.

The story was quickly exposed as a nonsense. Neeson and Richardson had been happily married for four years and had two sons, three-year-old Michael and two-year-old Daniel; neither partner was planning a divorce. Neeson was particularly concerned that the defamation would damage his work as ambassador for Ireland to the United Nations children's organisation, UNICEF.

The allegation had come from a source that was described as reliable, but the papers had not checked with Neeson and Richardson prior to publication. Martin Cruddance, the lawyer responsible for 'legalling' (providing legal advice) at the *Daily Mirror*, freely admitted that gossip/showbiz columns posed a special problem. The very nature of this category of story often means there is no admissible evidence available before publication. Cruddance recommends careful analysis of possible defamatory material before a final decision is taken to print. Showbiz columnists are still journalists and therefore should check out any allegation with the subject, or at least with the subject's PR officer. A summary of the response should be included in the article in order to ensure that a balanced opinion is presented.

Yet the truth is that no matter how many checks are made, no matter how previously reliable the source, mistakes are made. This is exactly what happened in the *Neeson* case. The source had mistakenly confused Natasha Richardson and her sister, actress Joely Richardson. It was Joely who was seeking a divorce and who had been seen entering the premises of a London law firm.

Most of what can be expected from responsible journalism was laid out in the ten points delineated by Lord Nichols in the judgment on the *Albert Reynolds v The Sunday Times* appeal. As Cruddance points out, 'They've always been reliable in the past' is not a defence against a defamation suit. The journalist should find out as much as possible about the source's information: how did he come by the information? Is it first-, second- or even third-hand? He adds that it is important that a journalist and lawyer maintain communication right up until the presses start rolling. Stories can be organic and have a life of their own, so any last-minute changes should be analysed carefully.

In the *Neeson* case, the *Daily Mirror* got it wrong – not slightly wrong, but totally wrong. Cruddance describes the telephone call he received from Keith Schilling of London solicitors Schilling and Lom. 'I act for Liam Neeson and Natasha Richardson,' Schilling announced. 'In the *Daily Mirror* today, Matthew Wright wrote that they are to divorce. They are not; they are perfectly happily married. You have published it in the *Daily Mirror*, *Irish Mirror*, *Northern Irish Mirror* and the *Daily Record*. One of Mr Neeson's elderly relatives read it on a billboard in Northern Ireland and nearly collapsed.'

The elderly relative was Neeson's mother, who had been shopping in Belfast. Cruddance made a quick calculation and concluded that the MGN group could be facing up to eight writs.

Schilling added: 'Most, if not all, newspapers have made a similar mistake. If you make a contribution of £X thousand to the fund for the victims of Omagh, pay my costs and publish a fulsome [sic] apology, that will be the end of the matter. This offer is open until 4 p.m.'

Cruddance immediately spoke to Matthew Wright and it was decided that the paper had indeed made a mistake and should make good. As Schilling had pointed out, the story was unfounded and hurtful. Some of the editors were unhappy with the grovelling nature of the apology Schilling had demanded be published. After further internal discussion, the apology was published and the sum paid to the fund for the Omagh survivors. It made sense to Cruddance to settle eight possible litigation actions at once.

Extracts from the retraction and apology read:

> MGN accept unequivocally that the story was entirely false and apologise for the embarrassment, hurt and distress caused to the couple.
>
> We entirely accept there is absolutely no truth in these allegations and they should never have been published. We have agreed not to repeat the allegations and to pay substantial damages.

Other newspapers that had repeated the defamation were not of the same mind, however. A few held out, but Schilling and Paul Tweed (a Belfast solicitor) persevered and ensured that the coffers of the Omagh fund were swollen considerably. It was estimated that some thirty publications had to pay damages.

* * *

Another illustration of the multiple claim in action is the case of Monica Leech.

Leech had been appointed Public Relations advisor to the Office of Public Works after being proposed for the post by Minister of State Martin Cullen. In 2004, there was a public outcry when it emerged in the Dáil that she was being paid €800 a day under contracts with the Department of the Environment, Heritage and Local Government. Taoiseach Bertie Ahern appointed Dermot Quigley, former chairman of the Revenue Commissioners, to carry out an inquiry into Leech's appointment and performance. His report, published 24 January 2005, found that there had been no impropriety in her appointment and that her duties had been fulfilled to a high standard. That should have been the end of the matter, but on 16 December 2004, during a live broadcast on RTÉ Radio One's *Liveline* show, presenter Joe Duffy took a telephone call from an irate member of the public. The caller, Ronan Petit, made lewd and offensive remarks on air, alleging that Leech had won the state contracts by granting sexual favours to Martin Cullen.

Although Duffy apologised to listeners for the scandalous comments, the damage had been done. Several newspapers reported at length on the radio show's gaffe, as did a number of internet blog sites.

Leech took swift legal action. Her solicitor, McCann Fitzgerald, issued warnings to the bloggers, insisting that the offensive material be removed. Defamation actions were launched against RTÉ, the Independent Newspaper Group and Associated Newspapers.

The first case to reach the High Court was Leech's suit against the national broadcaster. It seemed likely that RTÉ would base its defence on the right-to-know principle, which had been established in the Reynolds libel case against *The Sunday Times*; no Irish case had been defended successfully on that stance.

On 8 May 2007, the day the hearing was due to begin, RTÉ announced that a settlement had been reached with Leech. Counsel for RTÉ, Patrick Gageby, read out an apology in court, plus Leech would receive €250,000 in damages and her legal costs.

Leech's action against the Independent Newspaper Group started on 26 June 2007 and lasted three days. The jury found that Leech had not been defamed by the newspaper and Judge Peter Carleton awarded costs, estimated to be €350,000, against the plaintiff. Monica Leech declared her intention of appealing the verdict to the Supreme Court. She made no announcement in relation to her other libel suits.

This case is significant because it was the first time in Ireland that a libel defence had been won on the public's right-to-know. In the absence of defamation reform, the Leech multiple claims case has set an important precedent.

08 | A CLASS ACT:
BEVERLEY COOPER-FLYNN
v RTÉ AND ORS [2001]

L ibel litigants often display a reckless streak of arrogance.
Oscar Wilde had more than his fair share of it when he
instituted proceedings against the Marquess of Queensberry
in 1895 – did he honestly believe that his relationship with the
Marquess's son, Bosie, would not come to light and be used
against him? For damages to be awarded in a successful libel
action, it is necessary to prove to the jury that the plaintiff's
reputation has been damaged. Wilde's private life had been the
topic of Victorian scandalmongers for too long for that to have
been a realistic outcome.

Beverley Cooper-Flynn displayed a similar rash arrogance
when she decided to sue RTÉ, its reporter Charlie Bird, economics
editor George Lee and retired farmer James Howard over a series
of television reports broadcast between 19 June and 1 July 1998.
These reports implied that she had induced Mr Howard, among
others, to evade tax by investing capital offshore in a National
Irish Bank (NIB) scheme.

A Fianna Fáil TD since June 1997 and the first woman to
represent a Mayo constituency, Cooper-Flynn completely
misjudged the mood in the country at the time. A tsunami of
political corruption had swamped Ireland and hardly a month
went by without a further deluge of exposures. The tribunals of

inquiry were slowly but surely uncovering the depths of malfea-
sance in Irish political life. Reputations were being tarnished,
careers coming to a premature end, but it was widely believed that
there were others in Leinster House for whom the axe had yet to
fall. There was an air of expectancy, and of great disappointment
and anger. Nor was it a small number of avaricious politicians
who had been rumbled. The media was describing in detail how
some of the wealthiest people in Ireland had gone to incredible
lengths to evade taxation. Offshore Ansbacher accounts, Deposit
Interest Retention Tax (DIRT) evasion and bogus non-resident
bank accounts were just some of the scams the affluent had
resorted to in order to avoid the taxman. Many had been caught,
but few prosecutions were pending. Once again, Irish society had
been exposed as dual-layered: the haves and the haves-nots.

In this climate, to expect a jury to place a high value on the
reputation of a politician and former financial advisor was asking
a lot. Cooper-Flynn's misreading of the public feeling at the time
seemed all the more astonishing in light of the recent negative
experiences of other members of her family. Few people could
have been made more aware of the dangers of overconfidence
than Cooper-Flynn, whose father – former government minister
and EU Social Affairs Commissioner Padraig Flynn – had been
pilloried by the press after his appearance on *The Late Late
Show* of 15 January 1999. The show's presenter, Gay Byrne, had
questioned the then Commissioner over an alleged payment of
£50,000 given to him by property developer Tom Gilmartin. This
payment was allegedly intended for Fianna Fáil party funds, but
no record had been found at that time of the money being lodged
into any account.

Padraig Flynn spoke disparagingly about Gilmartin, in
particular about the developer's health and his wife – the reason
proffered for Gilmartin's failure to testify at the tribunal of
inquiry. Buoyed up by an inflated sense of self-importance, Flynn
then went on to boast of his own political prowess and success.
Obviously convinced that he was the fountainhead of a political
dynasty, he described his daughter Beverley as 'a class act'. His
belief in his daughter's loyalty was vindicated when Ms Cooper-

Flynn temporarily lost the Fianna Fáil whip a few weeks later, after failing to support a government amendment calling on her father to make a statement about the missing £50,000.

Padraig Flynn was not the only member of his family to display an astonishing pomposity. A sister, Audrey Flynn, the proprietor of a crèche, had appeared before Castlebar court in January 2000 on a charge relating to various traffic offences. The judge in the case described Ms Flynn as displaying an attitude of 'breathtaking arrogance' during the hearing. After a delay of a month, for the purposes of allowing Audrey Flynn to undergo psychiatric assessment, Justice Mary Devins handed down a nine-month custodial sentence, suspended for twelve months, and fines of £6,800.

Undaunted by the lessons contained in her family's various misfortunes, Beverley Cooper-Flynn decided to push ahead with her libel case. It eventually opened in a packed Court 4 in the High Court on 6 February 2001, before Mr Justice Frederick Morris, president of the High Court. Cooper-Flynn's leading counsel was Garrett Cooney SC, a veteran libel advocate, and he was ably supported by Hugh Mohan SC. Kevin Feeney SC and John Trainor SC acted for RTÉ and Charlie Bird; Paul O'Higgin SC acted for James Howard.

The court case was expected to take about ten days; in fact, it would last twenty-eight days – a record at that time. It was a case that portrayed a stratum of Irish society in a very poor light: grasping people, driven by avarice and duplicity. It would be a hard-fought and bruising encounter, with neither side emerging as a clear winner until the very last round.

Cooper-Flynn strode confidently into court. While she had many supporters on the public benches, she had no spouse by her side; she was separated from her husband, John Cooper. Known to her Fianna Fáil colleagues as a determined and ambitious woman who had her sights set on high office, there was no doubt that Cooper-Flynn had enormous self-belief and courage. On one widely reported occasion she had chased a handbag thief along Grafton Street. This time, however, she had a more daunting task on her hands, one that could not be won by pulling punches. The Dáil deputy was seeking 'swingeing' damages from the defendants, whom she claimed had portrayed her as a pariah to hundreds of thousands of people and from whom she had failed to secure an apology or retraction.

It had all started with a telephone call on 18 June 1998. Charlie Bird called Beverley Cooper-Flynn to tell her that RTÉ News was intending to broadcast a story within forty-eight hours regarding the National Irish Bank's use of Clerical Medical International (CMI) offshore investment schemes and how she had encouraged customers to evade tax. Their conversation was heated, but short. Bird read out extracts from a letter he intended delivering to her hand, detailing her part in the NIB's offshore scheme. It was disturbing news for the twenty-nine-year-old deputy.

Cooper-Flynn claimed that she had been in no position to meet the reporter because she was on her way to a two-day Fianna Fáil parliamentary party meeting at the Slieve Russell Hotel, Co. Cavan. She placed great emphasis on RTÉ's and Charlie Bird's failure to afford her the courtesy of an adequate opportunity to reply to their story.

In Irish law, defamation differs from other torts in that the relevant statement is presumed to be defamatory until proved otherwise. This is often a time-consuming and expensive process, and an injunction may be sought in the interim to spike a story. In other words, if, as a journalist sure of your facts, you are going to throw down a gauntlet, it is advisable not to give your subject a lot of notice. However, on this occasion Bird had indeed driven to Co. Cavan to seek a meeting with Cooper-Flynn, but had to return to Dublin without speaking to her. Bird left a letter outlining his main points with staff at the hotel, with the instruction to deliver it to Ms Cooper-Flynn.

The following morning Cooper-Flynn found the letter from Bird, which had been pushed under the door of her hotel room. Later on, in the foyer, her attention was drawn to a story in that day's *Irish Independent*: 'Flynn's TD daughter to face tax grill'. She left Cavan and drove to a hastily arranged meeting in Dublin with her solicitors, McCann Fitzgerald.

The story was the lead item broadcast on RTÉ's *Six One News* that same day. It was also the main item on the late evening news and the lead story in three daily newspapers the following morning. It was reported that Cooper-Flynn had encouraged a retired farmer to evade tax by placing his investments in the CMI scheme. Cooper-Flynn did not learn the identity of her accuser – James Howard of Wheaton Hall, Drogheda, Co. Louth – until a few days later, when journalist Jody Corcoran named him in a newspaper article.

The Clerical Medical International (CMI) scheme had proven to be a disaster for many NIB customers. The 1999 annual report of the Comptroller and Auditor General said that NIB had provided the Revenue Commissioners with the financial details of 429 individuals who had invested capital. Upwards of £20 million had been paid in tax settlement to that date. Despite this, Cooper-Flynn would persistently maintain that the scheme was a good medium- to long-term investment, and that she had not given taxation advice because she was not qualified to do so. Cooper-Flynn's basic annual salary while with the NIB was between £28,000 and £32,000, but she had averaged £50,000 a year after bonuses were included. She had joined NIB in 1989 and in her best year had earned £69,000. Commission paid on CMI Personal Portfolios was 4.4 per cent, slightly higher than many comparable investment vehicles. Ms Cooper-Flynn had also enjoyed overseas conferences in Australia and Hawaii.

First blood in the libel case had been drawn by RTÉ some nine months earlier, when it had succeeded in having the High Court order NIB to reveal details of other investors so the defendants could fully prepare their case. Charlie Bird had no intention of squandering this hard-won advantage and had done a lot of painstaking preparation for the libel case. He had spoken to a number of Cooper-Flynn's clients who had been netted in the Revenue Commissioners' trawl of tax-evaders. Although these clients had been 'named and shamed' by the Revenue, it did not mean that they would welcome further press exposure by appearing in a libel case. Some were eventually persuaded to do so. How important a role this early victory would play in the case could not be determined until the jury had handed down its decision.

Gary Skelton, a Co. Meath flooring contractor, was one such investor. Skelton met Cooper-Flynn on several occasions and told her he had some money to invest. He warned her that it had to be placed in an untraceable account, though the money had not been earned from drug trading. Cooper-Flynn assured him that a suitable investment could be found and that he could have his money back at any time, paid in cash in a brown paper bag if he so desired. Agreement was reached and Skelton's cash was counted out and a receipt given to him. Part of Cooper-Flynn's sales pitch to Skelton was that she had sold a similar scheme to her father.

Cooper-Flynn's recollections of her meetings with Skelton were very different from his. She denied knowing that the money was 'hot'. She denied taking cash from him and issuing him with a receipt. There was no receipt produced in court at that time. She denied telling Skelton that the scheme was very secure and that she had sold one to her father.

As it turned out, Skelton did not have the opportunity to produce the damning receipt. His investment had not gone into a CMI Personal Portfolio and the defence would not be allowed to stray at large into other policies sold by Cooper-Flynn. Judge Morris told the jury that the defence had 'nailed their colours to the mast' of the CMI Personal Portfolios and would therefore have to be confined to that. Cooper-Flynn must have felt like she had been given a Valentine's Day gift on 14 February when the jury was told to disregard any evidence it had heard relating to Skelton. She had won the first round on points.

Cooper-Flynn's credibility was sustaining other damage, however, much of it self-inflicted. She obstinately stuck to an explanation that the word 'hot' scribbled next to clients' names in her diary meant the client was hot to invest, i.e. that she could sign him up on the particular day. It was not that she was defending the indefensible, she was simply denying it altogether.

Skelton was not the only client who had done business with Cooper-Flynn. Seán Roe of Shercock, Co. Cavan, a car dealer, had invested £100,000 in a CMI Personal Portfolio through Beverley

Cooper-Flynn. His evidence had the potential to damage Cooper-Flynn seriously, especially in regard to a tax amnesty that had been discussed. Roe had earned undeclared money from dealing in cars and engineering plant, which he had placed in five different financial institutions, including an account in a Crossmaglen bank in Northern Ireland. He asked the NIB manager for advice in consolidating his capital and was put in contact with the plaintiff.

After a number of meetings with Cooper-Flynn, Roe was 'so happy' with her advice that he decided not to avail of the amnesty. Roe had asked Cooper-Flynn about the amnesty, wondering if he should pay the Revenue 15 per cent amnesty tax rate, thereby making his money legitimate. Cooper-Flynn said that since he had worked hard for his money, there was no point giving it away. He had no recollection of Cooper-Flynn urging him to seek tax advice, though if she had, he admitted, it would have 'gone in one ear and out the other'. It would not have been something he would have considered because he had no interest in paying tax.

Cooper-Flynn agreed that she had met Roe, but denied ever discussing the tax amnesty with him. To make any admission of having done so would have belied her earlier claim that she did not give tax advice because she was not qualified to do so.

A further three investors claimed, in a more certain manner, that Cooper-Flynn had told them not to give the Revenue Commissioners 15 per cent under the terms of the tax amnesty. Patrick Duff recalled that Cooper-Flynn had assured him, at the Bailieboro branch of NIB in Co. Cavan, that his investment would go into a numbered account in the Isle of Man. Duff, a farmer, building contractor and businessman, had declared his farming and building incomes to the Revenue Commissioners, but had concealed cash profits from his dealings in livestock. This money, along with some legitimate capital, had been placed in a bogus non-resident account. The account was held in the name of John Duff at a London address.

Duff and a group of other investors had issued proceedings against National Irish Bank because they felt they had been given bad advice. The basis of their claim was that Cooper-Flynn had persuaded them not to avail of the tax amnesty. Duff stated that he had been coaxed to invest in a scheme that would remain undisclosed to the Revenue. She had asked him why he would want to give away 15 per cent of his funds in the amnesty. This went against his instinct of coming clean, he said, primarily because a large proportion of the money was legitimate.

After a number of meetings with Cooper-Flynn between 1991 and 1996, which took place both at the Bailieboro branch and at his place of work, Duff finally invested £168,000 from his bogus non-resident account into a CMI Personal Portfolio. This was added to until a total of £308,000 had been invested. What had finally swayed him, Duff said, was that his name would not appear on any documentation and as he was a single man, in the event of his death the money would go to named beneficiaries. This would mean the money would not be declared in probate.

Duff was very insistent that Cooper-Flynn knew the source of the money and that some of it had not been declared. His primary purpose in first agreeing to meet her was to discuss the undeclared portion of his capital. He said that Cooper-Flynn had not told him to seek taxation advice. Duff had paid the Revenue over £350,000 to clear his tax debt. He had been taught a hard lesson, but he knew that few honest taxpayers would have much sympathy with him.

Retired businesswoman Joy Howe, of Co. Monaghan, had owned boutiques on both sides of the border for over thirty years. Undeclared income had been placed in two building societies in Enniskillen, Co. Fermanagh. Her first meeting with Cooper-Flynn was in the summer of 1992, when she had been persuaded to invest in a CMI portfolio, naming her husband as beneficiary if she should die. Cooper-Flynn had assured her that the Revenue Commissioners would not find out about this money.

In April 1998, the NIB told her to expect to be contacted by the Revenue. A letter arrived the next day. She later learned of a RTÉ advertisement in the *Anglo-Celt* newspaper asking CMI clients to contact Charlie Bird, whom she at first had taken to be a politician. Howe had eventually settled with the Revenue for £37,000 in 1999.

Next in a line of defence witnesses was Joan Quigley of Darver, Co. Louth. Quigley recounted her dealings with Cooper-Flynn. She had a sum of undeclared money in a Newry bank account, which she and her adult son had discussed at some length with Cooper-Flynn. Quigley said that Cooper-Flynn had advised her to go for the CMI Personal Portfolio, not the amnesty. Accordingly, she had placed £200,000 with CMI. When the CMI story broke, she contacted her accountant and later the Revenue Commissioners. Quigley confirmed to the court that she had paid £50,000 to the Revenue on account, but there would be a further amount to pay. She also said that she had issued legal proceedings against the NIB for wrongful advice.

Quigley admitted to counsel that she had not taken advantage of the earlier 1988 tax amnesty with its 10 per cent rate. She said that she had been dealing with a personal tragedy at the time and had not given the matter enough thought.

Appearing in the High Court is a nerve-wracking experience for anyone, but to find herself being put through such an ordeal must have been a nightmare for the Mayo deputy. In fact, what turned out to be a seven-day nightmare was one of her own making. When, in the previous summer, RTÉ had won the right to see details of other investors, Cooper-Flynn should have given serious consideration to discontinuing her litigation. She had been forewarned and knew what she was up against, yet it was her decision, and her decision alone, to press on. She could expect to be shown little mercy.

A person with undeclared capital faces a number of dilemmas. For starters, what is one to do with the money other than hide it under the bed? Investing it can draw unwanted attention from the Revenue Commissioners, as can spending it. Stricter financial regulations were introduced during the 1990s to thwart money-laundering, which means the options left to the holder of undeclared capital are few. Passing the money on in the event of death is also difficult. One of the greatest fears for such an investor must be the prospect of the money not being passed on to next-of-kin or other designated beneficiaries.

When a client of Cooper-Flynn's had died in the early 1990s, she said she had been horrified to discover that the £100,000 he had invested through her was undeclared income. She referred the matter to her senior staff within NIB. It was up to them, she stated, to resolve it. As the policy had not been put in trust, any proceeds would form part of the deceased's estate and be liable for tax. CMI was requested to pay the proceeds to the nominated beneficiaries without informing the Revenue Commissioners. CMI trustees advised against granting this unorthodox request.

Cooper-Flynn appeared to have taken a rather cavalier approach to the new banking procedures and regulations of the early 1990s. In the courtroom, her recollections of their introduction were vague, at best. She recalled a letter her bank had received from CMI and an internal memo urging employees to be alert to money-laundering. Cooper-Flynn was of the opinion that such matters should be dealt with by the bank's rigorous internal and external auditors and by its compliance departments. As a financial advisor, she felt that her job was to find a home for the money, not to account for it. Time and time again she denied that she knew she was investing undeclared capital. Although she had sold forty-seven CMI Personal Portfolios, not once had she enquired about the source of the investments.

What of James Howard, then? The well-dressed man who spoke in a strong brogue had become a familiar face around the Four Courts since the start of the hearing. Cooper-Flynn not only denied that she had ever met Howard, but insisted that it was someone else who had sold a CMI Personal Portfolio to Howard. According to her, another NIB employee, Patricia Roche, had sold James Howard a CMI Personal Portfolio.

Outside the Four Courts, the weather had turned bitterly cold, with heavy snowfalls bringing down many power lines around the country. To add to the gloom, the country was in the middle of a foot-and-mouth disease crisis. There was a clampdown on unnecessary travel from rural areas to the capital, which meant many of the listed court cases had to be postponed because witnesses were unavailable.

Cooper-Flynn must have been finding conditions inside Court 4 as bleak as those outside. The irony of the next witness being a retired farmer would not have escaped her: if Howard had still owned stock, he would not have been at court. But he was, and the question was: what damage would the co-defendant inflict?

In the 1980s, James Howard, then in his mid-fifties, had been diagnosed with high blood pressure and diabetes. He had farmed for most of his life at Ardcath, Co. Meath, but with forced retirement looming had started to put aside some undeclared cash from his cattle-dealing as a pension fund for himself and his wife. He also had some legitimate capital from the sale of his shares in Premier Dairies when it was acquired by Waterford Co-op. Cooper-Flynn had contacted him about investing this windfall, but he and his wife had decided to invest in property – apartments in Parnell Street, Dublin.

His next contact with Cooper-Flynn was three years later and came at the suggestion of his bank manager. He recalled his bank manager telling him that Beverley Cooper-Flynn was the best financial advisor in the country, and that her father was 'Pee' Flynn. Howard pulled no punches when he told the court about his appointment with the plaintiff in Balbriggan, in 1993. The sole purpose of the meeting, he said, was to discuss the investment of that portion of his money that had not been declared to the Revenue. He recalled how the meeting had been a hurried one; in less than ten minutes he had signed the papers to invest £83,000 in a CMI Personal Portfolio. Once he had given the matter more thought, however, Howard grew increasingly uneasy and rang Cooper-Flynn to ask for his money to be returned to him. He told her that he intended taking advantage of the 1993 tax amnesty instead. Cooper-Flynn replied that the money could not be returned and that there was no need to give the government 15 per cent.

Howard admitted that he had also met Patricia Roche, another NIB financial advisor. The first time was late 1993, approximately five weeks after he had asked for his money back. At that time she spoke to him about an insurance policy to cover a potential

inheritance tax liability on his estate at death. He had met Roche
on several other occasions and was certain that he would not have
mistaken her for Cooper-Flynn. The two women were not of
similar appearance, he insisted.

Howard learned from an early 1998 RTÉ news report of the
trouble with the CMI schemes. He contacted his bank manager to
express his growing concern. After seeing a second news report in
May, he contacted Charlie Bird of RTÉ and, following a meeting in
a Gormanstown public house, agreed to give a television
interview. In the initial interview, James Howard's face was not
shown and his identity not revealed. In a subsequent interview a
short time later, his identity was divulged.

Howard had received a letter from the Revenue Commissioners
in the spring of 1998 and eventually reached a settlement of
£54,000 in September 1999.

If Cooper-Flynn was to have any chance of winning the case,
Howard would have to be discredited. The glaring discrepancy
between their testimonies was the obvious starting point. Howard
was at a loss to account for Cooper-Flynn's claim that she had not
sold him a Personal Portfolio or indeed had met him. He also
strongly disagreed with counsel's contention that all the allegations he had made on television were wrong. It seemed like a
stand-off: his word against hers. Without concrete evidence, it
might boil down to what the jury made of James Howard's
assertions.

By his own admission, Howard had acted deceitfully over
decades in his dealings with the Revenue Commissioners and
had lied repeatedly to his accountant. He had developed, in
counsel's words, a 'well-oiled procedure for hiding his money'.
Howard also conceded that after receiving a letter from the
Revenue Commissioners in the spring of 1998, he had written a
letter of complaint to the NIB, alleging that he had been 'thrown to
the wolves'. He had also called at the bank's branch in Balbriggan
to voice his anger. Howard's motive was clear: having been caught
with his hand in the honey jar, he wanted someone to share the
responsibility. He threatened that he would go public if the bank
did not help him out to the tune of £50,000. Howard argued that

the bank had led him astray and he felt it should bear some of the financial burden for the poor advice he had been given. However, he was just one of NIB's many problems at the time, so any hope of a compensation offer was a long shot.

Howard insisted that he was not seeking revenge when he had contacted RTÉ. He was not waging a one-man vendetta against NIB. Insisting that he had nothing against Cooper-Flynn personally, he still felt that he had been advised wrongly. The NIB said that it would put him in contact with the best financial advisor in the country.

'If she was the best,' Howard said in court, 'I would hate to see the worst.'

Howard was not a man to give up without a fight. He recalled that in 1994 he had complained to Garry Connolly of NIB's Financial Services Division about the poor returns on his Personal Portfolio. Connolly agreed that the returns could have been better, but pointed out that heavy initial expenses on the policy had contributed to its dismal performance. When it was revealed that Howards's version of events could not be true because Connolly had not joined the Financial Services Division until the following year, Cooper-Flynn's counsel succeeded in calling Howard's memory of events into question.

Howard's credibility took a further knock when he admitted that he had secured an indemnity from RTÉ that would cover him for damages and legal costs if Cooper-Flynn won her action. Counsel suggested that this indemnity had been granted on the basis that he would maintain his story that it was Cooper-Flynn who had sold him the CMI Personal Portfolio, allowing him to walk financially free from court, irrespective of the outcome.

There was one point upon which Howard was insistent: 'Beverley Cooper-Flynn was the person that sold me the policy and I have no doubt about that.' He went on to deny an insinuation by counsel that he was a systematic fabricator of fables.

Marina Howard, James Howard's daughter, backed up her father, saying that she clearly remembered having met Beverley Flynn (as she then was) on her father's farm in 1990. The two women had talked at some length about her recent engagement to John Cooper, an Englishman, who was working abroad at that time. Beverley said that the wedding was set for January 1991. Miss Howard admitted to feeling a little in awe of this successful young woman, who seemed to have her life mapped out and had already attained some of her goals.

Miss Howard provided the crowded courtroom with some much-needed levity. She was asked about a television interview she had given Charlie Bird at her parents' home in Drogheda. At one point during the taped interview she had asked, 'Charlie, can she [Ms Cooper-Flynn] come back at me?' Expanding on this in court, she said she had been concerned that she could be sued. When asked if she believed anyone could be sued successfully for telling the truth in a court of law, she replied, 'Well, Daddy has.'

Cooper-Flynn responded to Miss Howard's testimony by saying that many people would have known of her plans, as several newspapers had written about her forthcoming wedding. She also denied that her father had been a CMI client. (It would emerge in February 2004 that half of the £50,000 given to Padraig Flynn by Tom Gilmartin had indeed been invested in offshore accounts.)

Two ex-employees of NIB, Deirdre Condron and Aidan McLaughlin, added credence to Cooper-Flynn's story, but surprisingly – and potentially damagingly – the key witness in the Howard affair would not appear at the Four Courts. Patricia Roche did not give evidence because of Cooper-Flynn's expressed reluctance to trouble her at a time of 'great trying personal circumstances'. It was left to the imagination what these 'personal circumstances' might be, since no further explanation was provided.

Deirdre Condron, a former administrative employee with NIB, supported Cooper-Flynn's assertion that some other advisor had signed up James Howard. According to Condron, who had spoken with Howard on several occasions, it was Patricia Roche who had dealt with clients of the Balbriggan branch from 1991 onwards.

Aidan McLaughlin, a tax consultant and former investment advisor with NIB, described the CMI Personal Portfolio as a 'sophisticated investment vehicle' that was still well ahead of similar schemes. He explained in some detail how the portfolio worked, and said that it had attracted capital gains tax from 1993 onwards. He confirmed that the CMI Trust Company was registered in the Isle of Man and that any investment returns accruing therefrom would be issued in cheque form from an Isle of Man bank.

McLaughlin insisted that the CMI portfolio provided confidentiality, but not secrecy. He stated that he considered secrecy to be more important to a tax-evader than confidentiality. It followed, he said, that after the 1993 Finance Act had imposed obligatory reporting on Irish financial institutions, the CMI portfolio would have been an unsuitable investment vehicle for tax-evaders.

The point being made was that if Cooper-Flynn had known that the money was undeclared, she would not have dreamed of using that particular investment vehicle. It was not the strongest of arguments: who has not, at one time or another, suspected that a salesperson is pushing a product that profits them most, rather than that best suited to the customer's needs?

That suspicion of opportunism was reinforced by evidence from a number of witnesses for RTÉ. Nigel Darcy had worked for NIB between May 1989 and September 1998. At one point he had been head of the Financial Advice Services Division and was line manager to five financial advisors, including Beverley Cooper-Flynn. He was appearing in court as a subpoenaed witness, and his time in the witness-box proved to be one of constant interruptions for legal argument. The jury was asked to troop in and out of the court on a number of occasions because Darcy wanted an assurance that nothing he said would come back to haunt him.

Darcy confirmed that National Irish Bank had started to promote CMI Personal Portfolios as a replacement scheme because its predecessor, the Emerald International scheme, had a poor sales record. His understanding was that the Emerald plan had been intended for non-residents. Counsel asked Darcy what type of investor the CMI schemes were intended for. After a dramatic pause, Darcy sought the protection of the court and claimed immunity because he feared his answer might incriminate him.

The jury was removed so the judge could hear counsels' arguments.

When the hearing recommenced, counsel referred the court's attention to an internal CMI memo, dated 28 September 1994, which mentioned that the bank and the family of a CMI policy-holder had put CMI on notice that the Clerical Medical International policy proceeds represented undeclared funds. The author of the memo had made it clear that the money had not been, and was not intended to be, declared to the Revenue Commissioners. Counsel asked the witness if the handwritten notation on the front page was in his handwriting, but Darcy refused to answer the question on the grounds that it might incriminate him.

The note read: 'Bev – for info. This case has taken up a considerable amount of admin's and my time. I've managed to sort this case out.'

Mr Justice Morris told Darcy that he would have to answer the question.

Darcy confirmed that he was the note's author and agreed that CMI was perturbed that the portfolio had been purchased with undeclared funds. He had written to his financial services managers two months later, instructing them to refrain from giving the impression that the bank, directly or indirectly, condoned or promoted tax evasion.

Another former employee of NIB, Patrick Cooney (no relation to the leading counsel), had been a financial analyst for the bank from December 1989 to July 1996 and was the author of an internal NIB letter that referred to people whose money was 'hot'. It was Cooney's recommendation that their investments be put into Emerald International. He claimed that the word 'hot' had a different subtext back then. When used in 1990, it suggested that the customer was a ripe prospect, whereas now it usually referred to 'undeclared capital'. Cooney said he would not use the term 'hot' today because it might cause confusion. The letter, dated 30 July 1990, should have gone out with that month's *Investment Bulletin*, but had not been sent because the Gulf War had put stock markets in turmoil.

Mr Justice Morris ruled that Cooper-Flynn could not be held to account on this letter since it was now known that she had not received it.

Patrick Cooney fielded a barrage of questions about offshore investments and if they had 'a smell' about them. He said that was not the case and stressed in his answers that the majority of offshore investments are perfectly legitimate. It was the non-declaration that was illegal.

Des Peelo, of Peelo and Partners accountancy firm, guided the court through the complexities of a CMI Personal Portfolio. It had sat through twenty-one days of divergent testimony and by now unambiguous statement of fact would be welcome. Peelo had been a chartered accountant for thirty-three years and a member of the Institute of Taxation for all but ten of those. He explained at length how clients' funds would be converted into sterling and transferred to the Isle of Man, then converted back into Irish punts and returned to Ireland in CMI's name. He found little logic behind it and had never come across a similar scheme.

The accountant also expatiated on the 1993 tax amnesty. People were given from 14 July until 30 November to come clean regarding their tax affairs. A 15 per cent charge had been levied on funds not previously declared, this to be paid within a few months.

The hearing then adjourned for the weekend. There was a buzz of anticipation as the public filed out through the doors of Court 4. It was rumoured that RTÉ's stalwart reporter and co-defendant, Charlie Bird, would be the next witness when the court reconvened.

Charlie Bird had held a number of jobs after failing his Leaving Certificate, before landing a research post with RTÉ's current affairs programme, *Seven Days*. After a six-month stint on *The Late Late Show*, he wound up as RTÉ's 'disaster' correspondent and had covered many of the big political stories of the last twenty years.

Bird's attention had first been drawn to the CMI scheme by an anonymous letter he had received and by a phone call from a leading trade unionist who did not wish to go on record. The letter claimed that EU Commissioner Pádraig Flynn and a former member of the judiciary were involved in the scheme promoted by NIB's financial advisors.

Bird had spoken to the retired judge mentioned, who had surprised him with his 'upfront responses'. However, Commissioner Flynn became angry when Bird contacted him. Some correspondence followed thereafter, in which Flynn denied that he or his wife were involved in the scheme. The Commissioner had wanted to know the source of Bird's information, but Bird did not reveal it.

Further enquiries led Bird to Cooper-Flynn, whom he had contacted twice in January 1998. The newly elected deputy referred him to NIB on the first occasion, but confirmed her involvement with the CMI scheme during the latter conversation.

Counsel put it to Bird that if Cooper-Flynn had not been a member of Fianna Fáil and a Dáil deputy, the story would not have received as much coverage. Bird agreed, adding that it had an added significance because the TD was a member of the Public Accounts Committee. It was a fact of life that public office brings with it greater public scrutiny. Nonetheless, Bird had made considerable efforts to get Cooper-Flynn's side of the story in an attempt to present a balanced report. Indeed, twenty-four hours after RTÉ had broadcast his report, Cooper-Flynn had issued a statement and he had incorporated much of it in his next news bulletin.

Bird again refused to name any of his sources, but maintained that none of them were NIB employees. He had contacted NIB in early 1998, but had received no response from the bank.

Bird knew that his news reports might sully Cooper-Flynn's good name and reputation. Despite being pressed on the degree of damage his report had inflicted, the most Bird would concede to was a 'serious impact'. He agreed that everyone had a constitutional right to have his/her good name protected.

Bird then found himself in the unusual position of defending a RTÉ bulletin broadcast on 28 June 1998, even though he had had no direct involvement in it. The news item reported Cooper-Flynn's denial of ever having met the man named in an article published in the *Sunday Independent*. RTÉ had chosen not to name James Howard in that broadcast, although his identity was in the public domain by then. Bird explained that Howard had been promised anonymity, and RTÉ was not prepared to break that promise until Howard had given it a release to do so. After further intensive discussions between Bird and Howard, the retired farmer stated that he was 100 per cent certain that it was Cooper-Flynn who had sold him the Personal Portfolio. Howard agreed to RTÉ broadcasting another interview in which his identity was revealed. Two days later Bird received a solicitor's letter confirming that Cooper-Flynn would be instituting legal proceedings.

Bird consistently denied having embarked on a six-month witch-hunt against the young Mayo deputy. He objected to a suggestion that he had gone after her rather than other NIB advisors because hers would be 'a big scalp' on his belt. Bird reiterated that he had spoken to a number of NIB employees off the record. He was not prepared to name his sources, although he did say that none of the bank's employees had led him to Cooper-Flynn. He also stated that at no point in his investigations had he come across CMI documents bearing the name Patricia Roche. He acknowledged that he had shown the script for the Howard broadcasts to RTÉ's lawyers.

The court rose. It would reconvene the following week. As Monday was the St Patrick's bank holiday, the jury would not start to hear the summations until two days later.

Kevin Feeney started his closing address to the jury with a brief history of the NIB's Financial Advisory Division. The 1980s had brought dramatic changes to the financial world, he said, and NIB had recruited a group of young, aggressive salespeople to take advantage of the bank's client base. Over the years the media had reported that the culture in similar sales-driven teams was one of competitiveness and greed, where best advice was often sacrificed to what was most advantageous for the advisors. Perhaps the same ethos had prevailed in the NIB? One advantage that an in-house sales team had over independent brokers, an advantage that would have been maximised, was that it was the branch managers who referred customers to the financial advisors. Those same managers would have intimate details of the clients' true financial background, and the clients would be only too aware of that. Yet Cooper-Flynn had not produced one witness to say that the CMI investors were telling lies. Indeed, one of the investors gave evidence that he had a bogus bank account and that the plaintiff was present when the details of the account were called up on a computer.

Astonishingly, Feeney said, Cooper-Flynn was asking the jury to believe that she had no idea where funds derived from nor of the tax implications thereafter, something any financial advisor would have to have known before offering best advice. Cooper-Flynn had also tried to minimise the relevance of CMI Personal Portfolios in the schemes available to her as a financial advisor, yet the jury had heard evidence that a substantial portion of her income had derived from the commission earned from sales of those portfolios. In terms of commission, what mattered was not the number of portfolios sold, but the size of the investment. Feeney asked the jury to consider whether a financial advisor could invest huge sums of money and not have any idea where those monies had derived from.

Paul Higgins SC, for James Howard, was next to make his closing address. He based much of it on Howard's remark that he had been 'thrown to the wolves'. Higgins's imagery ranged from Cooper-Flynn's portrayal of herself as an innocent Little Red Riding Hood to the defence's assertion that she was a female Kevin Costner – quite happy dancing with wolves. The jury would have to decide which version it believed.

Then it was Garrett Cooney's turn to address the court. He started by saying how extraordinary the case had been. A single individual had gone head to head with one of the most powerful organisations in the State. He asked the jury to send out a message that no citizen should be treated with such arrogant contempt as Cooper-Flynn had been treated. During the hearing, Cooney claimed, the defence had laid a smokescreen to camouflage the real issues. How plausible was it that James Howard had surrendered, in a matter of minutes, his nest egg of £83,000 to a girl in her mid-twenties whom he scarcely knew? There was ample evidence to prove that Cooper-Flynn had not been involved in the sale of the CMI portfolio to Howard. Nobody, he warned, should have their reputation tarnished because of their name and family connections.

Mr Justice Morris surprised the court by giving his closing address immediately after final comments of counsel for Cooper-Flynn. He instructed the jury to disregard the personalities in the case and make its decision solely on the evidence presented in court. Mr Bird was a well-known figure on their television screens and some might admire his work, while others might disapprove of his delving into other people's lives. Equally, some might admire Ms Cooper-Flynn and her work in the Dáil and with the Seanad Public Accounts Committee, just as others might see her as a busybody. However, no personal opinions should be allowed to colour the jury's judgment. Jurors could 'cherry pick' evidence, in that they could believe part or all of a witness's evidence. The judge advised that the jury could decide its verdict unanimously, or on a majority basis of nine or more.

So far there was nothing in the judge's address to unduly concern either side, but that was about to change. In a series of rhetorical questions, Mr Justice Morris seemed to sway heavily against RTÉ and Charlie Bird.

By the time the court rose that evening, the powers-that-be at RTÉ's Montrose headquarters had cause for concern. There would be a lot of late-night oil-burning for the defence's legal team. The outcome of the case could depend on how successful their pleas to the judge for even-handedness might be.

After a bout of intense legal submissions the next morning, Mr Justice Morris recalled the jury and told them that the defence felt he had not done justice to its side of the case. He said he wished to restore as much balance as possible and proceeded to do so.

The plaintiff's side had scored some points as well. The judge told the jury that his description of Cooper-Flynn as a salesgirl should be disregarded as inappropriate. She had been a financial advisor. The judge also granted a request from the jury that it be shown videos of RTÉ's 9.00 p.m. news broadcasts of 19 June and 28 June, and the 6.00 p.m. bulletin of 1 July 1998.

After deliberating for five hours, the jury returned. The issue paper on which the members had to reach verdicts contained five points:

1. Have the defendants proved that the plaintiff induced the third-named defendant to evade his lawful obligation to pay tax by not availing of the tax amnesty?

    If the answer is 'no', proceed to question 2.

    If the answer is 'yes', proceed no further.

2. Have the defendants proved that the plaintiff advised or encouraged other persons – being those referred to in the evidence – to evade tax?

    If the answer is 'no', proceed to question 4 to assess damages.

    If the answer is 'yes', proceed to question 3.

3. In view of the finding to question 2, has the plaintiff's reputation suffered material injury by reason of the matters published relating to the third-named defendant?

4. If the answer to question 1 and 2 is 'no', assess damages under the heading (a) general damages, (b) aggravation of such damages.

5. If the answer to question 1 is 'no', and 2 and 3 are 'yes', assess damages to the material injury to the plaintiff's reputation.

As the eight men and four women took their seats, the faces of all the main participants in the twenty-eight-day drama bore the signs of the ordeal. The coin was in the air, and few would be rash enough to predict on which side it would land. There was hardly a sound in the packed courtroom as the jury foreperson stood to relay the verdict.

On the first issue the jury found that the plaintiff had not sold James Howard an investment package that encouraged him to evade his lawful duty to pay tax.

On the second issue the jury found that the Fianna Fáil TD had advised or encouraged a number of persons to evade tax.

On the third issue, and in view of its findings, the jury had been asked if the plaintiff's reputation had suffered material injury by reason of the matters published relating to James Howard. It said it had not.

Finally, in response to the fourth and fifth issue, the jury had decided that no damages would be awarded to Ms Cooper-Flynn.

There was little jubilation in the courtroom as the significance of the verdicts slowly sunk in. RTÉ's economic correspondent, George Lee, hugged his colleague, Charlie Bird. There was the slightest trace of a wry smile on Kevin Feeney's face as he gathered up his papers. Cooper-Flynn and her legal team left quickly through a side door. Most people were a little mystified over the verdict: had Cooper-Flynn won or had she lost? It gradually dawned on them that the real victor in Ireland's longest-running libel case would be the side awarded costs. Those in the know estimated that the sum could be as much as £2 million. However, that crucial judgment would not be known for another eleven days. Mr Justice Morris would announce his decision on 5 April.

The political response to the verdict came quickly. The Labour Party leader, Ruairi Quinn, said the trial outcome had very serious implications for Cooper-Quinn as a member of the Dáil and also as a member of the Committee on Public Accounts: 'A jury of her peers has found that she advised and encouraged people to evade tax. There is now a clear obligation on her to consider her position as a member of the Dáil.'

Taoiseach Bertie Ahern, speaking in Stockholm during a break in an EU summit, promised to examine the judgment as soon as possible. He would not discuss the matter further at this time, citing the possibility of an appeal.

Cooper-Flynn issued a statement through her solicitors saying that it was a very disappointing result and that she and her legal team were actively considering an appeal to the Supreme Court.

Mr Justice Morris listened to lengthy legal submissions from all the parties before handing down his ruling on 5 April. He found that Beverley Cooper-Flynn was liable for all costs. It was the worst possible result for the Fianna Fáil TD. Her counsel had hoped to salvage something by asking the judge to award a portion of the costs in her favour. This was not entirely untenable because the jury had decided that the plaintiff did not sell the CMI Personal Portfolio to Howard. The judge sided with the defence, however, after Feeney argued that he was not aware of any case where a claimant had failed to get damages and had lost a claim and costs were not made in favour of the defendant.

Beverley Cooper-Flynn lodged an appeal on 11 May 2001. She did not give up the Fianna Fáil whip without a fight. She refused to resign it voluntarily, despite pressure from senior party figures. After a four-hour meeting of the parliamentary party, she was expelled by an overwhelming show of hands. Cooper-Flynn had claimed that losing the whip for the second time could well be prejudicial to her appeal, but her argument fell on deaf ears. The Taoiseach wished her well in her appeal, but believed the party and the government should be allowed to get on with its work without the uncertainty regarding Cooper-Flynn as a distraction.

Cooper-Flynn wrote to the Taoiseach to say that she would pay the costs, no matter how long it might take her. She had no intention of leaving politics, she told him, stating that her commitment has always been to serve the voters of Mayo and the Fianna Fáil party. In the letter she repeated her intention not to seek the protection of bankruptcy; that would mean the automatic loss of her Dáil seat.

A 'For Sale' sign was soon to appear at the Rathgar house Cooper-Flynn had once shared with her husband.

Beverley Cooper-Flynn fought the 2002 general election as an official Fianna Fáil candidate and retained her Mayo seat. She regained the Fianna Fáil whip when the new Dáil commenced in June 2002. In February 2004, more than three years after the historic libel case, Cooper-Flynn's appeal was heard by the Supreme Court. The mood in the RTÉ legal team was gloomy because it was generally believed that the appeal would be granted on a technicality. RTÉ had gone so far as to prepare a statement saying that the adverse result did not in any way affect the integrity of the stories that had led to the case. The despondency proved premature, however. In a reserved judgment the five judges returned an unanimous decision against Beverley Cooper-Flynn. Once again she was saddled with an enormous legal bill for an unsuccessful court action – an estimated €186,000.

In June 2005, Taxing Master Charles Moran approved almost all of RTÉ's and Charlie Bird's costs. He noted that justification had been pleaded as a defence and stated that it was a difficult plea to prove, calling for the highest degree or proof. RTÉ had had to take statements from sixty witnesses and retain five expert witnesses. It had also been necessary to obtain discovery against NIB – a difficult operation that had cost RTÉ €230,000. He was satisfied that the costs claimed were necessary and properly incurred, reflecting the enormous work done on behalf of RTÉ and Mr Bird.

RTÉ has indicated that it will pursue Cooper-Flynn for the full costs. As a state broadcaster, it was not considered appropriate that the public be asked to foot the bill. Should the libel case result in bankruptcy for the Mayo TD, she could of course forfeit the seat she retained in the May 2007 general election, when she stood as an independent candidate. She lost the party whip for a third time in the wake of her unsuccessful Supreme Court appeal.

On 18 June 2007, RTÉ brought a bankruptcy hearing against Cooper-Flynn, who on the same day initiated a High Court challenge to the constitutional ruling that no bankrupt person could hold a Dáil seat. Both cases were adjourned for a fortnight. A few days later, at a celebration dinner for her election supporters, Cooper-Flynn announced that she had made a full and final settlement with RTÉ and would be dropping her constitutional challenge. RTÉ had accepted €1.25 million, less than half the amount owed. The licence-payers of Ireland were left to fund the difference.

09 | A COURT TOO FAR:
SEÁN SHERWIN v SUNDAY INDEPENDENT [2001]

In libel hearings, it is rare for a witness for the defence to attract more attention than the plaintiff. However, this is exactly what happened when Fianna Fáil's national organiser, Seán Sherwin, brought a defamation case against the *Sunday Independent* newspaper to the High Court.

Sherwin was first elected to the Dáil at the tender age of twenty-three as a Fianna Fáil deputy for Dublin South-West in a 1970 by-election. He lost his seat three years later, after leaving the Fianna Fáil party to become the only deputy in Fianna Fáil rebel Kevin Boland's new party, Aontacht Éireann. Sherwin returned to the Fianna Fáil fold when Charles Haughey became party leader. He took over as national organiser in the mid-1980s.

The *Sunday Independent* had published a front-page article by Jody Corcoran, political editor, that Sherwin claimed was defamatory. Corcoran had written a follow-up article to the previous unmasking of Fianna Fáil's Padraig Flynn as the recipient of a £50,000 political donation from property developer Tom Gilmartin. Corcoran's story concerned a meeting that had taken place between Sherwin and Gilmartin, during which Gilmartin claimed he had first informed Sherwin of the donation. Tom Gilmartin claimed that towards the end of the meeting, Sherwin had solicited funds for his sister-in-law's political campaign as a Fianna Fáil candidate. Though this alleged request was not the main thrust of the article, the newspaper had used it as a 'pull quote' in a headline. The newspaper had acknowledged in the article that Sherwin had strenuously denied making any such request to Gilmartin, but this had not been enough to stave off a defamation suit.

While the spotlight would shine on Sherwin once the case started, there was never any doubt as to who the public really wanted to see and hear. The star of the hearing would be the white-haired Tom Gilmartin, a Luton-based developer who had been promising for a number of years to expose some of the skeletons in the Fianna Fáil cupboard. Thus far, the Irish public had been given only tantalising and indirect glimpses of a murky world of political corruption. After a period of relative silence since his original allegations of bribery and corruption against holders of public office, it would be a jury in a civil case who finally got to hear Tom Gilmartin's first public denouncements. The case opened in Court 4 of the High Court on 20 November 2001 in front of a jury and Mr Justice Philip O'Sullivan. Robert Dore, solicitors, had retained Garrett Cooney SC and Brian Lenihan SC to represent Sherwin; Kevin Feeney SC acted for the defence.

Independent Newspapers plc would deny that the words complained of were understood to bear the meanings claimed. Without prejudice to that denial, Independent Newspapers would also claim that the words were true in substance and in fact. The defence would further deny that the character of the plaintiff had been damaged or brought into public contempt, as alleged.

In outlining the case for Sherwin, Cooney took the court through Corcoran's contested article. It contained allegations of 'sleaze and guilt' and an assertion that Sherwin had solicited funds from property developer Tom Gilmartin for the local election campaign of his sister-in-law, Catherine Sherwin. The article was one of two Jody Corcoran had written that had appeared on the front page of the *Sunday Independent* on 14 February 1999. Entitled 'FF organiser sought election cash for his sister-in-law:

Gilmartin', it left much to be desired as a Valentine Day's message for Sherwin.

The key extract read:

> Tom Gilmartin claims that Fianna Fáil's national organiser Seán Sherwin asked him to make a financial contribution to his sister-in-law's election campaign. The property developer claims that the request was made during a meeting at party headquarters after he told Mr Sherwin about the £50,000 donation to Padraig Flynn, which was intended for Fianna Fáil.

Cooney put it to the court that any average reader of the article would come to the conclusion that his client had arranged a meeting with Gilmartin with a corrupt intention in mind. The story was false and had damaged his client. Cooney then called the plaintiff as first witness.

Seán Sherwin, of Cappaghmore, Clondalkin, Dublin, freely admitted that he had met Gilmartin on a number of occasions in late 1990. At the first meeting in October, at Fianna Fáil headquarters on Upper Mount Street, Dublin, arranged by Colm Scallon, brother of presidential candidate Dana, they had discussed the developer's plans for construction projects at Bachelor's Walk and Quarryvale (Liffey Valley Shopping Centre). Gilmartin complained to the Fianna Fáil organiser that the planning authorities were putting obstacles in his path. Sherwin said he could not be of assistance, but told Gilmartin to contact his public representatives in both wards.

At a second meeting, Gilmartin told Sherwin that he had donated £50,000 to Padraig Flynn, then Minister for the Environment and the Fianna Fáil's joint treasurer. Sherwin was alarmed by this announcement. He had heard no mention of it before – surely such a large sum of money would attract comment from the Fianna Fáil hierarchy? During the meeting, Sherwin recalled Gilmartin telling him of a conversation he had had with a councillor in Buswells Hotel, across the road from Leinster House. The two men had stood next to each other at the bar, speaking in furtive whispers. The councillor had allegedly told

Gilmartin that it would 'cost him' if he wanted his support for the building projects.

Gilmartin clearly thought that his £50,000 donation had 'cost him' enough already and he warned Sherwin that if no action were taken to smooth out his planning problems, he would go to the press. The developer promised to expose the unsavoury aspects of bribery and corruption in Irish politics. Sherwin repeated the advice he had given Gilmartin at their first meeting: talk to your public representatives.

The next day, Sherwin broached the £50,000 with a Fianna Fáil fund-raiser, who said there was no such donation on record. He also informed the new Taoiseach, Albert Reynolds, of the claim, as he thought Reynolds might intend appointing Flynn to his Cabinet and he did not wish any allegations to be left hanging over Flynn's head.

Catherine Sherwin had not stood in the local elections in 1990, though she was an unsuccessful Fianna Fáil candidate in the 1991 election. She polled 986 first preference votes and had paid her expenses (£500–£600) from her own pocket. Seán Sherwin believed that it would have been improper for him as national organiser to solicit funds for one party candidate ahead of others, even more so when that candidate was a close relative.

Under cross-examination, Sherwin repeated that he had been shocked by Gilmartin's claim that Flynn had donated £50,000 to the party. He had checked it out and, finding no record of such a large sum, assumed it was merely a scandalous allegation. Sherwin told the court that he could not be judge or jury over the allegation. It was not up to him to speculate about what had become of the donation, whether it had gone to Fianna Fáil and had been lost or whether Flynn had held on to it.

In time, Taoiseach Bertie Ahern laid a letter before the Dáil written by the Fianna Fáil general secretary to Flynn, then an EU Commissioner in Brussels. Flynn replied that he would explain the matter when he was called as a witness before the Flood Tribunal. Eventually Flynn said that £25,000 of the money had been a personal gift and the other half a political donation. The Revenue Commissioners did not believe his version of events and levied a £21,600 tax bill on the £50,000 'gift'. In February 2004, TV3 broke a story that claimed that a portion of the money had been invested offshore by Beverley Cooper-Flynn.

Catherine Sherwin's immediate reaction to the article was one of disgust and terror because it linked her to improper payments to politicians. She stated that there was no truth in substance or in fact to Gilmartin's claim.

The newspaper was dealt a serious blow by testimony from property developer Colm Scallon. Scallon related his memory of the meeting with Gilmartin at Fianna Fáil headquarters. At the time, he had a great admiration for Gilmartin and his two ambitious projects, not least for the employment opportunities they would bring. A mutual friend had introduced Scallon to Gilmartin, and it was Scallon who had suggested that the property developer meet Sherwin. The meeting had lasted about two hours and there had been a detailed discussion of the two proposed developments. It was Scallon's recollection that no donations of any kind had been mentioned at that meeting. Sherwin lived in Clondalkin, was familiar with the area's problems with high unemployment and poor housing and was keen to do what he could. However, he had told Gilmartin that he was 'in the wrong building', meaning that he needed to talk to the Dublin City councillors at Wood Quay.

Scallon also denied that there had been any mention of Sherwin's sister-in-law's political aspirations during the meeting. Neither had he any recollection of Pádraig Flynn's name being mentioned during the discussion, though he remembered there had been mention of Gilmartin running into difficulties with councillors and planning.

The first three days of the hearing had produced few front-page headlines. Seasoned court observers knew that what they had heard so far was merely a warm-up for the main performer. On Friday morning, Tom Gilmartin took the witness stand as the newspaper opened its case.

Gilmartin was born on a small farm in north Co. Sligo. He left school at fourteen to help his father on the farm. Young Tom had won a scholarship for a second-level education, but the family was too poor for him to take advantage of it. During the rampant unemployment of the 1950s, Gilmartin took a boat for England. He found work on the buses and in factories, eventually starting his own building business with just one worker. Twenty years later he had 500 men working for him, but a Labour government and militant unions were taking a heavy toll on building contractors during the recession of the early 1970s. Unfortunately, his business had folded.

The Thatcher years proved good for Gilmartin, however. He was now based in Luton and was back on his feet after building and selling a factory. He closed deal after deal, each one bigger than the last. He became a rich man. The Sligo native never lost his thick brogue and in many ways still regarded Ireland as his home. He was not afraid to put his hand in his pocket to help the less fortunate and funded a day-care centre for homeless Irishmen run by the Sisters of Clare in London.

Gilmartin had come across plenty of con artists and corrupt politicians in England, but told the court that his eyes had been opened when he had tried to do business in Ireland. His first project was a plan for a redevelopment at Bachelor's Walk, Dublin. His partners in London, Arlington Securities, with offices behind Buckingham Palace, thought a Dublin man with contacts would be an asset in this venture. Gilmartin needed someone to help him to locate the owners of near-derelict Dublin properties. A Blanchardstown bank manager suggested that a local man, Liam Lawlor TD, might be the person to consult. A meeting was set up in the Deadman's Inn, on the Old Lucan Road, Palmerston, and within a week the thrusting Lawlor had secured himself a £3,500-a-month post with Arlington Securities after gate-crashing a meeting in London. The Dáil deputy claimed that the government had given him authority to 'steer through the roadblocks' of the proposed development at Bachelor's Walk. Gilmartin was under no misapprehension as to what Lawlor was: in his opinion, he was a hustler, but he was Arlington's hustler.

Gilmartin and Lawlor did not work well together. The Sligo man thought the deputy had been rude and underhanded in the way he got himself involved in the project. Their relationship worsened when Lawlor tried to have himself recruited as a consultant on the Quarryvale project. In 1988, Lawlor introduced Gilmartin to a kindred spirit, George Redmond, then assistant Dublin City manager. (It was not the most propitious of alliances, as time would prove: Redmond was arrested at Dublin Airport some years later arriving in on a flight from the Isle of Man with a large amount of cash. He was eventually convicted of accepting bribes and jailed for one year. He was later freed on appeal, but the Supreme Court ruled against a retrial because he had served most of the sentence.) Gilmartin and Redmond discussed the development at Quarryvale. Lawlor said that the project would not get off the ground without his input – a snip at £100,000 – and that 'George had to be taken care of'.

This was what the public in the packed courtroom had come to hear. It was not exactly news – there had been acres of newsprint and weeks of broadcasts devoted to planning corruption and tribunals – but to hear it from the horse's mouth held a fascination for the court observers. Gilmartin had levelled many allegations over the previous fourteen years, some of which had been investigated by the Garda Síochána and the Flood Tribunal. He had been reluctant to co-operate with investigators, however, claiming that his wife's illness took priority in his life. He was expected to give evidence to the Flood Tribunal within the next few months. (It would, in fact, turn out to be years, rather than months, later.)

Once again, the jury was to hear how Pádraig Flynn had received a cheque for £50,000 in June 1988. Gilmartin was in such a hurry on the day he went to the Custom House to see Flynn that he handed him a cheque with just the amount and his signature completed. The Flood Tribunal had later located the cheque and had shown it to Gilmartin. It had been made out to cash and had been lodged in a bogus non-resident account held at a Castlebar bank.

Gilmartin recalled another meeting, in February 1989, which would have a significant impact fifteen years later on a future Taoiseach, Bertie Ahern. Gilmartin related how Lawlor had brought him to a room in the Dáil and introduced him to the then Taoiseach, Charles Haughey. Others allegedly attending that meeting were Bertie Ahern, Albert Reynolds and Seamus Brennan. Ahern would later deny any recollection of the meeting, despite Mary O'Rourke's testimony in spring 2004 during the Quarryvale module of the Mahon Tribunal (formerly Flood), that he was present. Mary O'Rourke had not taken part in the meeting, but had entered the room while it was in progress. Brian Lenihan, then Tánaiste and Minister for Foreign Affairs, was also said to have sat in, which was of particular interest to counsel for the plaintiff, who was his son.

Gilmartin went on to describe how a person Lawlor had spoken to after the meeting duly approached him and handed him a slip of paper bearing details of an Isle of Man bank account. A sizeable donation was expected, Gilmartin was informed. He replied to the unidentified man: 'You people make the so-and-so mafia look like monks.' Soon after, Gilmartin claimed, his projects began to run into serious difficulties. A media campaign was orchestrated by Frank Dunlop, Fianna Fáil press secretary. Gilmartin felt that the campaign had an anti-Tom Gilmartin agenda and soon produced its inevitable results: meetings were cancelled or disrupted, plans interfered with or lost.

In the spring of 1989, Gilmartin sacked Lawlor as a consultant after he had tried to put the squeeze on him for more money. The problems facing Gilmartin on his projects increased, and it was about that time that a councillor had asked him in Buswells Hotel for £100,000 to compensate for the 'damage to the little people' inflicted by his Quarryvale development. It was not all bad news, however. Gilmartin said that there were seventy-nine councillors in total, but he had never met 90 per cent of them or asked them for assistance.

The future of the Quarryvale project was in serious doubt by the turn of the decade. A scheduled meeting with George Redmond was cancelled at the last minute, and the Dublin City manager ordered Gilmartin out of his office. Gilmartin had £6–£7 million at stake in the project; Arlington had some £20 million. Arlington had previously pulled out of the Bachelor's Walk project because of the lack of co-operation they had encountered. Gilmartin had tried to buy land at Quarryvale from the Dublin Corporation for £30,000 per acre. After many false starts, he had successfully tendered for the land at £70,000 per acre.

There was no end to the problems Gilmartin faced with elected officials. He had met numerous councillors who had spoken with 'forked tongues', though he had dealt only with members of Fianna Fáil and could not comment on the elected representatives of other political parties. Then, in 1990, he met Colm Scallon, whom Gilmartin believed was an honourable and Christian man. Scallon thought Gilmartin had been treated shamefully and suggested he meet Sherwin. At the meeting, Gilmartin itemised the troubles he had been presented with by Lawlor, Redmond and others. He informed Sherwin that Lawlor had demanded a 20 per cent stake in the Quarryvale project.

Gilmartin thought Sherwin seemed sympathetic and that he said he would bring it to the attention of the 'powers-that-be'. Although Sherwin mentioned no names, Gilmartin took his phrase to mean the government, i.e. the Taoiseach and the Cabinet. He had no recollection of Sherwin saying that he was in the wrong place or the wrong building. Sherwin had asked him if there was any money going and if he would make a donation to the party. Gilmartin told him that he had already donated £50,000 through Pádraig Flynn. Sherwin claimed that he had not heard of the donation, excused himself and left the room for some minutes. When he returned, Sherwin was still of the opinion that there had been no such donation. As Gilmartin and Scallon were leaving, Sherwin said that his sister-in-law was running for election in 'his patch' and 'could do with a bit of help'.

At that request, Gilmartin closed his briefcase and left. He whispered 'déjà vu' to Scallon, meaning that it was the same old story: Fianna Fáil had the begging bowl out once again.

A further touch of intrigue was added by Gilmartin's memory of a second meeting with Sherwin. Sherwin had telephoned him in Luton, suggesting that Gilmartin meet an American businessman who was in Dublin to help salvage the Goodman meat empire. The American apparently had money to invest; a meeting was set up at the Conrad Hotel.

Sherwin and a man with a Northern Irish accent accompanied Gilmartin to the meeting, advising the developer to take the American seriously because he was a valuable contact, worth cultivating. The American, Edmund McMullan, was shown the plans for Quarryvale and seemed impressed. McMullan told Gilmartin that he represented a number of American banks and that if he managed to persuade them to invest £50 million, his finder's fee would be £120,000.

There were a number of follow-up meetings between Gilmartin and McMullan that Sherwin did not attend. Eventually, Gilmartin was given an offer-of-intent on Merrill Lynch-headed notepaper. McMullan was paid £36,000 for his work, but Gilmartin claimed that it later transpired that the offer had been a scam.

Gilmartin was asked to account for refusing to assist earlier investigations into alleged planning irregularities and political corruption. He said that the Flood Tribunal had tried to 'get me on board' in 1998, but he felt that it had the makings of a whitewash. His mind had been changed by a number of things. First, Frank Dunlop had launched a campaign to undermine his credibility. Secondly, Pádraig Flynn had demeaned him and his wife in January 1999 on *The Late Late Show*. Flynn, Gilmartin thought, had displayed a remarkable arrogance during the television interview.

The political journalist Jody Corcoran had earlier written a number of articles based on Gilmartin's information. He had told Corcoran that the £50,000 given to Flynn had been purely a political donation – a contribution that had been requested on a number of occasions.

To the best of his recollection, Gilmartin thought his first contact with Corcoran was probably in the late summer of 1998. Corcoran had eventually written a piece about the £50,000 that Flynn had been given, which had provoked a response from the

Fianna Fáil spin-doctors: they insinuated that Gilmartin had been attempting to bribe Flynn in return for political favours. After a number of defamatory articles had been published about him, Gilmartin felt he had no other option but to respond in like fashion by talking to one of the many journalists requesting interviews. He supplied Corcoran with additional information before Christmas 1998 and continued to do so until February 1999. It was his understanding that when they had talked on the phone, Corcoran was taking notes.

Gilmartin stressed that it had never been his intention to discredit Sherwin and he bore him no animosity. He had supplied the newspaper with information so that they could check it and help clear his name. Gilmartin insisted that he had not intended to convey that Sherwin was behaving in an improper manner. He himself knew all too well what an allegation like that felt like. He did not think it was illegal for anybody to solicit a donation to a political party. Gilmartin was adamant that when he had said 'déjà vu' as he left the Upper Mount Street meeting, he meant that once again he had been asked for a political donation. He did not mean that once again he had been asked for a bribe. At no time had Gilmartin been prepared to hit out at anybody just to clear his name. The suggestion, he said, was 'a damn lie'.

Reluctant to discuss any business problems he had experienced in 1990, Gilmartin insisted that that was a matter for the Flood Tribunal. When pressed on the subject, Gilmartin admitted that there was a need to advance the Quarryvale project. His company, Barkhill, had borrowed £8 million from Allied Irish Bank on short-term rates. Cooney wanted to know if the bank had been pressing for progress. Gilmartin once again told counsel that he was straying into tribunal territory and suggested that he pry no further.

Taken aback by this answer, Cooney asked the witness if he was threatening him. Gilmartin denied this, stating that he had merely been advising him. This comment raised a few eyebrows in the well of the court. Barristers are notorious for brow-beating witnesses, but only rarely does the reverse happen. But then, much in this libel hearing had strayed from the norm. By now Gilmartin had been giving evidence for four days – one day more than the plaintiff. To the regret of many in court, the judge ended further exchanges between Gilmartin and Cooney along these lines by admonishing the witness, reminding him that he was in court to answer questions posed by counsel.

Turning to a fresh line of inquiry, Gilmartin was asked to put a number on the people against whom he had levelled criminal and corruption accusations. About five, Gilmartin answered, making the point that he had made no accusation against Pádraig Flynn. Up until recently he had been confident that the £50,000 had been delivered, as intended, to Fianna Fáil party funds. When pushed a little harder, Gilmartin conceded that he had made allegations against ten people.

Gilmartin was finally allowed to leave the witness-box late on the seventh day of the hearing. He was replaced by Jody Corcoran, the *Sunday Independent*'s political editor and the journalist that had penned the contentious article.

Corcoran confirmed that in late 1998 Gilmartin had given him supplementary information about events in the late 1980s and early 1990s. The property developer was reluctant to talk at first, and it had taken a period of sustained pressure by him to secure Gilmartin's consent to an interview. The developer had told him how he had told Sherwin about the £50,000 donation he had made to Fianna Fáil through Pádraig Flynn. The journalist had contacted Sherwin to ask about his meeting with Gilmartin and for his views on Flynn. Sherwin confirmed that the meeting had taken place and that Flynn had been discussed. At Sherwin's request, the *Sunday Independent* had faxed a number of questions to the Fianna Fáil press office. In the interest of balanced journalism, Corcoran had included the party's reply in the contentious article. Fianna Fáil denied that Sherwin had solicited money from Gilmartin and stated that Sherwin had no recollection of introducing Gilmartin to an American businessman.

Corcoran told the court how he had watched Flynn's performance on *The Late Late Show*; he had telephoned Gilmartin during the show. Both of them had been unimpressed by the way Flynn had skirted around the core question. Gilmartin was incensed at derogatory references made to his wife and himself by Flynn. A few days later, Gilmartin gave an interview to Charlie Bird for RTÉ News. That was the first time the developer spoke publicly about the misplaced £50,000.

A few days before the publication of the controversial article, Corcoran had contacted Gilmartin and told him he needed to have him on the record. As Gilmartin talked, the journalist had typed contemporaneous notes directly onto a computer, and afterwards read back the statement for Gilmartin's approval. He tried to speak to Sherwin once again, but was unable to contact him.

Corcoran was asked if it was true that his article was dependent on the memory of a single man of events that had taken place some ten years before. That was the case, Corcoran admitted, adding that he had found Gilmartin to be a man of substance and of truth.

Counsel turned to the question of a fax sent to the Fianna Fáil press office. Had Corcoran not sent the fax to cover himself? Was it not the case that Corcoran regarded people as guilty if they did not plead their innocence? That was not so, Corcoran argued, nor did he believe that there had been any question of guilt raised in the article.

The jury of six men and six women listened to closing statements from both sides on the morning of the tenth day of the hearing. Of all the evidence they had heard in court, perhaps the most telling was that Catherine Sherwin had *not* been a candidate in any election in 1990. If Gilmartin's memory was so dependable, how could he have made such a mistake? Then there was the evidence of Colm Scallon, who had told the court that he had not heard Sherwin make a request for campaign funds at the meeting with Gilmartin. The developer himself had described Scallon as an honourable man and a Christian.

Feeney, for the defence, told the jury that the newspaper was pleading justification and, without prejudice, that if the article were true, it was not defamatory. The issue the jury had to focus on was simple: did Sherwin ask Gilmartin for money for his sister-in-law?

Cooney told the jury that the *Sunday Independent* had done a hatchet job on the plaintiff. They had chosen to put his denial at the end of the article, which meant many readers would have failed to read it. Counsel had no desire to be offensive to Gilmartin, but if he had been badly treated in Ireland, it was unfair of him to inflict revenge on Sherwin or on the latter's sister-in-law.

The jury retired after the judge's address and direction. It deliberated for three hours that first afternoon, until the forewoman finally told the judge that a majority had agreed on question one. Before proceeding further, she wanted to know what majority was required to reach a decision on question two. The judge replied that at least nine of the same majority who had agreed on the first question would have to agree a decision on the second. The forewoman then asked if the jury could adjourn until the following morning. The judge allowed the request and adjourned the court until 10.30 a.m. the next day.

The decision earlier that year in the *Cooper-Flynn v RTÉ* libel case would no doubt have been playing on the minds of the two opposing sides. It would be a long night for the principal combatants, one that would eventually end in possibly the worst moment of confused farce ever witnessed in an Irish court.

Even a cursory glance at the issue paper is enough to appreciate the difficulty of the task the jury had been set. This complex paper put a number of questions to the jury:

1. If the words complained of meant or was understood to mean:
   (a) Sherwin wrongfully solicited money from Gilmartin for his sister-in-law.
   (b) Sherwin was prepared to exert a political influence in return for a donation from Gilmartin for Sherwin's sister-in-law.

(c) Sherwin sought money from Gilmartin for personal use in return for introducing Gilmartin to a US businessman.

(d) Sherwin was aware that Gilmartin gave a US business-man £40,000 in circumstances which made it clear to Sherwin that Gilmartin was being treated as a 'sucker'.

(e) Sherwin, by seeking money from Gilmartin, abused his position as national organiser of Fianna Fáil.

If the jury answered Yes to any part of question one, the jury is then asked:

2. If the words complained of are substantially true in substance and in fact.

If it answers No to question two, the jury is asked:

3. Assess damages.

The jury returned its verdict at 3.00 p.m. on the eleventh day of the hearing. Mr Justice O'Sullivan read out the verdicts to a hushed courtroom. The jury answered Yes to section (a) of question one, and No to sections (b), (c), (d) and (e). So far the result was mixed for Sherwin. That outlook improved dramatically when the judge read out that the jury had replied No to the second question. The judge then read out that in answer to question three, the jury had awarded £250,000 to the plaintiff.

There were gasps around the court. Sherwin had hit the jackpot – not quite as much as Proinsias De Rossa, but pretty close. The size of the award meant that the plaintiff would almost certainly be allowed his costs. The gamble of taking a High Court action had been more than vindicated.

It took only seconds for the sweet taste of victory to turn sour. The jury forewoman drew the judge's attention to an error he had made. The jury had awarded Sherwin not £250,000, but £250! The High Court gamble had not paid off; Seán Sherwin could expect to be hit with most of the costs. He had cleared his name and won £250 in damages, but ultimately the case could end up costing him £500,000. The jury had decided that Sherwin's reputation was worth a miserly £250. The six women and six men did not believe Gilmartin's claim that Sherwin had solicited money, but the significance of his wider evidence had dramatically affected the amount of damages they had awarded.

As the uproar in the court began to settle down, Feeney got to his feet and asked the judge if submissions on costs could be left to another day. Counsel for the plaintiff had no objection, so the judge asked both parties to appear in front of him again the following Wednesday.

Outside the court, the opposing sides each claimed success of sorts. Sherwin told reporters that the case had never been about money. His good name and reputation had been vindicated in an action that he admitted had been an ordeal. He had taken the case as a private citizen and had not been influenced in any way by Fianna Fáil. He would be considering an appeal against the amount of damages awarded.

Michael Roche of Independent Newspapers plc said that the jury had found the article defamatory in only one of the five relevant matters: 'It is with the greatest regret that such costs and expenses had to be incurred over a three-week period to enable the *Sunday Independent* to substantially vindicate its article.'

Jody Corcoran said that he had been impressed by the way Gilmartin had given his evidence and would look forward to the developer's evidence at the Flood (later Mahon) Tribunal.

The Fianna Fáil press office refused to comment on the outcome of the hearing.

The following week, the legal teams duly made their submissions on costs to Mr Justice O'Sullivan. He ruled that Independent Newspapers plc was entitled to an order for costs for half the amount of the difference between its High Court costs and what it would have cost the newspaper group if the case had been heard in the Circuit Court. If the newspaper's costs were £250,000, then the Circuit Court costs would be around £50,000. Therefore, half the difference meant a £100,000 order of costs against Sherwin. The plaintiff would also have to pay his own legal team, an amount estimated at £200,000.

The judge awarded costs of £5,000 against the newspaper. Sherwin's legal team had argued that the plaintiff should be awarded full Circuit Court costs, but under the Courts Act 1991 Sherwin could have been awarded costs of as little as £250 – an amount equal to the damages award.

The judge chided Sherwin for bringing his case to the High Court. The issue could have been decided, the judge told him, in the Circuit Court, in proceedings that would have involved a much lesser outlay of costs and expenses, including, but not limited to, the extra amount incurred by bringing the case before the High Court.

One month later, Sherwin's solicitors confirmed that their client had informed the Supreme Court of his decision to appeal the order on costs. A cross-appeal was duly launched by the newspaper. Both were struck out after an agreement was reached, the terms of which remain confidential.

* * *

Politicians and property often make uneasy bedfellows, as the various libel cases heard in Irish courts attest. Seán Sherwin was not the only Fianna Fáil party member to defend himself against allegations concerning impropriety. The leader of the Fianna Fáil party, Taoiseach Bertie Ahern, was also forced to bring a defamation action in July 2001. His libel action was against businessman Denis 'Starry' O'Brien, and was, coincidentally, connected to the Quarryvale development. The action was unusual in that it was only against O'Brien, not against the publishers.

Denis O'Brien had accused the Taoiseach of accepting a £50,000 bribe some twelve years earlier, while sitting in a state car parked under the Burlington Hotel in Dublin. According to O'Brien, Ahern had been attending the hotel for a post All-Ireland Football Final dinner, and the alleged 'sweetener' was given to him by Owen O'Callaghan to facilitate planning permission for the Liffey Valley Shopping Centre.

Ahern brought the action against O'Brien only after a number of failed attempts to have the businessman withdraw his allegation, which had been published in the *Sunday Business Post* and the *Irish Examiner* in April 2000. The case opened on 10 July 2001, obliging Ahern to leave talks on Northern Ireland that were being held in Shropshire, England in order to attend court.

The Taoiseach and the witnesses called quickly exposed O'Brien's allegations as fabrications. At the time O'Brien claimed he had been handing over the £50,000, he had been seen fishing in Co. Waterford. There had been no GAA event in the Burlington Hotel on that evening: the winning Cork team had celebrated in the Royal Marine Hotel in Dún Laoghaire; the losing Mayo team had consoled itself at the Grand Hotel in Malahide. Most damaging of all was the fact that the Irish Nationwide deposit book examined during document discovery, and from which it was claimed the £50,000 had been drawn, was proved to be a forgery.

The defence put forward no case. Faced with such a barrage of incontrovertible facts, O'Brien had had little option but to withdraw his defence the week before. The judge declared that the claim had been utterly, completely and absolutely false and untrue and awarded Ahern the full limit of Circuit Court damages: £30,000. The Taoiseach said he planned to give the money to charity.

On 13 June 2007, during his evidence in the Quarryvale module of the Mahon (formerly Flood) Tribunal, Tom Gilmartin testified that he had told journalist Frank Connolly that O'Brien's claim to have bribed Ahern had been 'a set-up'. In July 2007, with just two days remaining of the six-year deadline for the enforcement of the award, Ahern's solicitors instructed the Cork County Sheriff to initiate collection of the outstanding sum.

10 FOR WHOM THE BELL TOLLS:
JUDGE JOSEPH MANGAN v SUNDAY INDEPENDENT & ANOR [2002]

It was something that was bound to happen sooner or later. Communications technology had made great leaps forward during the late 1980s and early 1990s and mobile phones, once the size of a brick and equally cumbersome to carry, had become as small as a cigarette packet. Mobiles were now pervasive in everyday life, spawning a new form of communication with their Short Message Service (SMS) capability. The ubiquitous mobile phone is the primary method of communication for the majority of people. Third-generation phones are capable of sending photographic images, which posed a new problem. Certain buildings, including hospitals, gymnasiums, libraries and schools, prohibited their use on the grounds of safety or etiquette. It was really a matter of common sense.

Imagine, therefore, the consternation on the faces of the assembled lawyers, clerks, gardaí and members of the public attending Judge Joseph Mangan's sitting of the District Court at Tallow, Co. Waterford, on 13 March 1998, when a mobile phone rang out loudly shortly after commencement, disrupting the proceedings. A few hearts probably stopped and more than prayers were said as a flurry of hands dived into pockets to check phones. If one owned the offending jingle, one could expect, at best, a dressing-down from the judge; at worst, a contempt of court charge. It would not be a good way to end the working week.

There was widespread relief when the ringing phone was discovered to be the judge's mobile. A few nervous laughs went round the courtroom as the judge rose and, accompanied by the district clerk, left the court to take the call. He returned five minutes later and recommenced the sitting, without offering an explanation for his absence.

There the matter might have ended – as an anecdote told at dinner parties – had it not been for an incident in another District Court on the same day. A mobile phone rang as the daily listings were being read out during Judge Terence Finn's sitting of Dublin District Court in Court 46. The hapless owner on this occasion was court reporter John Kilraine of *The Irish Times*. He tried to leave the court as quickly as possible, but unfortunately the side door he had made for was locked. Judge Finn brushed aside his explanation that he was a reporter on duty and ordered that Kilraine be held in the adjoining Bridewell garda station until he had decided what to do with him.

The Irish Times was alerted and immediately sent a solicitor to the court, but Kilraine spent over two hours in custody before he was permitted to return to the court to make an apology. The judge told Kilraine that, as an experienced court reporter, he should have been aware of court procedure. After the judge's reprimand, Kilraine was allowed to leave the court.

The General Secretary of the National Union of Journalists, Eoin Ronayne, later commented on the incident. He described it as a human error, which happened from time to time. He added: 'The judge's ruling was heavy-handed. No disrespect was intended to the court.'

So, on the same day, two very different mobile phone stories. Gene Kerrigan, a columnist for the *Sunday Independent* and author of the best-selling *Hard Cases*, a collection of stories from the courts, wrote an article about the coincidence of the two stories. His article was published on the front page of the *Sunday Independent* nine days later, under the headline: 'The Case of the Judge and the Clearly Visible Belly-Button'. It was intended as a humorous piece on three District Court judges, something to amuse the readers as they tucked into their leisurely Sunday breakfasts.

The article read:

The 'genitalia' judge [Paul McDonnell, who had imprisoned a woman because her genitalia could allegedly be seen] and the two mobile phone freaks [Terence Finn and Joe Mangan] may well have brought the courts into disrepute, but it's not entirely their fault … As for Judge Finn throwing a journalist into a cell because the poor hack's mobile phone rang and Judge Mangan, on the same day in a different court, leaving his mobile phone switched on so that he could take a call in mid-case; it is obvious that a little consistency is called for.

We suggest that mobile phones be banned from courts.

Judges were not the only target. Kerrigan continued:

Given the kind of dodgy characters you get in courtrooms, allowing the use of mobile phones could soon result in drug deals being arranged by mobile phones, right there in front of the judge. It is far preferable that barristers make their cocaine purchases in the usual places (a lane off Leeson Street and a car park not unadjacent to the Law Library).

Whether Judge Mangan choked on his breakfast as he read the article is not known. What is certain is that thirty-one months later, Mangan and Kerrigan faced each other across a courtroom when the libel action brought by the judge against the journalist started in the High Court on 8 November 2002.

Garrett Cooney SC was representing the plaintiff Mangan; Kevin Feeney SC was presenting for the defence; Mr Justice Barr was the presiding judge. Mangan's instructing solicitors were Ivor Fitzpatrick & Co., Dublin. The case had attracted a good attendance and several newspaper hacks were observed repeatedly checking that their mobiles were indeed switched off. The consensus from the benches at the rear of the court was that if

Mangan won, he would be guilty of lacking a sense of humour – a deficit of which few people would wish to be accused.

Mangan took the witness stand. He gave evidence that he felt the article insinuated that he was some sort of weirdo, some kind of eccentric. He had felt greatly embarrassed, upset, demeaned and denigrated by the article. It had angered him in its assertion that he had brought the court into disrepute. In his understanding of it, its accusation was that he was not fit to hold office.

The *Sunday Independent* and Kerrigan would defend the libel action on the grounds that the article was fair comment and justification on a matter of public interest, namely the discharge of their functions by members of the judiciary and their court conduct. They would deny that Mangan's character had been damaged or that he had suffered any distress or embarrassment, as alleged.

The exact circumstances that had led to Mangan having his mobile with him on the bench that particular day were outlined for the court. It transpired that the South Eastern Health Board was about to request a special sitting in front of the judge during which, he suspected, he might be asked to grant an emergency order. Mangan had telephoned the Clonmel District Court, but had been unable to speak to the person who had contacted him. He left a message for his call to be returned. The Tallow court accommodation was 'frugal', with no secretarial facilities, so the judge had taken his mobile phone with him into the courtroom. The Department of Justice had issued him the phone for contingencies like this. When the call came through, he had adjourned the court for a few minutes. As a result of the call a special court sitting had been arranged for later that day in Cahir, at which the judge had presided.

Mangan was asked what his views were on mobile phones in his courtroom. He replied that, in general, he was against them because their ringing would interrupt court proceedings. However, Mangan heavily criticized Kerrigan for making little effort to clarify the exact circumstances behind what was a highly unusual incident in a courtroom.

Kevin Feeney, counsel for the defence, asked Mangan if he knew of other occasions when a phone had rung on the judge's bench. He replied that the instance in question might represent the only occasion. Counsel pointed out that when the judge had left the court in these bizarre circumstances, no citizen could have been expected to know what exactly was occurring. The plaintiff did not concur. He claimed that by asking the court clerk to attend him, he had thereby made it evident that his withdrawal was on court business. He repeated that Kerrigan had not ascertained the purpose of his withdrawal from the court.

Mangan was then asked if it was usual for journalists to contact him regarding an incident that had happened in court. No, he replied, it would be more usual for them to speak to the court office, although he did have a vague recollection of a journalist ringing his wife on one occasion.

Under further cross-examination, Mangan confirmed that he had not complained to the paper for some seventeen months after the publication of the offending article. He disagreed that, after such an interval, the general public would have little or no memory of what had been written. As a result, he felt that the offer of an apology on page three of the newspaper was entirely inadequate. The article had appeared on the front page, so he felt the apology should also be printed there.

Before the court adjourned for the day it heard from Judge Peter Smithwick, President of the District Court, who said he believed that Mangan had acted correctly by taking the phone into court, and that it was quite proper in such a rare and unique instance. Later in his testimony, Judge Smithwick added that he had carried out no inquiry in relation to the newspaper's article.

There was an unexpected sensation for the assembled spectators on the morning of the second day. Feeney made his opening statement for the defence with a statement on law. He went on to say that controversy over mobile phone incidents had been in open arena for some time. It was against this background that Kerrigan had penned his article and that certain facts commented on had been shown to be true. After Feeney had concluded his opening, counsel for Mangan rose and requested the judge to hear a submission.

Mr Justice Barr had the jury removed before hearing legal arguments from both sides. Cooney requested that the jury be discharged over the statement on law made in his opening by counsel for Independent Newspapers. The point was made that the statement was incomplete. After the submissions had been concluded and he had taken a brief adjournment to deliberate, Barr called for the jury to be returned to the courtroom. He informed the members of the jury that he was discharging them and ordering a retrial. Costs were allowed to Mangan, but the defence was granted a stay pending an appeal.

Eight months later, the five-judge Supreme Court unanimously ruled that Mr Justice Barr had erred in stopping the libel hearing. The Chief Justice, Mr Justice Keane, said that he was satisfied that the action taken by the High Court judge was a disproportionate response. He went on to say that a more suitable response would have been for Mr Justice Barr to remind the members of the jury that they had heard a statement of law advanced by defence counsel, which counsel for the plaintiff contended was incomplete and partial and that they should bear that criticism in mind hearing the evidence.

The Supreme Court blackened the day further for Mangan by awarding costs, estimated to be close to £20,000, to Independent Newspapers, although it did order that the costs of the abortive High Court hearing should await the outcome of any new trial.

The new hearing commenced on 12 February 2002, with Miss Justice Mella Carroll presiding. It would last a week and would reach a conclusion on this occasion.

Mangan, who had been appointed Clare District Court judge the preceding year, gave evidence similar to that given during the aborted hearing. He said that the article's description of him as a 'mobile phone freak' was a scurrilous slur. The most damaging allegation, though, was that he had brought the courts into disrepute. He felt he had been accused unfairly of acting in a dishonourable way and of misconduct. The Tallow phone incident had been covered by the *Irish Examiner* and the *Irish Daily Star* newspapers, Mangan said, but they had not driven a stake through his heart. Once again his counsel, Garrett Cooney, questioned him, while Kevin Feeney, as before, represented the defence.

Feeney asked Mangan to explain the inordinate delay of seventeen months that elapsed before he complained to the newspaper, which seemed odd if he genuinely felt his reputation had been impugned. Mangan said that he was conscious that pursuing the matter meant taking on one of the wealthiest and most powerful newspaper groups in Europe – not something to take lightly. He stood to lose everything. 'I'm fighting for my life here,' Mangan emphasised.

Mangan was asked if he could recall disciplining a person whose phone had rung out about a year earlier in Wexford District Court. The judge said he remembered the incident on what had been a difficult day, when he had wanted to preserve control of the court. Feeney went on to ask if Mangan had asked that person whether the call had been an important one. The judge admitted that he had not; he had presumed that the person would have informed him if that had been the case.

Judge Patrick McCartan, a Circuit Court judge, said that he felt his colleague had been grievously wronged by the manner in which he had been presented in the article. Initially he had been astonished when he had read the article and had exclaimed of his colleague, 'What an idiot!' It was not until several months later, when he met the plaintiff at a conference and learned the true purpose of the judge having the phone in the court, that his opinion had changed. McCartan clearly remembered apologising to Mangan for his false presumption.

Gene Kerrigan was confident that he did not get anything wrong in his article. He claimed that the article was intended to be a semi-mocking, lighthearted, patronising piece on what he saw as a throwback to an era of pompousness and self-importance – aspects of the court system that had diminished over the years.

Kerrigan admitted that he had not been in attendance at any of the three courts during the incidents to which his article referred.

He explained that two people had been locked up for several hours by two judges, and he felt that if the persons who made the rules were not themselves subject to the rules, then those rules could not have a very high credibility. It was seventeen months after the article had been published that Kerrigan had received a letter from Mangan's solicitors.

When cross-examined, Kerrigan claimed that the purpose behind Mangan taking a call in court was not relevant. It was suggested that Kerrigan had deliberately suppressed that purpose to make a case against Mangan. Kerrigan strenuously denied this, adding that Mangan was suing him for not explaining what he had done in court, even though Mangan himself had not done so. Kerrigan was asking the jury to decide if the litigation was another example of double standards. Finally, Kerrigan disagreed with counsel's contention that what he had written was a dreadful and personal attack on Mangan.

The jury heard closing addresses from both sides. The newspaper's defence counsel asked the jury members to reflect on the background to Kerrigan's article. In the first case, a judge had imprisoned a woman because her genitalia could be seen; in the second, a journalist had been held in custody simply because his mobile phone had gone off. The jury was requested to consider what had been in Kerrigan's mind when he had penned the article. He had seen glaring inconsistencies in the manner in which the courts treated mobile phones and thought the best way to illustrate this was humorously.

Mangan's counsel told the jury that a very unremarkable series of events had been employed to hold his client up to the scorn and derision of more than half the adult population of the country. This had been done because a journalist had borne a grudge against a judicial system that had allowed a fellow journalist to be imprisoned. His client had, at all times, discharged his duties properly, with the unique feature that he had taken a call to deal with a pressing legal matter.

When the court reconvened after a weekend adjournment, Judge Carroll addressed the jury of six men and six women before it retired to consider its verdict. She told them that she had ruled out the defences of fair comment and justification and that it was up to the jury to decide if the words in their ordinary meaning, or in innuendo, were defamatory, as Mangan alleged. Five possible meanings were set out on the issue paper: that the article suggested that Mangan had acted in a manner inconsistent with the proper discharge of his judicial functions; that he had brought the court into disrepute; that he was not a fit person to hold judicial office; that he was a 'mobile phone freak' who was given to engaging in inconsistent behaviour; that he had engaged in ludicrous behaviour.

If the jury found one or more to be defamatory, then it was to award suitable damages. Judge Carroll added that there were no rules in relation to the use of phones in court and that it was for each judge to keep order therein. She had one final piece of advice for the jury: 'Be fair to everybody and do justice to the parties.'

After deliberating for two hours, the jury found that the article had indeed borne the defamatory insinuation that Mangan had behaved in a manner inconsistent with the proper discharge of his judicial functions. It did not find the article defamatory with regard to the four other implications.

The jury awarded Mangan €25,000 in damages. This was a considerable disappointment for the plaintiff's side, which would have wished for a higher sum. The threshold of damages for the High Court at that time was £30,000, so it seemed probable that Mangan would have been awarded costs equal to those that would have been awarded had the case been brought in the Circuit Court. Costs for both sides, for the three hearings, were estimated at €750,000. The thorny question of who was going to foot the bill was adjourned for one week.

After the verdict was announced, Mangan issued a statement saying that he and his family welcomed the findings of the jury, which had vindicated his reputation. He was pleased that the court had rejected the defences of fair comment and justification on the basis of deliberate omission.

A week later, Miss Justice Carroll gave her decision on costs. Mangan was granted costs on the Circuit Court scale: €100,000. It was thought that his legal team would absorb the difference between that and the normal High Court fees. Equally, the defence team may not have sought the full fees from Independent Newspapers because they acted regularly for the company.

Counsel for the newspaper made an application for a stay on the order of costs and award pending an appeal. A condition was imposed: should the appeal prove unsuccessful, interest would be paid from the date of the award.

Michael Roche, managing editor of Independent Newspapers, confirmed that the decision on costs would be appealed to the Supreme Court. He reminded journalists that this was the second recent case where plaintiffs had been awarded damages more appropriate to the Circuit Court. Once again, it begs the question: if a plaintiff is primarily interested in clearing his/her name and reputation, then would a Circuit Court action not suffice? When the costs of running a case in High Court, and a possible Supreme Court appeal, are taken into account, the risk a plaintiff runs is enormous.

On 31 January 2003, the Supreme Court denied the Independent Newspapers' appeal on costs, allowing Justice Carroll's decision to stand.

11 | FEAR AND LOATHING IN WEST CORK:
IAN BAILEY v THE IRISH SUN & ORS [2003]

The brutal murder of French film-maker and socialite Sophie Toscan du Plantier, near her isolated holiday cottage at Toormore on Mizen Head, Co. Cork, stunned the nation. She had been murdered three days before Christmas 1996 and as news of the discovery of her battered body spread like wildfire through West Cork, the initial reaction was one of disbelief. The local residents were deeply shocked; they thought their tranquil corner of south-west Ireland was a safe haven, far from the mean streets of Limerick and Dublin. How could anyone commit such a heinous crime on their doorstep?

West Cork is an area that has welcomed thousands of foreigners. Ex-pats from a wide range of nationalities live cheek-by-jowl with locals, usually in perfect harmony. Many of the early newcomers had a New World, bohemian spirit about them, often seeking a tolerance for their chosen lifestyle that they had not been able to find in their own countries. Some had chosen to settle in the area permanently, while others, like the murdered woman, kept a holiday home for short breaks away from their busy careers.

Diminutive Sophie Toscan du Plantier was a documentary film-maker and the wife of renowned film producer Daniel du Plantier. She had first come to Ireland as an exchange student in the late 1970s and was respected and liked by the many local friends she had made. Her husband was head of the French Academy of Cinema Art; Sophie was his third wife.

The Garda Síochána launched a major murder investigation, led by Superintendent Seán Camon, and within days a prime suspect for the killing had been identified. Ian Bailey, an Englishman, had been living with his partner, Jules Thomas, and her three daughters in Liscaha, Schull for a number of years. The Manchester-born Bailey was undoubtedly a handsome, hedonistic and slightly eccentric man. He wrote poetry and was trying to master the bodhrán, and was a relatively familiar figure in the area. His work as a freelance journalist did not bring in much of an income, so he would take odd gardening jobs here and there to supplement his earnings.

Residents of West Cork heaved a sigh of relief when, seven weeks after the killing, the gardaí arrested Bailey for questioning in connection with the inquiry. They had prayed for a quick breakthrough in the case so they could go on with their lives without fear that a killer was still in their midst. Their relief was short-lived, however. After twelve hours, Bailey was released without charge. Rumours and stories soon began to circulate: Bailey had been seen near the scene of the crime around the time of the victim's death; he had scratches on his face; he had been seen tending a bonfire a few days after the murder; he was known as a violent man.

Bailey was arrested a second time, but again he was released without charge. The stories that had begun as whispers were now being printed openly in the press. This public scrutiny of the prime suspect was widespread, and opinions differed. It was not unheard of for a crime to be committed by a journalist so he could make a scoop. Nor was it unknown for suspicion to fall wrongly on a journalist because he seemed to know too much, or had become too involved with the crime. Either way, it soon became apparent that the garda detectives were not seriously looking for anyone else in connection with the murder, but were concentrating most of their efforts on finding enough evidence to charge Bailey.

Months passed, then years, and still no one was charged and no new leads or suspects emerged. There was a growing realisation that the gardaí may have made some fundamental blunders in the investigation. The main obstacle stalling the murder inquiry was an inability to determine an accurate timeline of events, suspects and witnesses. The crime scene had not been preserved adequately, thus vital forensic evidence had been tainted. Gardaí had unwittingly permitted Bailey, in his role as stringer for the *Cork Examiner*, to visit the scene, therefore any physical evidence on his shoes or clothing linking him to the crime was worthless.

The timing of the murder also created problems. The investigation team had taken too long to reach full strength because of the Christmas break. Twenty-four hours had elapsed before state pathologist John Harbinson arrived to examine the body. His findings made for grim evidence at the inquest. Sophie Toscan du Plantier had been bludgeoned to death with a blunt instrument. Harbinson concluded that she had been struck up to a dozen times, though it was probable that it was the second blow, which fractured her skull and lacerated her brain, that caused her death in the early hours of 23 December. His conclusion relied on a forensic recreation of the layering of blows. The blood trails showed that she had been dragged some distance along the laneway in front of her dormer cottage. Her face had been so badly beaten, her features were almost unrecognisable.

Daniel du Plantier visited Ireland on a number of occasions to discuss the progress of the investigation with the gardaí. Initial optimism that the killer would be found gradually turned to frustration when no charges were brought. A simple stone cross was erected at the site of the victim's death. (Du Plantier later remarried and his new wife, a former personal assistant, bore him a child. In February 2003, France's leading film-maker died from a heart attack.)

Sophie's parents, George and Marguerite Bouniol, were determined to secure justice for the daughter they had lost. They eventually announced that they intended to bring a civil case against Bailey, as a form of closure. The Garda Síochána informed the Bouniols that, following two investigations and three reviews of the book of evidence, the State had no plans to bring a prosecution. Their action – under section 48 of the Civil Liability Act – would not be a civil prosecution, but rather a claim for compensation for the death of their daughter and for the distress and suffering inflicted upon them. It would be a difficult case to bring because it would be the first case of its kind in Ireland; they did not have full access to garda files; many locals who had spoken off-the-record to the newspapers were unwilling to come forward as witnesses; and members of the gardaí might not be allowed to give evidence because it might prejudice a future murder trial.

Then, the incredible happened. Ian Bailey announced that he was bringing a defamation case against eight newspapers. He would, to all intents and purposes, be putting himself on trial. Bailey's history of violence towards women and his often irrational behaviour made the odds for a win very long. Supposition was rife as to his motive for bringing the case. The main school of thought was that he must be deranged; a less vocal minority thought he may have been an innocent man pilloried falsely. At the very least, all sides agreed, the hearing would bring matters into the open and separate fact from fiction. The newspapers' defence team subpoenaed witnesses and a court order was obtained so that gardaí would have to give evidence. Amidst all the preparations for what would surely be a sensational trial, no one could have foreseen what lay ahead.

The hearing opened on 9 December 2003 in Court 1 of Cork Circuit Court, with Judge Patrick Moran presiding. Bailey had arrived earlier, clean-shaven and dressed in a double-breasted grey suit; he looked like a British Army officer in mufti. The hearing was to be heard in what had once been a garden supplies warehouse, now temporary home to Cork Circuit Court. Ian Bailey was taking seven actions against eight defendants: *Sunday Independent, The Times, The Sunday Times, Irish Daily Star, The Irish Sun, Irish Daily Mirror, Daily Telegraph* and *Independent on Sunday.* Paul Gallagher SC and David Holland SC would act for the joint defence; Jim Duggan BL and solicitor Con Murphy would act for the plaintiff.

The case attracted a large press corps, with some twenty-three reporters, eight photographers and two film crews in attendance on the opening day. The normal six-person bench reserved for the press was clearly inadequate, so eleven journalists took up seats in the empty jury box. Mr and Mrs Bouniol had declined to attend the hearing.

The first morning of the sitting was dominated by a final application from the State for twelve gardaí to be excluded from giving evidence. It was argued that garda evidence being placed in the public domain at this time might weaken the chances of a successful prosecution being brought in the murder case at some future time. Judge Moran took submissions from the State and from the opposing parties before ruling that the gardaí would have to give evidence.

Later that day, the case proper got underway, with both sides outlining their arguments. The newspaper reports – described contemptuously by Bailey's counsel as pure lies and figments of the imagination – had contained allegations that Bailey was near the scene of the murder at the time; he was responsible in some way for du Plantier's death; he had a history of violence; he was hated by West Cork locals; he may have destroyed evidence. His counsel told the court that Bailey was living a nightmare, had been demonised and was frequently called 'the murderer' in West Cork.

The newspapers would deny that any defamation had taken place. It was their contention that what they published was justified, had qualified privilege and that there was an element of contributory negligence on Bailey's part in his agreement to grant interviews as a prime suspect. They would seek to prove that Bailey was a very violent man and had courted adverse comment by the manner in which he covered the crime, that he was, in other words, the author of his own misfortune. If Bailey were to win all seven actions included in his case, the newspapers could potentially face a maximum damage award of €38,000 each: a total of €266,000.

Bailey's journalistic involvement subsequent to the murder of Sophie du Plantier began when Eddie Cassidy – *Cork Examiner*'s West Cork correspondent – contacted him around midday on 23

December 1996. Cassidy had told him that there had been reports of a murder close to where he lived and asked him if would cover the story. It was thought the dead woman was French. Cassidy always insisted that he had not known at that time that the death was a murder, and would never have described it as such without official confirmation. Bailey had taken the call from Cassidy just after he had killed and cleaned a number of turkeys, during which he had sustained some scratches to his face. He had also trimmed a fir tree to decorate his home and bore additional scratches from that activity.

After speaking to Cassidy, Bailey drove to the murder scene, accompanied by Jules Thomas, his partner of thirteen years, and gathered as much information as he could. He spoke to a few gardaí and interviewed a couple of the local residents to garner further details about the victim. Bailey later passed the information on to the *Cork Examiner*. He also wrote follow-up stories that were published in the *Irish Daily Star* and in a number of French periodicals.

Bailey stated that he had never been introduced to the Frenchwoman, but had seen her around. He thought her quite plain. He denied that her death had in any way helped further his career as a journalist. He also rubbished a claim that after he had cashed the £25 cheque paid to him by the *Cork Examiner* in a local shop, he had remarked: 'There's no money in knocking people off. That's all her death is worth to me.' Reports of him having a premonition of her death were wrong, he said, although he did experience 'a feeling' when he stopped his car on a mountain road near to where du Plantier was killed.

Bailey seemed hell-bent on drawing attention to himself. Time and time again he did or said something that jarred with the people of West Cork. Some off-colour remarks could be put down to his twisted sense of humour, but his other actions were less easy to excuse. When covering the story, he had filed reports of du Plantier's sexual promiscuity. The gardaí would later reject these reports as baseless.

It was said that mid-morning on 23 December 1996, he had told three people that a murder or some other big story had happened – this would have been just a short time after the body had been found and before the awful truth of du Plantier's death had become common knowledge. Bailey insisted that he had not done so, that the three people must have been mistaken about the timing. He repeated that the first he had known of the murder was when Cassidy had telephoned him at midday.

A Goleen fruit and vegetable stall-holder, James Camier, recalled how Jules Thomas had spoken to him at 10.30 a.m. on 23 December and told him of the murder. She also made several references to the terrible state the body had been in, as though she had seen it from close up. Thomas disputed this, saying she had gone to Goleen on Christmas Eve, not the day before. Camier was certain that it was 23 December.

Bailey had provoked further suspicion when he lit a bonfire on St Stephen's Day. Louise Kennedy and Brian Jackson saw Bailey tending the fire at his house. Jackson, a neighbour, said he found Bailey to be a strange man. He had been told that Bailey's hobby was the destruction of religious artefacts and that he had a reputation for walking alone at night with his, in Bailey's words, 'thinking stick', and that he would occasionally howl at the moon.

Bailey could not account for what they had seen: 'That is a complete mystery to me. There was no fire. I am one hundred per cent certain it was not started by me and not started by Jules.' He recalled a fire in that spot some time in November when he and Jules had been clearing old papers from the house.

Another local resident claimed that he overheard a telephone conversation between Bailey and Thomas. He said that Bailey had stopped his car on Hunt's Hill on 22 December to tell Jules Thomas that he intended to call at an address close to the du Plantier house.

The gardaí had become interested in Bailey a fortnight after the murder. He was questioned informally on a number of occasions, then arrested for the first time on 10 February 1997. He was driven to Bandon garda station and was astonished to see that a party of some twenty to thirty journalists were awaiting his arrival. At least one television crew was also present.

Bailey's name and photograph appeared in print the following day in an article published in *The Irish Sun*. He was described as a 'suspect'. From that day forward, newspapers and reporters maintained a great interest in Ian Bailey and carried photos and articles about him, mostly of an accusatory nature. Bailey insisted that his motivation in bringing the case was not financial gain; it was to convince the public that he was innocent of the horrific crime.

In court, Bailey had earlier given his name, address and oath in a steady, unruffled manner that gave no hint of what was to come. His testimony was to be a series of accusations and shocking revelations. The first target on which he vented his spleen was the Garda Síochána.

Bailey described how the arresting gardaí had at first been courteous to him outside his home in Schull. He was handcuffed and placed in the rear of a garda vehicle. But 'shortly after we were on the road, the atmosphere towards me changed to what I can only describe as one of great hostility. I was bombarded with verbal claims and allegations.' He went on to allege that minutes after he had been arrested in connection with the murder, gardaí warned him that if he did not co-operate, he would be found with 'a bullet in the back of the head'.

A garda told him that even if they could not pin the murder on him, he was finished in Ireland. He was told that everyone, even his partner, accepted that he was the killer of Sophie Toscan du Plantier and he should confess to clear his conscience.

Bailey felt that the gardaí had made little effort to conceal his identity when they helped him from the squad car at Bandon garda station. He felt the station gates had deliberately been left open so that the press corps could follow him into the yard. Inside the station, he was asked to undress and provide hair and blood samples and his fingerprints were taken. He co-operated fully at all times, and no fingerprint or DNA match linking him to the crime scene was ever found. During an intense interview, the gardaí warned him that there was a 'hanging mob' waiting for him outside.

After his second arrest, on 21 January 1998, Bailey admitted he had felt he was in a 'fight or flight' dilemma. He decided that he would have to stay in West Cork and prove his innocence: 'Wherever one went in the world, it was never going to disappear. There was no question of running away from this.'

Bailey outlined how some of the articles had come to be written. Paddy Clancy of *The Irish Sun* and Senan Molony of the *Irish Daily Star* had asked him to give interviews so he could put his side of the story. He agreed, going so far as to pose for photographs to accompany the articles. He was outraged when both papers subsequently published defamatory allegations about him and accused him of domestic violence against his ex-wife, Sara Limbrick. It had been a stormy and acrimonious marriage, he conceded, but he had never struck her. However, former Skibbereen neighbour Peter Bielecki contradicted this by saying that Bailey had once confided to him that he had once blacked out and that when he came to, he had his hands around Sara's throat and was attempting to strangle her.

'Absolutely not. It never happened,' Bailey insisted. He eventually divorced Sara Limbrick when they moved to a new house and he discovered that his name was not on the deeds.

There was no hiding the fact that Bailey had a fiery temper as far as women were concerned. His current relationship had lasted for thirteen years and had been stormy at times. There had been occasions when he had physically fought with Jules Thomas, and he accepted that he had been at fault. The worst of these incidents occurred on 1 May 1996, when Thomas had had to receive medical attention after an altercation. She received eight stitches to a mouth wound, and bite marks to her hands and scratches to her face were also treated. Two clumps of her hair had been pulled out. She had been found at her home by Peter Bielecki, curled up at the foot of her bed, screaming like an animal in pain. Bielecki drove her to hospital and stayed in the house for three weeks in case Bailey tried to return. He slept on a sofa on the ground floor and kept a hammer under his pillow.

Bailey insisted that Thomas had started the argument but, although he was intoxicated at the time, he agreed that that could be no excuse and that it was an appalling attack. He denied that the row had erupted when he had attempted to assault Thomas's eighteen-year-old daughter, Virginia. A barring order had been placed on Bailey after the 1996 incident.

There were two other occasions when violence had occurred and, in the wake of an assault in August 2001, a District Court prosecution had been brought. The gardaí had arrested Bailey on that occasion at Cork Airport, as he was about to board a flight to England. Bailey insisted that his intention had not been to flee, but simply to allow Thomas and her family some breathing space. His appearance in court on that charge had handed the press a golden opportunity to further demonise him.

Saffron Thomas, a daughter of Bailey's partner, recalled how Bailey and her mother had wept every day for two years after he was named as a prime suspect in the du Plantier case. The media coverage had affected her family deeply: 'It was disgusting. I was sick to my stomach. I just couldn't believe it. It was just that my family was implicated in the matter. It's like a big, heavy weight on us all. It's like a dark cloud that just never goes away.'

Saffron Thomas claimed to have known little of the domestic violence to which Bailey had subjected her mother. She had heard nothing about allegations that one of the most traumatic rows had started after he had tried to assault her younger sister.

Beryl Ann Thomas, Jules Thomas's mother, described the newspaper coverage of the murder investigation as a ghastly and crushing ordeal for the family. Her daughter had been the victim of physical abuse in a previous relationship.

Jules Thomas, a fifty-four-year-old Welsh-born artist, was extremely critical of the way in which the media had blown out of proportion the domestic violence she had suffered. In thirteen years with Bailey, there had been only three violent incidents: 'The devil drink was the cause of it. It's like a temper flash. It's not something that goes on. It's always like two minutes and that's it.'

The first incident, Thomas said, had occurred in 1993 and was more of a tussle than a violent fight. It had taken place while they were visiting friends in Cork. Thomas tried to gloss over her treatment at a hospital: she had gone there simply to be checked out and to reassure herself that any injuries were superficial. Bailey had been remorseful in the aftermath of the attack.

In the 1996 attack, Thomas did suffer some injuries that required hospital treatment. The attack happened as she was driving herself and Bailey home after a friend's birthday party. 'What happened was that we were in the car,' Thomas said. 'I was a bit wobbly. Ian took over the driving. Ian then started swerving a bit and I got angry with him when he did not stop the car.' She had grabbed Bailey and he had grabbed her back, his finger catching in her mouth and tearing the flesh at the gum. It was this injury that had required stitches. It had been a regrettable incident, but one she felt sure would not be repeated now that Bailey was abstaining from alcohol.

Thomas described the seven years since the first press allegation as a living hell. The pain and suffering from the press mauling had been a million times worse than any beatings she had endured. Thomas believed that the press was sabotaging their lives. She no longer had a regular sleep pattern and suffered frequent nightmares. Her painting had deteriorated and friends and neighbours would shy away from her and Bailey: 'Some people actually cross the road so as not to make contact with us.'

Thomas went on to describe how, when the gardaí had arrested her for questioning, she had had to ask for a coat to shield her head. But when released twelve hours later, she was left to run a gauntlet of reporters alone. They laid siege to the house in Schull she shared with Bailey and disrupted her family life. She insisted that subsequent newspaper articles were sensationalised and inaccurate.

Skibbereen newsagent Brendan Houlihan and Schull businessman Thomas Brosnan provided character references for Bailey. They had both noticed a dramatic change in the plaintiff in the wake of the media reports naming him as a prime suspect. Bailey had been branded a murderer and whenever he walked into Houlihan's shop there would be a knowing reaction, a 'hush-hush' from customers. The men's evidence highlighted how many people of West Cork – despite Judge Moran's strict admonitions to the contrary – had taken to calling the defamation hearing 'the murder trial'.

The press article that had caused Bailey the most distress was written by Brighid McLaughlin of the *Sunday Independent*. She had contacted him with regard to writing a piece. He had been hesistant at first, but she had promised that it would have a sympathetic slant. They took a drive together and talked at length, McLaughlin asking him at one point if it was possible to get hold of some hashish locally. They left on good terms and McLaughlin gave him her mobile telephone number for contact on future stories. When the article was published, however, under the heading 'Investigating with the Prime Suspect', she had accused him of taking her on a terrifying journey and of trying to intimidate her. She claimed he had told her that he had burned clothes because they were stained with turkey blood and that he had been seen washing his wellington boots in a stream near the murder site.

Bailey also believed that his professionalism had been defamed by a claim made in the *Daily Telegraph* that he was a rejected scriptwriter. Just a year before, he had completed a script for a West Cork community film project whose patron was Sir David Puttnam, who has a home in the area.

Incredibly, Bailey had admitted to a number of people that he had killed Sophie du Plantier, but now insisted that he had done so in jest. The first occasion was when the news editor of the *Sunday Tribune*, Helen Callanan, had told Bailey that suggestions were being made that he was the murderer. He had responded: 'Yes, that's right.'

Bailey claimed that his 'admission' was a piece of banter. He had heard that some journalist was saying that he was the killer, but it was nothing he took seriously. The incident with Callanan was the cause for him later telling a local woman, Yvonne Ungerer, that he had done it and had used a concrete block as the murder weapon. He was, he said, simply reiterating the accusation Callanan had passed on. He had not been serious and he did not think Ungerer had thought he was being serious.

A New Year's Eve party in Bailey's home in 1998/99 was the scene of the next 'confession'. Bailey showed his guests a scrapbook he had kept of information relating to the du Plantier killing. Two guests, Ritchie and Rosie Shelly, found the production of the scrapbook to be in poor taste. In court, husband and wife related their memories of the party. Bailey had followed them into the kitchen and seemed very upset. He cried as he put his arms around Ritchie Shelly and said, 'I did it, I did it.'

'You did what?' Shelly had said.

'I went too far.'

Shelly assumed that Bailey was talking about the murdered woman, as that was the only topic they had discussed all that evening. Bailey seemed obsessed by it, he recalled, and had collected almost every article published on the subject.

The next day, Shelly met Bailey in a pub and became even more convinced that he was the murderer. Bailey insisted that all he had been doing was repeating a 'mantra' that the gardaí had put to him repeatedly. The couple, he said, had picked up on something they had heard out of context. Jules Thomas also said that the couple had got the wrong end of the stick and had misunderstood Bailey's comment.

The next person to be subjected to one of a plethora of admissions from Bailey was fourteen-year-old schoolboy, Malachy Reed. He accepted a lift in Bailey's car. Bailey had been drinking and seemed upset, and Reed heard him admit to the murder. Bailey confided in the young boy that he had smashed the victim's head with a rock. Afterwards, Reed had been so terrified that his parents had to fit deadbolts on every door of their house.

Reed admitted that he had asked for the lift and had been known to Bailey through his friendship with Funella Thomas, youngest daughter of Bailey's partner, Jules. Reed did not like Bailey and would avoid him as best he could. When asked why he had accepted lifts from Bailey on a further two occasions if he had been so terrified, Reed replied, 'Because I didn't have the opportunity to jump over the ditch.'

Reed insisted that his story was the truth and that he had no reason to lie. His mother corroborated her son's evidence. She confirmed that her son had been in an agitated state after getting out of Bailey's car. Her son, she said, was not a liar.

Bailey agreed that he had given the youth a lift, but that in speaking about the du Plantier murder he was merely repeating rumours that were in circulation about him and that there had been no reference to a rock being the murder weapon.

Bill Fuller, a gardener and former work colleague of Bailey's, told of seeing Jules Thomas near the murder site at approximately 11.00 a.m. on 23 December. He also gave evidence of how Bailey, speaking rhetorically in the second person, had said, 'Yes, you did it, didn't you? You saw her [Sophie] in Spar and she turned you on, walking up the aisle with her tight arse. You went there [Toormore] to see what you could get, but she wasn't interested. You chased her and then something stirred in the back of your head and you went a lot further than you intended to.'

Fuller had said to Bailey, 'Sounds like something you would say.' Bailey had replied, 'Funny you should say that. That is how I met Jules. I saw her tight arse. But she let me in.'

Fuller strongly rejected a suggestion that he had made up the incident to incriminate Bailey in the murder. Bailey denied having addressed himself in the manner quoted. He pointed out that repetitions of allegations did not constitute an admission of murder.

It is understandable how a weak man, lacking purpose and seeking celebrity, could be drawn like a moth into the spotlight of a high-profile murder investigation. The glut of reality shows on television demonstrate all too vividly what ignominy people will expose themselves to in order to have their fifteen minutes of fame. Bailey certainly enjoyed, in the early days at least, being the centre of attention, going as far as courting publicity over his arrests. He gave a television interview to RTÉ News immediately after his release from the initial arrest. Pat Kenny also talked to him at length on his radio show. During the Kenny interview, Bailey had said that it was quite reasonable for the gardaí to suspect him because he had scratches on his hands. This interview had been broadcast before all but one of the allegedly defamatory articles had appeared in the newspapers.

Bailey admitted in court that, in hindsight, he had not handled the matter very well: 'But the pressure was incredible. What was one supposed to do? We were under siege. And knowing that these people [the media] were there to get information, the best way to get rid of them was to give them some information.'

Bailey's use of drugs was also called into question during the trial. He had once opened his door to Fuller in a black kilt, smoking hash and drinking cider. There was a suggestion that he was a regular drug-user, a claim Bailey has consistently denied. An extract from Bailey's personal diary read out in court seemed to contradict this, however. The entry, made in 1993, read: 'I am totally obsessed by sex – I love drugs and I adore my drink.' Bailey said the note was a poetic allusion to lyrics written by Ian Dury, an English rock singer. He insisted that he had been clean and sober for some time.

During the course of the libel trial, Bailey made an official complaint of intimidation against Fuller. It would be the first of several such complaints. He told the gardaí dealing with his complaint that Bill Fuller had approached him and said, 'I have got you now.'

The following day, Bailey also made a complaint against Peter Bielecki. Both Bielecki and Fuller were ordered to leave the courtroom and not to return until called to give their evidence. The judge noted that his directions should not reflect on the good name of both witnesses.

Bailey then launched a fresh tirade against the investigating gardaí. He accused them of conspiring to pervert the course of justice, of trying to 'stitch him up', of hounding him and even claiming that they had gone so far as to say that he had acted like a werewolf monster because the moon was almost full on the night of the murder. He further claimed that one woman, local shopkeeper Marie Farrell, had been put under duress to implicate him. She had told him about this in a Schull pub, explaining that she did not want to see an innocent person accused.

Judge Moran stemmed the flood of accusations by telling Bailey that this was a defamation hearing and that if he had a complaint to make against the Garda Síochána, he should do so via the proper channels.

Unquestionably one of the most crucial testimonies was Farrell's memory of her meeting with Bailey, but her version was very different from his. She complained that Bailey had been trying to intimidate her to withdraw her statement, in which she had said that she had seen Bailey near Cealfada bridge, on the Schull–Goleen road, in the early hours of 23 December. She and a former boyfriend had been driving around and the sighting, she recalled, would have been at about 3.00 a.m. Farrell also said that a few days before du Plantier's murder, she had seen Bailey watching the Frenchwoman as she left her shop. She had made a statement to the gardaí mentioning both sightings of the plaintiff. It was shortly after this, she said, that things had taken a nasty turn. Jules Thomas had informed Farrell that Bailey wished to talk to her. Later, Thomas invited her to her house so she could record a statement accusing the gardaí of prompting her to make a false statement and thus protect an innocent man. Farrell declined both invitations.

Bailey had eventually appeared at her shop in person, opened his coat and told Farrell that he was 'all wired up'. It was her understanding that he meant he had a microphone and tape-recorder concealed about his person. Again she was asked to say that the gardaí had coerced her into making a false statement. Her anxiety turned to fear when Bailey stood on a chair and started to wave his arms about. Farrell immediately thought how easy it would be for him to kill her. Incredibly, Bailey seemed to know a lot about Farrell, making references to her partner's London address and her own former addresses in Longford.

After the incident in the shop, Bailey's attitude towards her changed dramatically. He now acknowledged that she had indeed seen him at Cealfada bridge, but that he had not killed Sophie. He also told her that if she scratched his back, he would scratch hers. He would make cut-throat gestures at her, or point an extended first finger at his temple as though he were firing a gun at his head, execution-style. The terrified woman began to receive threatening phone calls. She became afraid to be in her shop alone and as a result hired three extra staff members she did not really need and the business could not support. On the previous Sunday before being called to give evidence, an anonymous female caller had told her to keep her 'bloody mouth shut'.

Farrell claimed that she had been living a nightmare. She accused Bailey of mental torture and of making her afraid to let her children out of her sight. It was suggested by Bailey's counsel that Farrell had invited Bailey into her shop. She denied this: 'I don't think any woman in her right frame of mind would invite Ian Bailey to her shop, especially when she is on her own. It's a well-known fact that he is abusive towards women.' She also denied that she was put under pressure by the gardaí regarding what she had seen in the early hours of 23 December.

Jules Thomas was Bailey's alibi for that night and she insisted that he had not left the house. She refused to speculate on the implications of Farrell's sighting, however, and denied knowing the woman. Bailey had got up during the night, she admitted, but had stayed in the kitchen, writing. In the morning she had found a lengthy handwritten article on the table. She disputed the wording in her statement to gardaí claiming that Bailey had 'tossed and turned' in bed. Thomas also vigorously disowned an allegation, made in her statement, that Bailey had duped her.

'They didn't seem to want to believe what I was saying. They kept putting words in my mouth,' Thomas said.

Thomas had been so unhappy with her statement that she later contacted a solicitor with instructions that the gardaí be informed that she could no longer accept several items in her signed statement because she had not been thinking clearly after the ordeal she had been put through. Her arrest, along with Bailey, had quite overwhelmed her; she could hardly speak. It was then that three detectives had subjected her to a harrowing interview. She had been arrested a second time, in September 2000, and she alleged that on that occasion she had been coerced into signing a second memo stating that the first statement was correct.

Judge Moran expressed unease over the purpose of the second arrest. He instructed that Thomas should not be questioned about her second arrest.

Ian Bailey had not finished lambasting the gardaí, however. He went on to accuse them of being involved in an operation at the temporary Cork residence he was renting for the duration of the case. He believed that things at his residence had been moved and altered during his absence. Bailey complained that the gardaí were conspiring to implicate him in the murder. He could not be more precise than that, but he felt that what was happening was not legally sanctioned. Bailey's protestations were starting to sound like the ranting of a paranoid conspiracy theorist, and they did not help his case. Even if there was any truth in his allegations, the libel hearing was not the correct forum for airing them.

Bailey had remained composed during his four days of cross-examination – a tough ordeal for anyone – losing his composure only when told by defence counsel that he was a failed poet and a poor musician. Thus far the hearing had occupied the best part of five days, and most of the court pundits agreed that the odds had swung strongly in the defence's favour. The plaintiff had been branded a woman-beater, a fantasist, a drug-user and a heavy drinker. Bailey would have an uphill struggle to convince the court that he was not a 'Billy Liar' character.

Bailey's case took a further downturn when the newspapers began to put their case. A very strange picture of the man began to emerge. Fourteen witnesses testified, the majority giving evidence that directly contradicted Bailey's assertions. There was also a great deal of evidence to support the claims that Bailey's behaviour was aberrant.

Shirley Foster, the woman who had made the horrific discovery of du Plantier's body, told the court that she had seen Bailey drive up the laneway outside her house, at speed, on the day before the murder. There were only three houses along that lane, including the du Plantiers'. Bailey said that he had met Foster on the main road, but she remained unshakable in her claim that it had in fact been in the laneway.

Alfie Lyons, Sophie du Plantier's next-door-neighbour, told the court that he had introduced Bailey to the Frenchwoman when she had called to his house in June 1995. Bailey had sworn he had never met the murder victim.

Paul Webster, a journalist for the *Observer* who had been working in Paris for the *Guardian* at the time of the murder, said that Bailey had contacted him in France with information about the investigation: 'He made it absolutely clear that he had talked to her before – there is no doubt about that at all – and seen her on the day she died.'

Local woman Caroline Leftwick also found Bailey a rather bohemian character. She had been due to meet with Bailey on the morning of 23 December, but he had telephoned her at around 11.00 a.m. to cancel, explaining that he had a murder to cover. She found his excitement distasteful. Paul O'Colman, a West Cork writer, had also received a call between 11.00 a.m. and 12.00 and had been told of the gruesome murder. Ceri Williams thought Bailey could be very intimidating at times. At a party, held before Bailey's initial arrest, fellow guest Diane Martin had put it to him that he was the murderer. He had made no response, made no denial.

Paul Gallagher's closing statement lasted almost five hours and was a scathing, piece-by-piece demolition of Ian Bailey's evidence. He accused Bailey of misleading the court regarding the domestic violence to which he had subjected his partner, Jules Thomas. There was an overwhelming body of testimony to prove that Bailey had lied about the attacks on Thomas. He was a man capable of menace and intimidation. The jury was asked to bear in mind that many of the witnesses had had to be subpoenaed for the libel trial because their fear of Bailey was so great, they may not have given evidence voluntarily.

Turning to the murder, Gallagher pointed out that Marie Farrell had sworn that she had seen Bailey on the Goleen road on the night Sophie Toscan du Plantier was killed. Farrell had since been subjected to a campaign of harassment and intimidation. Almost every point the plaintiff had made had been contested by witness evidence: Bailey had known Sophie du Plantier, he had lit a bonfire on St Stephen's Day, the gardaí had not pressurised witnesses into making statements.

Such was Bailey's reputation in West Cork, Gallagher argued, that it was absurd to claim that the press articles had damaged it.

The greatest damage had been done by his two arrests, on proper cause.

The judge interjected to remind defence counsel of what he regarded as the core issue of the hearing.

'The citizen's good name is what this case is all about,' Judge Moran said. 'Just how far are they [the media] allowed to go?'

'A person is entitled to a reputation,' counsel countered, 'but no person has the right to come into court and tell lie after lie.' He reminded the court that Bailey had played a pivotal role in the publication of the facts. He was the prime suspect and seemed almost to bask in that moniker, an attitude apparent in the interviews he gave to the Pat Kenny radio show and other press members and organisations.

Jim Duggan, counsel for the plaintiff, began his closing address on Friday morning, the tenth day the court had sat. He described how Ian Bailey's life, career and reputation had been destroyed by the media coverage that had branded him the killer of Sophie Toscan du Plantier. At times, counsel's performance edged towards the theatrical as he spun his reading glasses around to make his point. The plaintiff, he said, had been lambasted and demonised. It was bad enough that acres of newsprint had already been devoted to him, but, to add insult to injury, the papers had been giving the hearing unprecedented coverage.

Judge Moran commented wryly, 'Well, you are suing seven newspapers.'

Bailey's demeanour became more bowed with each day of the case. Perhaps he had not realised the full implications of a libel hearing. The defence had left no dirt unthrown, and Bailey had an abundance of dubious incidents in his history that might have been better left in the dark. On the evidence of domestic violence, Duggan said: 'It does happen. It's a fact of life. It did happen, but they got over it. They are getting on with their lives, but these people [the media] won't let them. These people want to bring it up at every hand's turn.'

Duggan was scathing about the defence's decision not to call a single journalist who had written the relevant articles. He claimed that this had greatly hampered the court and had ensured that specific information could not be obtained. He was also critical of the close links between the gardaí and the defence: 'Nobody could fail to be impressed by the level of co-operation between the gardaí and defendants.' To drive his point home, he questioned the presence throughout the hearing of retired Superintendent John Courtney, a former member of the murder squad, asking if it was guilt by association. Judge Moran interrupted counsel on this, telling him it was not fair to make such an assertion.

Duggan moved on, admitting that he himself had been troubled by the discrepancies between testimonies. However, if the court ruled that the twenty witnesses were telling the truth, it could affect the potential damages open to the plaintiff. Counsel for the defence, David Holland, opposed this, saying that if the court held that Bailey had not told the full truth, then his entire action should be struck out.

Duggan closed his relatively short address with a quote from Stanley Baldwin, made in a 1931 by-election speech when Baldwin was speaking of the newspaper magnates, Beaverbrook and Rothermere, who, he said, wanted 'power without responsibility – the prerogative of the harlot throughout the ages'.

Holland replied for the defence. He also chose to end with a quote, one from the plaintiff's barrister: 'Nobody has any regard for a person who beats their partner or wife.'

Judge Moran then announced that his judgment would be delivered on 9 January 2004. This was later delayed, without any reason being given, until 19 January. It was thought that the judge's workload and the sheer bulk of evidence may have contributed to the delay.

The parties reassembled in a temporary courtroom on Camden Quay on 19 January to hear the forty-minute judgment. Judge Moran dismissed five of the actions, ruling that no defamation or damage to reputation had occurred in the coverage of the murder and its investigation. However, he upheld two of the plaintiff's actions, against the *Irish Daily Mirror* and *The Irish Sun*. Those two papers had accused Bailey of unproven violence against his ex-wife, Sara Limbrick. Damages were set at €4,000 in each case. No order on costs was made at that point, as counsels for both sides requested an adjournment. It was thought that costs could reach as high as €500,000.

During the delivery of his judgment, Judge Moran said that he found it quite unusual that a person arrested on suspicion of such a serious matter should grant interviews and pose for photographers: 'One can only presume Mr Bailey is a man who likes a certain amount of notoriety, likes to be in the limelight, and likes a bit of self-publicity.'

The judge also commented on the arrests of Ian Bailey and Jules Thomas. He said that when the gardaí make an arrest for serious criminal offences – particularly murder – they usually do so for very good reasons, based on a strong suspicion of involvement. He was sorry that the hearing had at times taken on the mantle of a murder trial, despite his best efforts to prevent it. Bailey and Thomas had made good witnesses, staying cool under the most intense pressure. On the balance of probability, however, he accepted the evidence of the witnesses for the defence. There were gasps from the assembled public when the judge said he believed the Shellys' testimonies that Bailey had said, 'I did it. I did it.' The judge recognised that if it had been a criminal trial, some of the evidence would have been ruled inadmissible.

Outside the courtroom, newspaper executives queued up to hail the judgment. Michael Roche welcomed the verdict, saying he felt the decision reflected the facts. Other media executives agreed that it was a just and moral victory, and a great day for newspapers. Representatives of the *Irish Daily Mirror* and *The Irish Sun* said that an appeal might be lodged on their behalf. The Director of Public Prosecutions would later ask for a transcript of the hearing in case any new evidence could aid the bringing of a criminal prosecution.

The gardaí cleared a path through the throng of journalists for a haunted-looking Ian Bailey. For the first time since the case had begun, Jules Thomas was not by his side. He was bundled into a car and driven to a secret location. A few days later, Thomas would claim that she had been subjected to a Klu Klux Klan-type intimidation when petrol had been thrown at her house. A dead rat had also been put through her letterbox and she said she was receiving threatening phone calls.

On 13 February 2004, Judge Moran announced his ruling on costs. The *Irish Daily Mirror* and *The Irish Sun* would pay Bailey's lawyers €20,000, while Bailey would have to pay five other newspapers about €200,000. The €8,000 awarded to Bailey would be frozen until it was paid against the €200,000 owed. Judge Moran stated that 'the main prize' had gone to the newspapers and that Bailey's team would receive 'the runner-up prize or even third-place prize'. It would be unfair to award full costs against Ian Bailey, the judge conceded, adding that he thought the newspapers could have done more in pooling their resources to reduce costs.

Bailey remained in hiding for some time. As, in legal parlance, he was 'a man of straw', without assets, the newspapers might decide not to pursue costs against him, but they could still make life very uncomfortable for him financially. The man who had once allegedly declared that there was no money in bumping off people had learned the hard way that libel actions do not pay that well either.

Just as the dust was beginning to settle on the Bailey libel hearing, a sensational development threw it wide open once more. In early October 2005, Marie Farrell's solicitor wrote to the gardaí, withdrawing his client's evidence. A sworn statement to this effect was also handed to Ian Bailey's legal team. Ms Farrell claimed that she had been induced to make certain statements about Bailey; the gardaí strongly denied her accusations. In the wake of the star witness's dramatic withdrawal, the Bouniol family had little choice but to drop its civil action against Bailey.

By withdrawing her evidence, Farrell may be leaving herself open to a charge of perjury, something her solicitor would have made very clear to her. It is not yet known if this option will be pursued by the Director of Public Prosecutions.

Bolstered by Farrell's retraction, Bailey returned to the courts in February 2007 and commenced his appeal against the unsuccessful libel actions. Judge Brian McGovern and the Cork High Court listened to three days of testimony as Bailey was questioned by his legal team. While giving evidence, Bailey levelled accusations against the Garda Síochána and against the press, claiming that there had been a conspiracy to frame him for the murder of Sophie Toscan du Plantier. The hearing ended abruptly on the fourth day when it was announced that Bailey was withdrawing his appeal. The newspapers claimed it as a clear victory, but an out-of-court agreement that they waive their Circuit Court costs and contribute towards Bailey's High Court costs may have been as good a result as the 'man of straw' could have expected.

One thing is certain, however – justice for Sophie Toscan du Plantier looks further away than ever.

12 | **CYBER-LIBEL:**
DEFAMATION IN THE
TWENTY-FIRST CENTURY

In Britain, the Defamation Act 1996 was expected to bring libel litigation into the modern era. Publishers in Ireland carefully monitored the early workings of that Act, so that someday its successes might be enacted in this jurisdiction and its failures avoided. It soon became clear, however, that the Act left many dilemmas unresolved, reducing it to minimal value as a possible blueprint for legislation.

Underlying the British Act was a wish to modernise and untangle libel law, with the stated aims of making litigation less expensive, fairer and more efficient. Unfortunately, the Act was not well drafted and its many flaws have had to be addressed by later legislation. Lord Wolfe, master of the rolls, recommended several proposals, which were adopted in the Civil Procedure Act 1997. His protocols provided alternative, less costly routes to settlement of libel disputes in an attempt to render litigation a last resort. His aim was also to provide a more equal forum for litigation by keeping costs down and ensuring that the process was commensurate to what was at stake.

To complicate matters further, the incorporation of the European Convention of Human Rights into English law, by means of the Human Rights Act 1998, greatly reduced restrictions on free speech while at the same time exposing the need to safeguard a right to privacy. Article 10 of the Convention states that everyone has the right of freedom of expression, which shall include the freedom to hold opinions and to receive and impart information and ideas without interference by public authority and regardless of frontiers. In effect, English courts would have to expand the principles first laid down in the *Reynolds* case, with reference to their obligation to European decisions.

Article 8 outlines a right of privacy, under which every person is entitled to respect for his/her private life, home and correspondence. One of the first cases to test the right to privacy was *Douglas v Hello!*. In that case, the courts decided that *OK!* magazine had a right to enforce its exclusive right to photographs of the film stars' wedding.

The Irish government made its first tentative steps towards new legislation with the drafting of the Defamation Bill 2002, which was not expected to become law until the after the next election. Unfortunately, Michael McDowell's proposed changes failed to win Dáil approval and were duly rejected in June 2005. The main changes that the Bill proposed were the abolishment of a differentiation between libel and slander and a discontinuation of the system whereby juries assessed damages awards. The media would benefit from clearer parameters being laid down, while there would be a wider range of redress options than at present. The limitation period would be reduced from six to three years.

The National Newspapers of Ireland (NNI) had expressed concern that the burden of proof still lay with the defence and not with the plaintiff, as in other civil cases. The NNI had also hoped that the limitation period would be reduced to one year, as in the UK, but this had always seemed unlikely. The limitation for books in the UK was set at three years, reflecting their longer shelf life.

McDowell made a further attempt to modernise Ireland's libel laws by presenting another Defamation Bill to the 29th Dáil in July 2006, this time addressing most of the flaws exposed in the Defamation Act 1961. At first glance the Bill seemed to correct many of the weaknesses inherent in defamation legislation: plaintiffs and defendants would have to submit sworn affidavits; an apology would no longer be construed as an admission of guilt;

defendants would be able to lodge a sum of money into court to limit liability; juries would be retained but the judge could issue directions on damages; a limitation period of one year; and the provision for new remedies and defences.

The new legislation may have proved a poisoned chalice for some if another general election had not stalled its progress. The freedom of the press came close to being shackled, and it could blame no one but itself. The NNI had planned to establish its own Independent Complaints Commission, comprising a Press Ombudsman and a Press Council. The Independent Complaints Commission would be a cheaper alternative to the courts for anyone who thought they had been maligned. It would draw up a code of practice, be staffed by people from within the media and would rule on breaches. However, the irresponsible reporting of disgraced politician Liam Lawlor's death in a Moscow traffic accident (the translator accompanying Lawlor was erroneously described as a prostitute) and the unsavoury allegations levelled at Monica Leech, advisor to Minister for Transport Martin Cullen, provided the government with the perfect excuse to introduce a statutory-recognised Press Council. In other words, the newspaper industry would be regulated by a State body run by State appointees: hardly a healthy combination for a modern free press.

Making the outlook even gloomier for the Irish press corps was the possibility of a privacy law being introduced in the wake of ever-growing tabloid domination and Naomi Campbell's successful House of Lords appeal against the *Daily Mirror,* which had published a photograph of the model leaving a Narcotics Anonymous meeting. This move to protect privacy seemed very conceivable, as there is an implicit right to privacy in the Irish Constitution, coupled with the distaste over recent objectionable press intrusions – such as the *Sunday World* publishing details of an illness suffered by a family member of u2's The Edge, and *Ireland on Sunday* photographing the son of double-killer Malcolm McArthur. Once the media had shot itself in the foot with unacceptable conduct, it seemed acceptance of a statutory-recognised Press Council and stricter privacy rights would be the asking price for reform of the libel law.

Fortunately, wiser heads prevailed and the privacy element of McDowell's reforms was quietly dropped before going to the Seanad. The May 2007 general election prevented the Defamation Bill 2006 reaching the statute books. Despite twenty-five years of intensive lobbying to bring it about, change to defamation law is still in the pipeline. During that time, successive governments have shown little real enthusiasm for progress.

While Ireland awaits new legislation, the courts have turned to common law to protect its less well-heeled citizens from defamation, often relying on the Non-Fatal Offences Against the Person Act 1997 to bring criminal prosecutions. Dubliner Michael Walsh was jailed for two years for writing defamatory libels on the walls of public toilets in Dún Laoghaire and Blackrock. His libellous comments were directed at a local garda, whom he falsely accused of being a child molester. After the graffiti appeared, the local garda station was inundated with callers offering sexual favours. The victim was devastated, forced to endure jibes from his colleagues and from local hoodlums.

Walsh also pleaded guilty to sending an obscene libellous letter and an indecent photograph to a woman at roughly the same time as writing the graffiti. Walsh alleged that the woman's children were being abused and that he wished to abuse her. Prosecution counsel stated that the letter had been sent in an Oireachtas Éireann envelope.

When he was arrested, Walsh was found to be carrying handcuffs and a replica gun, apparently for a robbery he was planning of an amusement arcade on Eden Quay. He had served an earlier sentence for the theft of a violin from the Royal Irish Academy of Music. Judge Elizabeth Dunne suspended fifteen months of the sentence, as Walsh had been in custody for nine months.

Hopefully the inordinate delay in enacting fresh legislation will yield a benefit by allowing the drafting of suitable measures to deal with a new form of libel that could tie up the courts for years.

December 1999 brought the first Irish prosecution for criminal libel on the internet. A twenty-six-year-old Dublin man was accused of posting messages on bulletin sites alleging that a former teacher was a paedophile. He had also sent an e-mail with similar content to a school colleague of the teacher.

The case was heard at Dublin Circuit Criminal Court, with Judge Elizabeth Dunne presiding. She made an order that the accused could not be named. Prosecution counsel, Una Ní Raifeartaigh, told the court that the man had made three allegations of abuse to the gardaí and a file was prepared for the Director of Public Prosecutions. It was at a late stage in the proceedings that the allegations were discovered to be false. Subsequently, the complainant was charged with libellous defamation and released on bail. Doubts about his allegation had arisen when other students alleged to have been abused by the teacher denied that this had happened. While on bail, the man had twice posted offending messages on the internet from a computer at the Cyber Café in South Great George's Street, Dublin. The dates were given as 3 December 1997 and 22 June 1998.

The victim gave evidence that his life had become a nightmare since the allegations had appeared. One of the messages gave an alleged account of how the teacher had asked up to ten people, over a number of years, to pose for nude films and that he had been the subject of an international investigation into child pornography. The accused had written that he too had been asked to pose for such a film.

Passages of the messages were read to the court: 'It is about time that he stopped. For God's sake, somebody do something. The kids are not safe with him about.'

The accused pleaded guilty to two representative counts of criminal libel and apologised to his victim, saying he was deeply sorry for what he had written and now wanted to start his life over again. The accused had been in custody for nineteen months and a jury had found him fit to stand trial. Later, he changed his plea to guilty.

Defence counsel, Erwin Mill Arden SC, referred to a report from psychiatrist Dr Tom McGonagle, which stated that the defendant suffered from Asperger's Syndrome, a form of autism, the main symptom of which is an inability to act appropriately in social situations. A sufferer would, for example, be unable to comprehend another person's tone of voice or body language, which in turn could lead to inappropriate behaviour.

The judge sentenced the accused to a two-and-a-half-year prison term. She said that the offences had been near the top end of the scale; nothing worse could have been said about the teacher.

A second case of defamation on the internet that reached the Irish courts was the prosecution of Francis Kenny, a forty-year-old father of two from Ballyhaunis, Co. Mayo. The case opened at Westport Circuit Court on 27 March 2001.

The court heard that Maureen Walker, of Castlerea, Co. Roscommon, began to receive humiliating calls on her mobile phone after 4.00 p.m. on 6 March 2000. Walker had become greatly distressed after receiving over 100 calls in forty-eight hours from men requesting various sexual favours. The calls would come at all times of the day and night, and the callers often became abusive when told of the deception.

Walker visited an internet café in Sligo and, with assistance from the proprietor, attempted to track down the site that was advertising her name and phone number. Unfortunately, she had no success on that occasion and the calls did not cease.

Then Walker had a stroke of luck. One caller omitted to remove caller ID from his phone, so she was able to phone him back and convince him that her details had been given by someone wishing her harm. The caller eventually consented to assist Walker, and showed her and the internet café-owner the website. It was the Escort Ireland website, which is commonly used by prostitutes to advertise their service. Within the site, Walker's name, age, description and telephone number were given, along with a catalogue of the sexual services it was said she was willing to perform. The advertisement was headed 'Exclusive Maureen'. The trio was able to trace the advert back to the defendant.

Walker contacted the Castlerea garda staion and on 8 May Sergeant John Hynes called to the home of Francis Kenny. Initially, Kenny denied any involvement, but when the sergeant announced that he intended to seize his computer, Kenny confessed.

Kenny was charged under Section 12 of the Defamation Act 1961 and pleaded guilty. Judge Moran heard that Walker had been in tears when reporting the offence to the gardaí. She had been afraid that her children, aged seventeen and fifteen, would learn about what had happened. Walker ran a sandwich-making business called Exclusive Sandwiches; Kenny had a similar business called Fresh Cuts, which he ran from his home in Ballyhaunis and had first begun trading in 1998. In a statement, Kenny accused Walker of having poached some of his customers and of spreading malicious rumours concerning his business, namely that he was not registered with the Western Health Board and that he was a cowboy who provided an inferior product. When he began to lose orders, he had sought revenge against his rival.

Kenny admitted [mistakenly] that he saw an advertisement in the *Sunday World* newspaper for an escort service, and it gave him the idea. He set up an account with the Yahoo search engine using an e-mail account in Walker's name. A forged letter was sent to Escort Ireland, detailing the alleged services and costs that his business rival would provide, including S&M, water games and threesomes. The advert ran for a short time, but succeeded in generating an enormous response.

In his defence, Kenny stated that he had not really understood the full implications of what his actions would subject Walker to. There had been no intent to subject her to such a harrowing ordeal. He admitted that he had been under pressure and feeling very stressed at the time, but now deeply regretted what he had done and had apologised for it.

Padraig O'Higgins SC, for the defendant, told the court that his client had no previous record and, although a man of no great means, had offered compensation of £10,000 to Walker. Counsel noted that Kenny had been given several exemplary testimonials by local, eminent Mayo people.

Judge Moran, acknowledging that Walker had agreed that Kenny's guilty plea had saved her the further distress of a trial, ruled that the compensation was insufficient and adjourned the hearing for a week. On that subsequent court appearance the defendant was told to pay a higher amount – most probably £35,000, the Circuit Court limit – within seven days. A week later the judge applied the Probation Act after hearing that the required compensation had been paid into court.

Accompanied by her solicitor, Walker read a statement to journalists after the landmark case concluded: 'I am pleased this saga has come to an end with Mr Kenny pleading guilty to his disgusting offence.' She hoped that what had happened to Kenny would deter others from engaging in this type of sordid behaviour.

*　　*　　*

It is not just individuals who face litigation over misuse of the internet. The case between Western Provident and Norwich Union provides a salutary warning to Irish firms regarding the liabilities they could face. In this landmark case, the plaintiff was a provider of private medical insurance. In 1995, unfounded rumours started to circulate around the insurance world about financial irregularities at Western Provident, along with the equally unfounded suggestion that the company was being investigated by the Department of Trade and Industry. These rumours were traced back to the internal e-mail system for Norwich Union employees.

Libel litigation was initiated by Western Provident, which sought to hold Norwich Union liable for the defamatory messages sent by its employees. Prompt action in obtaining court orders, which allowed Norwich Union's e-mail records to be searched and defamatory messages preserved, helped Western Provident to build a strong case. The case was eventually settled for an apology read in court and damages of £450,000, plus costs.

*　　*　　*

It was also in 1995 that an Asda customer, PC Eggleton, was awarded significant damages against the supermarket giant after he discovered it had been sending e-mails to branches erroneously accusing him of fraud. The policeman came upon the e-mails when he was advising an Asda store on crime prevention.

* * *

The first blogger to be sued for libel was Tracy Williams, in March 2006. She was ordered to pay £10,000 to Michael Keith Smith, a UKIP parliamentary candidate. On a right-wing group discussion website, Williams had falsely accused Smith of being a sex-offender and a racist bigot. Despite using a false name on the site, Williams was identified.

Dublin blogger Seán O'Sullivan pleaded guilty to defamation at a hearing in Dublin Circuit Court in February 2007. The €38,000 he was ordered to pay in damages set a new record for Irish online defamation awards. Judge Jacqueline Linnane made the award against the fifty-four-year-old retired tax inspector and also granted a permanent injunction prohibiting him from making further defamatory publications. A series of articles posted on www.corrupt-lawyers.com had accused Orpen Franks, a Burlington Road legal practice, of incompetence, negligence, lying and arson. O'Sullivan had waged a twenty-year campaign against the law firm after a dispute arose over a house purchase. In court, he had used justification as a defence, but failed to provide proof of his claims.

The dangers of open communication are clear, and internet service providers have made strenuous, although largely unsuccessful, attempts to disassociate themselves from liability for defamatory messages posted on websites. They claim that they are not responsible for content, but are merely conduits of information. *Godfrey v Demon* [1999] did much to clarify the situation in the UK. Dr Laurence Godfrey sued internet service provider Demon after it failed to comply with his request to remove squalid, obscene and defamatory postings from websites. In an interlocutory ruling, the judge refused to strike out Godfrey's claim on the basis of Demon's argument that it could have no liability as a mere transmitter of messages. The suit was eventually settled in Godfrey's favour, for damages and costs exceeding £230,000.

The advantage for the plaintiff in involving an internet service provider in internet litigation may serve any one, or all, of three purposes: the plaintiff may not be able to identify the author; the internet service provider may have more financial resources to meet awards; or the author may be resident in a country with a more liberal legal system. So, for example, a Spanish victim of alleged defamatory material could sue an impoverished French author in an Irish court by including an Irish internet service provider as co-defendant. The French damage awards for libel are notoriously low, while Irish awards are perceived as more generous. Under the Brussels Convention on the enforcement of judgments, an award made in any EU Member State is automatically enforceable in any other Member State.

In Europe, a distinction has been accepted between three types of internet provision and, therefore, each type's liability to libel suits. An internet service provider that acts as a 'mere conduit' will not be liable for damages or prosecution as a result of information transmission. Internet service providers that cache information may be liable if they do not act quickly to remove a web page when ordered to do so by a court. The third category, hosting, also has immunity, but this may be lost if the provider is aware of defamatory material and fails to act expeditiously to delete or block the content.

A case that helped to define the position of an internet service provider was heard in October 2000. The court heard that David Frankl, a former employee of Takenaka (UK) Ltd, had been sending defamatory e-mails under a false name, Christina Realtor, to Takenaka. Several allegations were levelled against the company and against Frankl's former boss, Brian Corfe. Corfe was accused of having had an eighteen-month affair and of fathering a child, of domestic violence, of lying and of threatening to have 'Christina Realtor' killed.

After legal submissions, several encompassing orders were made against the internet service provider for disclosure. This enabled the company to trace the e-mails to the man's laptop in

Turkey. Mr Justice Alliott did not accept the defence's claim that someone else had used a computer programme called Black Orifice to access Frankl's computer and send the e-mails without his knowledge. The judge awarded £100,000 costs to the company and £26,000 to Brian Corfe.

The first Irish case in which a court had to consider jurisdiction was USA *Rugby Football Union Limited v Ivan Calhoun.* The case arose from an article written by Calhoun and posted on his popular rugby website. In the article, Calhoun had been highly critical of the management structures of USA Rugby, although he voluntarily withdrew the offending article after representation made by officers of USA Rugby.

However, USA Rugby was concerned that substantial damage had been done to the organisation and feared an unfavourable response from sponsors. As the headquarters of the International Rugby Board (IRB) is located in Dublin and USA Rugby received much of its funding from the IRB, it was decided that litigation should be initiated in Ireland. The notorious difficulty of successfully pursuing a libel case in the USA may have had some bearing on the choice.

Calhoun lodged an application challenging the jurisdiction of the Irish courts. It was his contention that there was no evidence that anyone in Ireland had accessed the article; the case was *Forum Non Conveniens,* i.e. Ireland was not the correct forum to hear the case and USA Rugby was indulging in 'Forum Shopping'; and both plaintiff and defendant were America-based, as were the majority of the witnesses.

USA Rugby argued against Calhoun's application, stating that publication had occurred once the article had been put on the website; USA Rugby had a reputation in Ireland; and should the case be heard in the USA, it would still mean witnesses having to travel great distances, as the plaintiff was based in Delaware and the defendant in Texas.

The defendant's application was denied by the Circuit Court at the first time of asking, but an appeal to the High Court reversed this decision. Mr Justice White, in an *ex tempore* judgment given on July 2002, said it was unsafe to assume that access implied publication, and he agreed with Calhoun's assertion over *Forum Non Conveniens* and the issue of extra costs that would be incurred should the case be heard in Ireland.

* * *

Another landmark case, which took place in Australia just five months after the *Calhoun* case, ended with a slightly different judgment that provides some insight into the complexities facing judiciaries when dealing with internet disputes. In December 2002, the Australian High Court ruled that a man resident in the state of Victoria could sue a non-resident business. In October 2000, Dow Jones, publishers of *Barrons Online*, a web-based subscription version of *Barrons Magazine,* accused mining magnate Joseph Gutnick of posing as a law-abiding citizen while being a tax-evader and a money-launderer. Dow Jones sought to have the subsequent libel action heard in New Jersey, USA. It was their contention that the libel action should be heard where the company had its internet service provider (and where there was a much greater duty on the plaintiff to prove libel). They further argued that publication had occurred when Dow Jones's internet service provider had received a request from the subscriber's computer and had, at that point, gained control of the article.

The court disagreed, holding that there had been no publication in a readable form until the plaintiff had downloaded the article onto his computer in Australia. Therefore, the plaintiff had the right to sue either in America or in Australia, where the damage to his reputation had occurred.

This decision has obviously opened up a can of worms that will take years of international discussion and agreement to resolve. Until then, defendants may not bother to fight a libel action if they have no assets in the country where the case is to be heard. Any attempt to enforce damage awards would then be fought in courts more to their liking.

Should the thorny problem of jurisdiction not prove enough to keep international legislators busy for years to come, there is also the question of how exactly defamation should be defined. At present, what might be recognised as clearly libellous in one country could well be perfectly acceptable in another. An obvious disparity could therefore arise between Christian and Muslim countries, between free economies and communist states, or between democracies and dictatorships.

Increased international publication, either by way of the internet or the globalisation of media companies, will create an avalanche of libel wrangles well into the twenty-first century. While world harmonisation of libel law is an impossible dream for the distant future, the internet is already bringing litigation nightmares to many. While UNESCO has debated the problem, it has yet to propose little more than some form of self-regulation. Inevitably there will be those willing to cash in on this vacillation. Perhaps even now, some opportunistic-minded country is considering introducing a punitive libel forum as a lucrative income source. This cannot be allowed to happen, yet delaying legislation almost guarantees that it will. Time will tell.